Looking after Children in Primary Care

A companion to the Children's National Service Framework

Edited by

Ruth Chambers

and

Kirsty Licence

Foreword by

Al Aynsley-Green

Radcliffe Publishing

Oxford • San Francisco

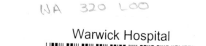

D1147702

Radcliffe Publishing Ltd
18 Marcham Road
Abingdon
Oxon OX14 1AA
United Kingdom

www.radcliffe-oxford.com
Electronic catalogue and worldwide online ordering facility.

British Library Cataloguing in Publication Data

A catalogue record for this book is available from the British Library.

ISBN 1 85775 888 9

Typeset by Anne Joshua & Associates, Oxford
Printed and bound by TJ International Ltd, Padstow, Cornwall

Contents

Preface

How this book fits with the Children's National Service Framework

This book has been written as a companion to the Children's National Service Framework (NSF) to help you to put the NSF into practice in primary care. Most of the chapter authors chaired or participated in one of the eight External Working Groups (EWGs) of the NSF. The book includes much of their background material and evidence that went into the evolution of the final Children's NSF as it relates to primary care. The authors have taken the opportunity to expand on the vision, themes and goals within the published NSF and recommend tried and tested ways for implementing best practice in primary care settings.

The vision and standards of the various themes of the Children's NSF are reproduced in the Appendix at the back of this book. The chapters are written around the themes and priorities for primary care so you will need to refer to the relevant standards that underpin each chapter as you read through the book.

We hope that by reading and using this book, you will be able to improve the children's services you provide in your everyday work in primary care, whether you are a health professional, support worker, manager or policymaker. The scope of each chapter is applicable to children's healthcare anywhere in the Western world, so although the Children's NSF relates to England, those in other countries in the UK or beyond will be able to generalise from the contents of this book to their own workplace.

Gathering the evidence for the Children's NSF

The NSFs set the standards for the provision of NHS care in key clinical areas, alongside the work of the National Institute for Clinical Excellence (NICE) and are based on the best available evidence. 'National Service Frameworks will bring together the best evidence of clinical and cost-effectiveness with the views of service users to determine the best ways of providing particular services.'[1]

The evidence base for the interventions set out in the Children's NSF was collated by a small team of researchers, who gathered evidence to meet the generic guidance set out in *A First Class Service*,[1] including:

- the rationale behind each key topic or standard. This included the importance of the topic in determining health, prevalence of associated health effects, issues of inequality and current provision of services
- the evidence for the effectiveness of interventions set out in the NSF, including the populations and settings in which different interventions have been shown to be effective and the potential size of the effect. Evidence of cost-effectiveness was also sought
- gaps in the evidence base to guide future research.

A categorisation of evidence was agreed by all the researchers contributing to the Children's NSF (*see* Box P.1). This was based on the system used in the Older People's NSF.[2] This categorisation is used in Chapters 6, 8, 9 and 12, the four chapters that present the evidence base commissioned from the healthy child and young person EWG.

Box P.1 Categorisation of evidence used in the Older People's and Children's National Service Frameworks

A1

Systematic reviews which include at least one randomised controlled trial (RCT) (e.g. systematic reviews from the Cochrane Library or the NHS Centre for Reviews and Dissemination)

A2

Other systematic and high-quality reviews which synthesise references

B1

Individual RCTs

B2

Individual, non-randomised experimental/intervention studies

B3

Individual well-designed non-experimental studies, controlled statistically if appropriate

C1

Descriptive and other research or evaluation not in B

C2

Case studies and examples of good practice

D

Summary review articles and discussions of relevant literature and conference proceedings not otherwise classified

---

CE

Evidence from economic studies, including cost-effectiveness analysis, cost-benefit analysis and option appraisal

Evidence from expert opinion

P

Professional opinion, including reports of committees, inquiries, Social Services Inspectorate (SSI) reports

U1

User views – children

U2

User views – parents/carers

Where available, NSF researchers used recent high-quality reviews as the main sources of evidence. On topics where no good recent review could be identified, the primary literature was searched and appraised. Members of the NSF EWG (*see* www.dh.gov.uk for membership) also contributed evidence from their own areas of expertise. Because of the scope of the Children's NSF, the evidence base for different sections comprised different amounts of published and unpublished, primary and secondary, professional- and user-derived evidence.

In the areas of the NSF relating to health promotion for children and young people, the evidence base presented in this book relies principally on reviews and syntheses of primary and secondary research ('reviews of reviews'), which were readily available for most topics. These were identified from major quality assessed databases (Box P.2). Where primary research was used or where more formal bibliographic searches were carried out, the database used was PubMed. The evidence presented here does not profess to be a critical and systematic review of the available evidence. Instead, it brings together the conclusions of past reviews, systematic and narrative, identifying the interventions that are consistently supported by analysis of primary trials.

Many of the papers referred to are available on the Internet through sites such as the Cochrane Library, the Health Development Agency evidence base, the NHS Centre for Reviews and Dissemination, the National Guidelines Clearing House and other sources (Box P.2).

> **Box P.2** Website addresses for main evidence sources and databases
>
> - Cochrane Library www.nelh.nhs.uk/cochrane.asp
> - UK Department of Health www.dh.gov.uk
> - Health Development Agency www.hda-online.org.uk
> - Health Education Board for Scotland www.hebs.scot.nhs.uk
> - NHS Centre for Reviews and Dissemination www.york.ac.uk/inst/crd/ (for Health Technology Assessments, the Database of Abstracts of Reviews of Effectiveness, the NHS Economic Evaluation Database, Effectiveness Matters and Effective Healthcare Bulletins)
> - National Guideline Clearinghouse www.guideline.gov
> - PubMed www.ncbi.nlm.nih.gov/PubMed
> - Scottish Intercollegiate Guideline Network www.sign.ac.uk

Ruth Chambers
Kirsty Licence
October 2004

References

1 Department of Health (1998) *A First Class Service: quality in the new NHS.* HMSO, London. www.dh.gov.uk/assetRoot/04/04/48/91/04044891.pdf

2 Department of Health (2001) *The National Service Framework for Older People.* HMSO, London. www.dh.gov.uk/assetRoot/04/07/12/83/04071283.pdf

About the authors

Editors

Professor Ruth Chambers has been a GP for over 20 years. She was the co-chair of the Children's NSF External Working Group (EWG) on the healthy child and young person and is a member of the Children's Taskforce. She is currently a part-time GP, head of the Stoke-on-Trent Teaching Primary Care Trust (PCT) programme and clinical dean at Staffordshire University. She has published widely on healthcare topics including teenage pregnancy and sexual health and other clinical fields.

Dr Kirsty Licence is a specialist registrar in public health who was seconded part-time to the Department of Health (DH) to work on the Children's NSF. Her main role was to gather evidence for interventions across the key topic areas of the NSF that related to the healthy child and young person. Kirsty was a GP before switching to public health in 1998. She has worked on various initiatives during her public health training, in particular prevention of road traffic injuries, services for children and adolescents with mental health problems, local area profiling and health protection.

Contributors

Dr Ruth Bastable is a GP in Cambridgeshire, where she has worked for 25 years. She has always had an interest in children's issues and recently became interested in children in special circumstances. She works with or for GPs, general practices, PCTs, the Area Child Protection Committee, the Eastern Deanery and the Royal College of General Practitioners (RCGP).

Francine Bates is chief executive of Contact a Family. The organisation was set up in 1979 to help families with disabled children. Francine is a member of the Children's Taskforce and was chair of the NSF EWG on disabled children. She is a non-executive director of the Royal Marsden NHS Trust and a long-standing governor of an inner-city school for children with severe learning difficulties.

Dr Helen Bedford is a lecturer and researcher in children's health and Director of Child Health Monitoring at the Institute of Child Health. She has a background in nursing and health visiting. Her main interest is childhood immunisation, particularly the determinants of vaccine uptake. She is a member of the Standing Committee of the Royal College of Paediatrics and Child Health on immunisation and infection. She writes and lectures widely on the subject for audiences of parents and health professionals.

Rob Chambers is employed as an apprentice joiner in industry. He works and socialises with teenagers and young adults from whom he collated insights about teenagers' personal habits and lifestyles and adolescent healthcare, for this book.

Dr Dick Churchill is a practising GP and part-time lecturer in primary care at the University of Nottingham. He has undertaken and published research in the areas of teenage health, teenage pregnancy, glue ear and the management of depression in general practice. He runs a clinical skills centre for undergraduate healthcare students in the medical school and is vice chair of the RCGP Adolescent Task Group.

Mary Crowley MBE is chief executive of the Parenting Education and Support Forum. Before she joined the Forum she was head of the adult education service of the London Borough of Waltham Forest. Mary created and directed the European Socrates *Dialogue* parenting education project with partners in six EU countries. In 2000, she was awarded the MBE for services to parenting education and family learning.

Dr David Elliman is a consultant community paediatrician working at Islington PCT and Great Ormond Street Hospital for Children. He is Chair of the Child Health subgroup of the National Screening Committee and co-editor of the fourth edition of *Health for all Children*. David sat on the healthy child and young person EWG. His main interest is immunisation and he has authored many papers on the subject, a large number in conjunction with Helen Bedford.

Dr Amanda Hampshire qualified as a GP in 1991. For the past 10 years, she has been a lecturer in primary care at the University of Nottingham and worked as a GP. She has been a job-share principal in a suburban practice working with a closely knit primary healthcare team. Mandy's clinical and research interests include child health and she has recently completed her doctorate, based on an evaluation of child health surveillance in primary care.

Dr Caroline Lindsey is a consultant child and adolescent psychiatrist and systemic family therapist at the Tavistock Clinic, London. She has been co-chair of the CAMHS EWG. She was previously chair of the faculty of Child and Adolescent Psychiatry at the Royal College of Psychiatrists. Caroline has a special interest in fostering and adoption and child protection work. She is also involved in training GPs and primary health professionals and specialist registrars in child psychiatry using a systemic/narrative approach.

Professor Margaret Lynch is professor of community paediatrics at Guy's, King's and St Thomas's School of Medicine. She is the designated doctor for child protection for Southwark PCT. Margaret is a member of the Children's Taskforce and co-chair of the EWG on children in special circumstances. She has provided professional advice to the Department of Health as a member of the Climbie Response Team and to the Department of Education and Skills' (DfES) Child Death Screening Groups. Her work on child protection and children's rights has received national and international recognition. Margaret chaired the Royal College of Paediatrics and Child Health's Child Protection Committee until 2003 and continues to chair their advocacy committee.

Dr Ann McPherson is a GP in Oxford and lecturer in the Oxford University Department of Primary Care where she runs a research team looking at patients' experiences of health and illness. These are available on the website www.dipex.org. Ann writes books for teenagers with Dr Aidan Macfarlane, including the best-selling *Teenage Health Freak Series* and the www.teenage-healthfreak.org website. She chairs the RCGP Adolescent Committee, which is dedicated to improving teenager services in primary care.

Miss Heather Mellows has been a consultant obstetrician and gynaecologist at Bassetlaw Hospital since January 1998. She was previously clinical director for maternity and has been postgraduate clinical tutor since 1997. She has been the regional obstetric assessor for the Confidential Enquiry into Maternal Deaths since 1993. Heather has been involved in RCOG affairs for over 10 years and among other positions has been chairman of the Hospital Recognition Committee for three years. She is now junior vice president in charge of home affairs and has particular interests in maternity services as well as the assessment of competence and assisting doctors in difficulty. Heather was co-chair of the *maternity* EWG of the Children's NSF.

Professor Leon Polnay has worked in Nottingham since 1978 and is professor of community paediatrics. He was assistant secretary to the British Paediatric Association from 1990 to 1995 and chair of the British Association for Community Child Health from 1994 to 1998. Leon chaired the National Working Party on Health Needs of School Age Children from 1992 to 1995 and was the workstream lead for Secondary Care Services for the fourth edition of *Health for all Children*. He was one of the first two consultant community paediatricians appointed in the UK and works in the inner-city area of Nottingham. He is the author of two textbooks: *Community Paediatrics* and *Manual of Community Paediatrics*.

Meryl Thomas was co-chair of the maternity EWG. She has been a practising midwife for 35 years, holding a variety of posts in midwifery practice, management and education. For 13 years, until its demise in 2002, she was the director of midwifery education, supervision and practice at the English National Board (ENB). Meryl devised and led the development of the National Audit and Annual Report on Visits to Maternity Services across England for the ENB. She led the establishment of midwifery education within the university sector and the development of the new curriculum. Meryl was made an honorary vice president of the Royal College of Midwives in 2000 and was awarded an Honorary MSc by the University of the West of England in 2002.

Marilyn Toft is head of the Schools and Young People's Health Team at the Health Development Agency and co-ordinator of the National Healthy School Standard. She is currently on secondment from Lewisham Education and Community Services, where her role is senior adviser for Personal, Social and Health Education (PSHE), which includes managing a local healthy schools programme, involving a partnership between three local education authorities (LEAs) and local PCTs, as well as leading continuing professional development services for teachers.

Acknowledgements

We are grateful to all those who have participated in the developing work programme of the External Working Groups (EWGs) of the Children's NSF from whom we have derived much of the material for this book. We have included examples of good practice sent into the Children's NSF teams from professionals working in health and social care – users and carers – from around the country.

We should particularly like to acknowledge the contribution of the Department of Health team that worked on the healthy children and young people module, led by Cathy Hamlyn and supported by Ruth Stanier, Geoff Rayment and Jane Rumble. Paul Ennals co-chaired the module, consultation with young people was enthusiastically organised by Jo Butcher and the overall compilation of the NSF was ably led by Claire Phillips.

CHAPTER 1

The Children's National Service Framework and the vision for primary care

Ruth Chambers

The vision of the Children's National Service Framework (NSF)

The Children's NSF sets out a vision and range of national standards for children's and young people's health and social services, outlining what support should be available to children and their parents in managing and preventing a wide range of conditions and problems.[1] (*See* Appendix 1 at the back of the book.) This should drive up the quality of services, promote general health improvement and redress health inequalities.

The Children's NSF emphasises the promotion of evidence-based clinical guidelines and provides examples of good practice for children and young people, whatever their circumstances. The NSF addresses health inequalities – between various groups of children and young people and their parents or carers, in different settings. In addition, exemplars use particular problems to illustrate what the standards mean for children and their families and health, social services and education sectors working together with voluntary organisations and the public themselves. The Department of Health (DH) will publish exemplars and other examples of good practice on related websites and as toolkits, as more material is developed to support the NSF.

Implementing the NSF will require great changes in our attitudes towards children. The NSF is a 10-year direction of travel designed to revolutionise the care of children in England. Some of the changes, such as changes to the law to aid information sharing about risk factors between staff working in different organisations, will need action by the government. Others, such as issues around accountability, will need action to be taken by strategic health authorities (SHAs) and primary care trusts (PCTs) or individual practitioners. The formation of children's trusts will need action on a countrywide basis and not just from those working in the health sector, but also from education and social services. It is important not to be overwhelmed by the scale of these changes; real lasting change will depend on each of us playing our part.

The Children's NSF is the way by which the government's Children's Taskforce will deliver the NHS Plan in England, in respect of the quality of children's services.[2] The overarching aim for the NSF is to enable 'all children and young people to develop healthy lifestyles and to have opportunities to achieve optimum health and wellbeing within the context of high-quality preventive and treatment services if and when they need them. Children and young people should be supported/enabled to have the resilience, capacity and emotional wellbeing that allows them to play, learn, relate to other people and resolve problems in life'.[3] Broadly, the NSF will put children, young people and pregnant women at the centre of their care – building services around their needs.

This NSF is different from the previous disease-based NSFs in that it relates to a large section of the population – children and young people and their families. Health, social care and education sectors and voluntary sector organisations will all be responsible for implementing the NSF, which concerns children and young people from pre-birth to their nineteenth birthday, covering the transition into both adult life and services. PCTs will be instrumental in achieving the standards of the NSF, supported by SHAs. The Children's NSF aims to describe outcomes, what good children's and young people's services look like, leaving practitioners to devise local arrangements to achieve good practice. This will take time though – the NSF is a means to an end and not an end in itself.

The principles upon which the policies and services for children and young people should be based were derived from the Children and Young People's Unit (www.cypu.gov.uk):

- centred on the needs of the young person
- high quality
- family oriented
- equitable and non-discriminatory
- inclusive
- empowering
- results oriented and evidence based
- coherent in design and delivery
- supportive and respectful
- community enhancing.

No one could argue with these ambitions for children's services. Children's services have been ignored for too long. Some question whether these ambitious proposals are realistic and achievable for GPs and their primary healthcare teams without hypothecated funding (that is, funding additional to the core NHS budget). There is little additional funding specific to children's services contained in the quality framework of the new General Medical Services (GMS) contract.[4]

There is a strong emphasis on services being designed around children, young people and their families and their needs. It is expected that PCTs will work with local authorities to develop multiagency preventive services that meet the needs of this sector.

The first part of the NSF was published in advance of the full NSF in 2003, describing three standards for hospital services for children concerning:

1   child-centred hospital services
2   quality and safety of care provided
3   quality of setting and environment.[5]

Strong local leadership and children's champions with the ability and commitment to influence and drive change in partnership with local people (including children and families) are seen as key to the success of implementing the hospital standards.[5]

How the Children's NSF has evolved

The Children's NSF was drawn up in a similar way to the other NSFs, by professionals in the field working with public sector officials to recommend an NSF to government ministers. Eight EWGs composed of over 250 professionals were drawn from across health settings, social services, education and voluntary sectors, including service users and carers and key advocates for children's services. Many of the EWG members worked in practice and were in regular contact with patients or clients as well as having relevant senior or expert roles of some sort. The EWGs focused on: children who require acute or hospital services, maternity, child and adolescent mental health (CAMHS), children with disabilities, children in special circumstances (for instance, looked after children in local authority care), medicines management, the ill child and the healthy child and young person. Each group was supported by teams of experienced staff from the DH and other sectors, who undertook the drafting of documents and compilation of the overarching NSF.

In addition, parallel working groups focused on information, research and development/evidence, workforce and the built environment. These parallel groups considered the practice implications of the draft recommendations in the NSF, such as changes in skill mix or the need for premises and resources in order to improve access arrangements. As the interventions in the NSF became more defined, experts gathered evidence of their effectiveness and undertook an economic analysis.

Proposals in other key documents relating to child and public health were carefully considered and incorporated into the NSF's ongoing development.

There were local and national consultations between professionals from the NSF and the general public, throughout the drafting of the NSF. Consultations were undertaken that involved children and parents from vulnerable groups and not just those who were relatively easy to access. A primary care advisory group provided a reality check for the application of the evolving NSF in the primary care setting which led to a nationwide consultation. A consultation organised by the Royal College of General Practitioners (RCGP) considered final drafting of the NSF in relation to primary care.

Addressing health inequalities

Promoting health and wellbeing and preventing illness means tackling the root causes of inequalities to enable all children and young people to achieve the best health possible. The main causes of mortality in the adolescent age group are accidents and self-harm. Injuries, self-harm and other risk-taking behaviour all show marked social class gradients in incidence and prevalence, for example increased risk of injury to child pedestrians and from fires and increased prevalence of smoking with lower social class. Addressing health inequalities requires a multiagency approach. Interventions profiled in the Children's NSF include helping children and young people to manage health-related risks, e.g. from smoking and substance misuse; preventing injuries and accidents; providing healthy settings in schools and other locations used by children and young people.

Box 1.1: Campaign targets second-hand smoking[6]

More than 40% of children and 20% of non-smoking adults are exposed regularly to second-hand smoke. The second phase of a campaign aimed at encouraging parents to give up smoking around their children and raising general awareness about second-hand smoking risks was launched at the end of 2003.

The campaign featured billboards, TV spots and cinema and press adverts with a slogan that appears to be written by a child in crayon: If you smoke, I smoke. It also included the distribution of bibs with the same slogan to all babies born in December 2003 and the promotion of survey results that show the majority of children dislike exposure to second-hand smoking.

Over the last century the risk of dying in infancy has fallen dramatically. In 2002, the infant mortality rate (the number of deaths of children under one year of age per 1000 live births) was 5.3 per 1000 live births in England and Wales. But infant mortality rates are 70% higher in the most deprived areas than the most affluent areas.[7] The wider determinants of health such as income, employment, education and other social and environmental factors such as housing conditions all contribute to the relatively poorer health of children and young people whose families fall into social class 4 or 5 categories. This is why it is important to use the NSF to improve conditions for all children and young people to reduce health inequalities.

There are some practical examples of government initiatives to address inequalities, as with the free fruit initiative described in Box 1.2.

Box 1.2: Free fruit as part of healthy eating in schools

A free fruit drive is part of the government's '5 A DAY' programme, a plan aimed at increasing fruit and vegetable consumption. All children aged 4–6 years old in state schools in England are entitled to a free piece of fruit or vegetable each school day, according to the NHS Plan. This will involve the distribution of about 440 million pieces of fruit and vegetables to over 2 million children in some 18 000 schools across England. The programme has been rolled out across various regions of England with funding of £42 million from the National Lottery.

The government has also set aside £2 million for the new Food and Schools Programme, which will promote healthy-eating tuck shops, vending machines with less sugary products and improved nutritional content in packed lunches.

The aims of increased consumption of fruit and vegetables should be realised in terms of benefits in relation to heart disease and cancer as well as combating obesity.

Support for children and young people, their carers and families

The Children's NSF stresses the extent of good information, education, ongoing support and services that parents and carers need to help them to bring up healthy children. It has put an emphasis on helping hard-to-reach groups of parents and carers.

There has been widespread concern about the health and wellbeing of young people who provide informal care for family or friends with chronic illnesses. Around 114 000 children aged 5–15 years old act as informal carers in the UK. One study estimated that nearly 9000 children provide at least 50 hours of care per week and 18 000 provided at least 20 hours of care per week.[8]

Improving access to primary healthcare

Improving access to healthcare requires a more holistic approach than has been conventionally adopted in the past, concerning basic practice issues applicable to any healthcare environment.

- Assurance of confidentiality.
- Appointment systems.

- Staff training to be more receptive or responsive.
- Resources to address young people's health issues (e.g. free condoms).

Improving access might concern specific initiatives, for example:

- invitations to attend, such as via sixteenth-birthday-card invites to health review clinics
- special services for rural locations to overcome transport difficulties
- health clinics held on school or youth club premises (such as those described in Box 1.3)
- drop-in sessions in GP surgeries.

Box 1.3: Clinic in a box

Clinic in a box is a nurse-led service that was launched in 2000 and operates in 25 youth-friendly venues across North Staffordshire. The service was established to provide sexual health and contraceptive supplies to young people and, in response to requests from young people, has expanded to provide a general health service. Clinic in a box nurses provide information and advice around issues such as diet, relationships, alcohol and drug use, as well as support for safer sex and good sexual health. The teenage pregnancy team in North Staffordshire set up the scheme to reduce the rate of unwanted teenage conceptions in line with national targets.[9]

Improving access should result from better collaboration between public sector organisations (especially health, education, social care and youth services) or groups of general medical practices. For instance, core interventions in the treatment and management of anorexia nervosa, bulimia nervosa and related eating disorders require initial assessment by GPs followed by the coordination of care across primary and secondary care. Good practice is to make a clear agreement about the responsibility for monitoring a patient with, for example, an eating disorder among individual healthcare professionals, which is put in writing and shared with the patient and, where appropriate, his/her family and carers. Good information and support in this case will include education and information on the nature, course and treatment of eating disorders and contact details of self-help and support groups.[10]

Some groups of young people have particular difficulties with access to services associated with issues arising from disability, poverty, ethnicity, being looked after and sexual orientation.

School nursing

School nurses are involved in a wide range of health-promoting and public health activities. A school nurse is a registered nurse who has additional training, skills and knowledge that enable them to work competently with school-age children and young people in a range of settings, including schools. School nurses work in different ways to improve the health of individual schoolchildren and of whole school communities. In some areas school nurses work closely with primary care teams, collaborating over the organisation of GP surgeries held in schools or in relation to drop-in clinics for teenagers held in local GP surgeries. Some school nurses are involved in coordinating local healthy schools programmes (*see* Chapter 7), through school nurse secondments, while others have a more peripheral role.

Some of the work undertaken by school nurses in relation to local healthy schools programmes includes:[11]

- confidential, one-to-one advice for young people, provided in a convenient and acceptable way to support them in managing their own health needs
- contributing insights into the health needs of the school community
- clinical knowledge and expertise that support school staff across themes
- linking schools with primary care – helping PCTs to understand the priorities and language of the education sector; helping schools to understand their contribution to addressing local and national targets
- their working knowledge of the NHS and local services.

Links with the General Medical Services GP contract

Child health surveillance provides the only additional funding for children's services within the quality framework of the new GMS contract.[4] That includes child development checks and follow-up of problems identified. The quality points offered for these indicators are minimal (6 points), compared with the rest of the quality framework. Some other quality indicators are relevant, but not specific, to general practice provision of children's services, such as those relating to organisation, records, information and communicating with patients. Consequently, there is a risk that ensuring high-quality services for children and families will not be an immediate priority for primary healthcare teams.

Medicines management

Children having ready access to safe and effective medicines in formulations that can be easily administered to different age groups is an integral component of the vision of the Children's NSF (*see* Appendix 1).

Those working in primary care should enable parents, young people and children (as appropriate) to take an active role in making decisions about options for treatment and investigation of their condition. To do that they need up-to-date, comprehensive and timely information about the safe and effective use of medicines in children and young people. Risks and benefits of treatment should be discussed, so that parents and children/young people understand what health gains can be achieved by complying with the treatment recommended by the doctor or nurse they are consulting, e.g. in the treatment or self-management of diabetes, epilepsy or asthma.

Effective provision of child and young people's services

The Intercollegiate Working Party on Adolescent Health convened by the Royal College of Paediatrics and Child Health chimes well with the vision for healthcare for adolescents conveyed by the Children's NSF. Recommendations in the Executive Summary[12] state that:

> 'All healthcare providers should plan, support and monitor (child and) adolescent services within GP and other primary care, school-based and secondary care services.
> * These services should enable all (children and) young people to have good information and easy access to services of appropriate quality where consent and confidentiality issues have been resolved.
> * Effective provision requires coordination across different specialties specifically for (children and) young people.
> * Health commissioners should ensure that (children and) young people who are "difficult to reach", such as those in pupil referral units or not in school, receive health services on an equitable basis.
> * Every healthcare organisation should have a policy for and identified professional lead for the provision of services for young people.
> * Good practice guidelines should be followed by all practitioners in relation to (children's and) adolescents' rights and professionals' responsibilities in the areas of consent and confidentiality.'

Links to other government strategies

There are many other national initiatives in health and social care and education that are relevant to improving the quality of children's services. Some are described below, but there are many more such as the Planning and Priorities Framework for 2005–08 which sets out what the NHS and social services need to achieve in order to deliver the national Public Service Agreement targets for 2005–08. Proposals in the Green Paper *Every Child Matters* were carefully considered and incorporated into the NSF's ongoing development.[13]

The national programme for information technology

The national IT programme will improve electronic communication[14] by:

* creating an electronic NHS care records service to improve information sharing relating to patients' records across the NHS (with consent)

- making it easier and faster to book hospital appointments for referrals from primary care
- providing a system for electronic transmission of prescriptions.

Learning together, working together

There are a variety of initiatives to accelerate the priority given to the training and development of the NHS workforce.[15] Trusts are expected to work to develop a learning organisation culture, where investment in staff knowledge and skills is a priority for service development.[16] The NHSU provides a corporate learning resource for the NHS that is already raising the profile of mandatory training, induction, personal development of non-professional staff and health professionals who provide a first contact service.[17] Trusts and SHAs are busy supporting changing workforce programmes and redesigning staff roles to provide more modern services, including those for children and young people.

Standards for better health[18]

The 24 core and 10 developmental standards proposed to cover the entire spectrum of NHS work apply to primary care services. They have been designed to ensure that all healthcare provided under the NHS is to acceptably safe and effective levels. The standards cover seven domains:

- safety
- clinical and cost-effectiveness
- governance
- patient focus
- accessible and responsive care
- care environment and amenities
- public health.

Most of the standards refer to patients in general, that is, all age groups. Children are mentioned specifically in one of the core standards for safety: 'Healthcare organisations (should) comply with national child protection guidance within their own activities and in their dealings with other organisations'.

References

1 Department of Health (2004) *The Children's National Service Framework.* DH, London.
2 Department of Health (2000) *The NHS Plan.* DH, London.
3 Department of Health (2001) *Terms of Reference and Working Methods. National Service Framework for Children. Healthy Children and Young People External Working Group.* DH, London.

4 General Practitioners Committee/The NHS Confederation (2003) *New GMS Contract. Investing in general practice.* British Medical Association, London.

5 Department of Health (2003) *Getting the Right Start: the National Service Framework for Children, Young People and Maternity Services – Standard for Hospital Services.* DH, London.

6 Petersen S and Peto V (2004) *Smoking Statistics 2004.* British Heart Foundation (BHF), London. www.heartstats.org

7 Wanless D (2003) *Securing Good Health for the Whole Population.* Population Health Trends. HMSO, London.

8 Doran T, Drever F and Whitehead M (2003) Health of young and elderly informal carers: analysis of UK census data. *BMJ.* **327**: 1388.

9 www.clinicinabox.co.uk

10 National Institute for Clinical Excellence (NICE) (2004) *Eating Disorders.* Clinical Guideline 9. NICE, London. www.nice.org.uk

11 Jones C and Webster D (2002) *School Nursing. National Healthy School Standard.* Health Development Agency, London.

12 Tripp J (2003) *Bridging the Gaps: health care for adolescents.* Royal College of Paediatrics and Child Health, London.

13 Cm 5860 (2003) *Every Child Matters.* The Stationery Office, London. www.dfes.gov.uk/everychildmatters

14 NHS Information Authority (2004) *makingIThappen. Information about the National Programme for IT.* Reference number 1501. NHS Information Authority, London.

15 Department of Health (2001) *Working Together–Learning Together.* DH, London.

16 Davies HTO and Nutley SM (2000) Developing learning organisations in the new NHS. *BMJ.* **320**: 998–1001.

17 www.nhsu.org.uk

18 Department of Health (2004) *Standards for Better Health. Health Care Standards for Services under the NHS.* DH, London.

CHAPTER 2

Involving children and young people in how healthcare is organised

Ruth Chambers

The impetus to involve children and young people in health policy and initiatives

Consultations with children and young people were undertaken in relation to each of the seven module components of the Children's NSF, as it was put together. In recent years there has been a move to involve children and young people in various national health-related policies and guidelines and initiatives.[1] For instance, the National Children's Bureau (NCB) was funded to work with children and young people in developing the first ever children's version of the drugs strategy and a national seminar on volatile substance misuse. The NCB also runs a young people's involvement and consultation project in teenage pregnancy policy, with a young people's forum and targeted consultations, which have informed the healthy child and young person perspectives in the NSF.

The involvement of children and young people is an integral part of the work of the Commission for Patient and Public Involvement in Health (CPPIH). The Commission or its successor arrangement is expected to ensure that children's and young people's views are represented in local patients' forums and that children are supported so that they are able to be effective members of patients' forums.[2]

Good examples of involving children and young people from social care

Councils around England have spent about £10 million on listening to children programmes and advocacy/children's rights work under the Quality Protects initiative. Box 2.1 conveys some examples of the messages young people give to those who will listen.

Box 2.1: Ten messages from looked after children[3]

- **Listen to me**. Listen to what I say about my care and involve me in my care planning and reviews. Help me get an advocate if I want one and if I make a complaint, don't just write a report – sort it out!
- **Don't bin bag me**. When I move placements my belongings are sometimes bundled into rubbish bags. That makes me feel rubbish! I want to know someone cares enough to pack my things in some proper luggage.
- **Give me a choice**. Give me a choice about my placement and, unless it is an emergency, let me meet my new carers before I move. Things can work out better if we are a good match.
- **Let me keep in touch with my last carer**. If I move, I want the chance to keep in touch with my last placement – with my carer and other young people fostered with me. I also want to stay in touch with my family and friends.
- **Let me sleep over without police checks**. I can't feel normal with my friends if you police-check their families when I stay over. Just use your judgement like any good parent would.
- **Give me a filofax about services**. I need an easy way to find out about services I can use. A filofax all about local services would help me find my way around.
- **Let me help train carers**. I want to help train foster carers so they understand what young people in care really need. And I want the chance to talk to councillors and managers about life in care, to help them make services better for young people.
- **Support me if I am bullied at school**. Being in care can make me a target for bullies. I want my teachers to understand this and support me.
- **Help me meet other young people in care**. Sometimes it's good to meet people who understand my situation and how I feel. Whether I am in foster care or residential care, I would like the chance to join an in-care group so I can meet other young people like me.
- **Understand my cultural needs**. I want my carer to understand if my skin and hair need special care and if I eat different food because of my religion or background.

In social care, the government has created teams of young inspectors to undertake children's services inspections with the SSI. Hertfordshire County Council, for instance, has an interactive package that helps some 500 looked after young people a year prepare for their statutory reviews, making children's participation in their reviews more meaningful.[3]

The Hertfordshire County Council strategy aims to:

- involve young people informally in daily decisions about their lives and more formally, for example in reviews
- consult on how services should develop

- support young people to train and recruit staff
- provide independent advocacy to take up complaints
- ensure looked after children participate in sports, arts, leisure and cultural activities
- provide direct work that young people need and want, such as life-story work or counselling.

In Hertfordshire young people directly influence the policies of the county's social care services and units. The leaving care policy is informed throughout by young people, giving their views as to better accommodation, out of office hours support and healthcare for care leavers. A small group of looked after young people have been trained to take part in the authority's recruitment and selection process. Looked after young people are involved in developing arts, sport and leisure activities.

What is child and young person involvement?

The vision of the Children's and Young People's Unit is for all children and young people to have a fulfilling and enjoyable childhood and adolescence, to achieve their full potential, to be respected, to have their voices heard and to make a positive contribution to the world in which they live. The Unit has developed core principles for young people's participation, which were integral to the Children's NSF as it evolved. The principles state (in brief) that:

- children and young people should be treated honestly
- the contributions of children and young people are proportionate to their age and maturity, are taken seriously and acted upon
- feedback on the impact of children and young people's involvement is timely and clear
- children and young people are not discriminated against or prevented from participating effectively on grounds of race, religion, culture, disability, age, ethnic origin, language or the area in which they live
- departments and agencies take a proactive approach in targeting those facing the greatest barriers to getting involved
- where necessary, support and opportunities for training and development are provided to children and young people so that they can contribute effectively
- relevant information is available to children and young people in good time and in appropriate formats – jargon free, culturally appropriate and accessible.[4]

Involvement is the term that is often used by those in the NHS to imply that some activity happened that brought the public or individuals into contact with those working in the particular healthcare organisation to hear or receive views or information on a particular matter. There may not be true participation – that is, not only being consulted or listened to but also influencing decision making and change. The terms participation, consultation and involvement tend to be used interchangeably in popular parlance in the NHS. But participation encompasses the progressively more participatory stages[5] of:

1 information exchange: we give the public information, they give us information, but we do not negotiate or develop a shared view
2 consultation: the public and patients express their views but the organisation makes decisions about developments
3 support: the public decides what to do and others support them in doing it
4 deciding together: thinking and planning together
5 acting together: putting plans into action together.

For children, non-participatory behaviour may include manipulation by adults or token involvement, while participatory behaviour may be mediated by adult-initiated shared decisions with children or, better still, child-initiated shared decisions with adults.[6] Although it may seem that there is child or young person involvement on paper, those involved may have little influence in reality, as the study reported in Box 2.2 relays.

Box 2.2: Extent of child and young person involvement 'in the real world'[7]

A study in North Staffordshire looked at the extent of young person involvement and youth participation in strategy or delivery of services in various sectors that included education, health, social services, youth services and leisure. Involvement ranged from inviting children's and young people's views, to involvement in decision making, to responsive changes to policies and procedures. The majority of organisations could give at least one example of where they encouraged children and young people to give their views. Around half to two-thirds could cite an example where they involved young people in decision making and about one-third to a half reported that they had made changes to policy or procedures due to involvement. Respondents from the health sector were least likely to involve children and young people in giving their views or in decision making and in making changes to policy or procedures as a result. Only one-fifth of general medical practices, for example, stated that they involved young people in decision making, compared with three-quarters or more of youth clubs, projects and high schools and two-thirds of voluntary groups.

But there seemed to be a gap between professionals' reports and reality. Professionals interviewed in the course of the study reported that they had set up young people's forums, involved young people in management committees and had set up channels of communication so that young people were free to make choices about their club or organisation. But some young people interviewed in the same organisations were unaware of the existence of the kind of youth involvement cited by the professionals. The types of changes that had been made as a result of youth involvement in decision making often concerned relatively trivial matters, such as youth membership of a youth club committee (without decision-making powers) or choosing where to go on a trip. There were no examples of young people having significant impact on decision making or priority setting about the operation of the services or allocation of resources. There was little or no systematic or meaningful involvement of young people in reality.

Ways in which those in primary care can empower young people with patient and public involvement

What individual practitioners can do

You can achieve a great deal by demonstrating a consistently child-friendly manner – as in the dos and don'ts given in Box 2.3. This will encourage the child or young person to become involved in their care, grasp the information you offer and be ready to share decisions with you.

You can act as a champion for child and young person involvement in your practice, team or workplace. Find out more about best practice in how to do involvement by reading up on the methodology[8,9] or attending a workshop or visiting a general practice or social care unit where they do it well, to shadow others or attend a pertinent review meeting, for instance. Talk to the young people who consult you, to get their ideas on how they might be more involved in giving their opinions about your services or advising on changes or educating staff. When asked to comment on draft strategies or reports, ask why children or young people have not been involved in its formulation or the planning.

Box 2.3: Tips on how to be child friendly[10]

'Do:
- smile (or look saddened) as appropriate. Maintain good eye contact. Being calm shows you are in control
- acknowledge and greet the child. Talking to parents or carers first gives the child time and space to relax
- observe, wait, listen (OWL). Careful observation and attentive listening can provide valuable information and improve cooperation

- give simple and clear information. Take time to state your expectations. The enemy of cooperation is hurry
- act out. Imitating with a doll what you want the child to do can be helpful
- giving them choice empowers children: "Do you want me to examine you on mummy's lap or on the bed?"
- play. Adapt yourself to the situation. Children engage better while having fun
- distraction. Talk about their interests, their school, their likes and dislikes, etc. while you examine them. Make use of play therapists, nurses, parents or carers, etc. to play and distract
- children like to hear positive things about themselves. By giving enthusiastic praise you hit the emotional jackpot
- acknowledge the child's feelings. Appreciate his or her struggle with a word, for example, "Mmm", "I see", etc. Congratulate him or her on their effort
- have some quick fixes up your sleeve – give rewards like stickers or superstar certificates, play with a special toy, etc.

Don't:
- stand over a child. Do not use force
- promise things you cannot deliver (Do be truthful.)
- express your frustration (Do avoid blame and criticism.)
- expect the same things at different ages (Do communicate on the child's level.)
- rush with answers. (Do avoid asking too many questions.)'

You can involve children and young people as active partners in making decisions about their healthcare. As children grow in confidence and competence, they will ask their own questions and you should answer them in ways they understand, as in Box 2.3.

What primary care teams can do

Practices could make it clear how they want to interact with patients of any age – for example, can patients email in suggestions or comments about services (to report delays, suggest convenient times, etc.) and if so, how and to whom?

The General Medical Services (GMS) contract encourages patient and public involvement as part of its quality framework.[11] A general medical practice that undertakes an approved patient survey each year will receive 40 quality points and if they have reflected on the results and made changes as a team and involved a patient group or non-executive director of a primary care organisation, they will receive a further 30 points. And points equate to income, to reward the effort and resources expended. So it makes business sense for general medical practices to invest in patient involvement and include children and young people in that involvement programme.

Other primary care practices such as dental, optometry and pharmacy practices can learn from colleagues in general medical practices and explore the extent to which they can mirror their activities with children and young people.

Practices can learn from others who have set up a dedicated teen website as an advice forum (*see* Box 2.4 for an example). Using an electronic medium that young people are used to overcomes one of the barriers to young people accessing healthcare – their lack of transport, especially relevant for practices in rural locations.

Box 2.4: Helping teenagers to access advice[12]

The Teen-Scene forum set up by one practice in Staffordshire is built into part of the surgery website (www.hazeldenehousesurgery.org.uk). It offers the 15% of patients on their practice list who are aged 10–20 years old a means to obtain answers to health concerns in a secure environment. The website is one of a series of measures to cater for young people's needs for healthcare – the practice has tried young persons' clinics and visits to youth clubs.

Teen-Scene contains information on common health issues, links to other websites and the forum. Online questions can be put to the doctor on health-related issues and answers are delivered within 48 hours. Site users enter personal identifying data in such a way that all references to the user are deleted in making replies and a third party could not identify the questioner. A database is being created of teenager-related queries and a bank of answers.

A further step that could be used by practices such as this would be to invite teenagers to contribute comments and suggestions about their services and plans. This interactive approach has been a main feature of the acclaimed national website www.teenagehealthfreak.org, which regularly runs teen surveys and disseminates the information and teen opinions widely.

What primary care trusts can do

Most of all, primary care trusts can encourage a patient and public involvement culture with a child/young person focus. They can provide resources for learning activities and organise educational events in respect of best practice. They can train and support individual patients of all ages to be ready to join and influence policy-making committees or performance management meetings within the PCTs.

PCTs and other trusts should provide accurate information to patients, carers and families about trust services and other health-related issues. They should improve and produce information specifically for children and young people. To do this, they may usefully run focus groups for young people to find out how teenagers would like primary care services to be improved. Teenagers are unlikely to respond in great numbers to a postal survey but one that is completed in school during school hours may have a good response rate.[13] Discussions at a focus group can reveal dissatisfactions with services that would not be revealed by a posted or school-based questionnaire and such qualitative methods are invariably worth the effort of recruiting young people and organising the events.[14]

Trust's Patients Advice and Liaison Groups (PALS) should be accessible to everyone, including children and young people.[15] So PALS should be proactive in approaching children and young people to obtain their views of health services through: email, working through and with others, e.g. youth workers, childcare facilitators, visiting and talking to children and young people, via parents and young people groups or councils or advisory panels (combined patient/child or individual groups) or schools councils (SC) or healthy school partnership models.

Expert Patients programmes are envisaged for teenagers too.[16,17] This would build upon the national initiative relating to chronic disease self-management courses, where a group of people with long-term medical conditions learn to solve their own problems in dealing with the day-to-day emotional and physical impact on their lives of their health condition. Teenagers with long-term medical conditions need information on how to deal with the impact of a chronic condition on their daily life in a suitable language and format likely to facilitate their behaviour change.

References

1 Department of Health (2003) *Listening, Hearing and Responding. Action Plan 2003/04.* DH, London.
2 Department of Health (2003) *Strengthening Accountability.* DH, London.
3 Anon (2003) Listen up! *Choice Protects.* **15**: 6–8. www.dfes.gov.uk/choiceprotects
4 Children and Young People's Unit (2001) *Learning to Listen. Core principles for the involvement of children and young people.* Department for Education and Skills (DfES), London. www.cypu.gov.uk
5 Taylor M (1995) *Unleashing the Potential. Bringing residents to the centre of regeneration.* Joseph Rowntree Foundation, York.
6 DfES (2003) *Involving Children and Young People – where to find out more.* The National Youth Agency, DfES, London.
7 Chambers R, Linnell S and Meah Y (2001) *Good Practice in Young People's Involvement in North Staffordshire.* Staffordshire University, Stoke-on-Trent.
8 Teenage Pregnancy Unit (2001) *A Guide to Involving Young People in Teenage Pregnancy Work.* Teenage Pregnancy Unit, London.

9 Chambers R, Drinkwater C and Boath E (2004) *Involving Patients and the Public. How to do it better.* Radcliffe Medical Press, Oxford.

10 Gada S (2003) Tips on how to be child friendly. *BMJ Careers.* **327**: s126.

11 General Practitioners Committee/The NHS Confederation (2003) *New GMS Contract. Investing in general practice.* British Medical Association, London.

12 McWilliams H and Bishop P (2003) Helping teenagers access advice. *GP.* **22 September**: 49.

13 Burack R (2000) Young teenagers' attitudes towards general practitioners and their provision of sexual healthcare. *Br J Gen Pract.* **50**: 550–4.

14 Jacobson L, Richardson G, Parry-Langdon N *et al.* (2001) How do teenagers and primary healthcare providers view each other? An overview of key themes. *Br J Gen Pract.* **51**: 811–16.

15 Department of Health (2002) *Supporting the Implementation of Patient Advice and Liaison Services.* DH, London.

16 Phillips J (2003) *Developing the Expert Patients Programme for Teenagers.* DH, London.

17 Department of Health (2001) *The Expert Patient: a new approach to chronic disease management for the 21st century.* DH, London.

CHAPTER 3

Getting it right in primary care: creating a child and young person friendly environment

Dick Churchill and Ann McPherson

Introduction

Children and young people are the next generation of health service users. Provision of accessible, safe, confidential and user-friendly services for them will not only help their health needs to be addressed in the short term but also have the potential of enormous gains in the future. Producing a child and young person friendly environment in health settings can be done at minimal cost in terms of money, time and disruption and, at the same time, create great benefits for many of the practice population.

The *Concise Oxford Dictionary* defines an environment as 'the physical surroundings, conditions and circumstances, etc. in which a person lives'. It encompasses both the physical aspects of the built environment as well as all other external influences. It includes factors such as the temporal environment (e.g. when the service is available) and the personal environment (e.g. the characteristics and expressed attitudes of staff).

The NSF Standard for Hospital Services states that 'Care should be provided in an appropriate location and in an environment that is safe and well-suited to the age and stage of development of the child and young person'.[1] This is no less important in primary care and, although this chapter mainly considers general practice premises, the principles described here apply equally to other health and social care settings.

When a person (old *or* young) approaches primary care, they are often unwell or anxious and thus more vulnerable to environmental influences than they might normally be. Children and young people tend to be more sensitive than adults to the cues that they receive from their surroundings. Subtle changes to the environment may therefore have a significant impact that can be used to positive or harmful effect. Children and teenagers can be unforgiving in their opinions and are frequently not willing to give a second chance to anyone or anything.

Confidentiality is the key issue mentioned by young people in surveys as to what they want from their primary healthcare services. Although it is difficult to provide direct evidence of the effects of the environment on clinical outcomes, there is indirect evidence to suggest that teenagers' concerns about embarrassment and confidentiality do actually influence consultation rates about sensitive topics by young people. Teenage conception rates have been shown to be associated with differences in age, gender and skill mix of healthcare professionals in general practices.[2,3]

Primary healthcare settings for children and young people

Traditionally, primary healthcare for children and young people has been provided in health centres and general practices, with some specific functions carried out in the school. These settings can each have characteristics that may hinder or facilitate the process of care.

General practice surgeries are designed for the needs of a wide range of patients of different ages and backgrounds, with different expectations of healthcare and health services. While both the physical setting and staff attitudes are important, it is unlikely that most practices will have scope for significant physical alterations in order to create the ideal child and young person friendly environment, unless they are involved in a new build or major extension. Even if some alterations can be made, the requirements of all service users need to be balanced against each other – for example, what is music to the ears of one group may be a nightmare to others!

Dedicated community-based child health clinics are less common now than in the past, with responsibility for most child health surveillance and immunisation having been transferred to general practice. However, there may be increased interest in developing such facilities now that the new GMS contract allows GPs to opt out of such provision, passing the responsibility to primary care organisations.

Box 3.1: A general practice clinic sited in a school in a rural area

4US is a general practice clinic held in a senior school in rural Herefordshire. It was set up because most young people in the area are dependent on their parents to get them to their registered general practice under normal circumstances. The solution was to bring the practice to the patients, with support from all stakeholders, including parents and school governors. It is jointly run by a GP and practice nurse. It has its own prescribing budget and has been rolled out to two other localities.[4]

There is increasing scope for providing primary healthcare, particularly for teenagers, in a school-based setting (see Box 3.1). This has several potential advantages: there is no need for the young person to travel; the service can be provided at a convenient time; and the surroundings are familiar and designed for young people. To increase the chances of the service being valued by the potential clientele, it must be held in an area with sufficient privacy that pupils cannot be seen to be waiting for it by their peers and the consulting room must be adequately equipped, including space for secure records storage. If suitable on-site facilities cannot be found, then it might be possible to offer similar care from adjacent premises (e.g. youth club, hospital, surgery), providing access is accepted as secure from the school perspective.

Specific clinics for young people outside the school setting have the advantage of being dedicated to the needs of the particular age group and the environment can be designed solely for this purpose. Consultation with potential users is essential to success, so that the location, timing and physical facilities can all be optimised to being young person friendly – as in the example reported in Box 3.2. Currently many such clinics are intended principally to provide sexual health services and there is a danger that teenagers themselves feel stigmatised by being seen attending them. Young people recognise that their personal needs are much broader than health and so the concept should and could be extended to clinics that provide not only a wide range of health services but also advice about housing, jobs, etc.

Box 3.2: Organising healthcare for young people at convenient times

Burnham Medical Centre Clinic was started by the practice nurse.[5] The aim is to give young people in the area ongoing support and education so that they can take responsibility for their healthcare and lifestyle. The clinic is open one evening a week from 6.00pm to 8.00pm and is available to under 20-year-olds, regardless of whether they are registered as a patient. The clinic is staffed by a practice nurse – who is also a counsellor – two GPs and a friendly receptionist.

Out-of-hours care is increasingly being provided away from the traditional general practice setting. Out-of-hours and drop-in centres are being established to deal with urgent problems at these times. Children's illnesses account for a relatively high proportion of out-of-hours consultations and yet there is a danger that the needs of children are forgotten in the design of such facilities. There is a genuine risk that a sense of security and trust engendered in children by a well-designed friendly local general practice could be unduly damaged by a journey to an insensitively designed and organised out-of-hours facility at a time when they have an acute illness and are vulnerable.

An accessible environment

Practical access to any healthcare setting requires a location that can be reached with minimal difficulty by those for whom it is intended. Infants and children are usually brought along by parents or carers. However, with home visits for children being a rarity, false assumptions are often made about the mobility of families under difficult circumstances, such as illness. For example, it is not always easy for a single parent or a parent whose partner is at work to travel on public transport with an ill, miserable young child, together with any siblings. Falling levels of family and peer support exacerbate such difficulties while isolation in rural surroundings and increased centralisation of primary healthcare centres further aggravate the situation.

Similar problems exist for young people wishing to seek health advice on their own and, perhaps, without parental knowledge. Their mobility will often be restricted, not only because of distance and availability (if necessary) of public transport but also by time. In this instance, easy access at certain times of the day is not simply a matter of convenience but more of a necessity. It is unlikely that the young person would be able to negotiate legitimate time off school and availability of appropriately timed surgery appointments outside school hours may be restricted. Practices should consider the needs of such patients, who will rarely have the ability or opportunity to highlight this problem for themselves.

Rapid access is an important feature of services designed for children and young people. Symptoms can develop rapidly among infants and young children and parental concern and anxiety follow suit. Research with teenagers repeatedly demonstrates their perceived need for easily accessible appointments or drop-in sessions. Although 48-hour access has been identified as a convenience target by the government, young people have a particular sense of urgency or immediacy in relation to their health concerns.

Provision of appropriately timed and rapidly accessible services is only effective in meeting healthcare needs if the users are aware of them. Young people, in particular, need clear, accessible and consistent information about availability of services and how to approach them. There are many ways of advertising local health services to young people. Web-based information, specifically designed practice information leaflets and booklets, notices in local libraries and credit-card sized information sheets have all been produced by some general practices for this purpose.

Additional physical aspects of accessibility include the need for convenient access for pushchairs and prams, together with safe storage areas for them. Clearly marked doors and directions reduce embarrassment for young people who may be using the service for the first time and are often acutely aware of other people watching them!

Reception desks and areas are usually designed with the needs of staff in mind, rather than those of users. For children and young people the desk provides a barrier that is sometimes insurmountable, particularly as it may be at a level over their heads! Multilevel reception desks without glass screens or windows are a better option, though the attitude of the staff to all ages of patient is still of primary importance!

A user-friendly environment

An environment that is perceived as friendly by those who use it is one in which an effort has been made to create some familiarity for them, with elements of homeliness and comfort. There is considerable information available about what different user groups want in their practice waiting rooms. For example, parents of infants need access to baby-changing facilities and comfortable privacy when breast-feeding. Younger children respond to interesting toys and books, covering the age range likely to be encountered. Toys need to be in good condition, washable and well maintained. Appropriate magazines for young people include *Sugar*, *Bliss*, *J17*, as well as older titles such as *Elle* and *Cosmopolitan*. Magazines for young men are often overlooked but include some about football (e.g. *Shoot*), computers and computer games. Whatever magazines are available need to be relatively current and in good condition.

Young people prefer surroundings that are modern and bright, with pictures and natural light (although windows should be protected with blinds to avoid young people being seen by passers-by). Carpeted floors are more welcoming and provide a warmer atmosphere (carpet tiles can easily be replaced) and are better for crawling on by toddlers! Seating needs to be comfortable but cleanable. Individual seats are often preferred by teenagers so that they do not have to sit immediately next to someone else. Young people welcome drinks machines in the waiting area but these may present a potential safety hazard to younger children.

Providing music can assist in creating a welcoming environment but this also presents difficulties in view of the range of tastes encountered. However, background sound is recognised as helping to ensure privacy at reception and some young patients have suggested that singing along with the music can have a calming effect. Television provides a useful distraction and, although there is a potential problem of choice, most teenagers are not averse to watching younger children's programmes surreptitiously! Computers and computer games can provide endless entertainment for a range of age groups but have the disadvantages of cost and usually being accessible to only one user at a time.

It is the attitudes of staff themselves that provide the greatest opportunity for creating a welcoming atmosphere. The negative effects engendered by unwelcoming and/or paternalistic reception staff are a repeated theme with young people, who cite this as one reason that they find general practices difficult to access. Young people are sensitive to non-verbal cues. Reception staff are usually the first point of contact and need to provide a friendly welcome and try to make the young patient feel at ease, with a non-judgemental approach and a smile! Staff training is important in this respect and applies equally to clinical and ancillary staff.

A safe environment

Safeguarding is a key theme within the NSF. At a fundamental level, any healthcare environment must be designed to ensure the safety of those using it. Common practical issues concern the position and protection of electrical sockets, the heights of climbable surfaces, the stability of nappy-changing facilities and dangers of closing doors on little fingers. Separate toddler enclosed play areas can often provide the solution to these problems.

Of particular concern for young people is the confidentiality or safety of the information that they provide and revelations that they make. Young people repeatedly report that their major concern when consulting health professionals is that the consultation will remain absolutely confidential. They have difficulty understanding the concept of confidentiality as they are not used to their secrets being kept – either at home or at school! General practices need to have a written statement of confidentiality that all members of the practice team are signed up to and which is advertised in the practice's waiting rooms in youth friendly language (*see* Box 3.3). In an ideal world the concept of confidentiality also extends to not being seen by people who know them while in the waiting room or not being heard making an appointment or talking to a receptionist – however, this is not normally possible within the bounds of most contemporary practice premises, especially in rural areas. A reception area separate from the waiting room is ideal and limiting waiting time between arrival and being seen reduces the risk of being observed.

Box 3.3: Promoting confidentiality

Here to Listen, Not to Tell is a poster, produced by Brook, which promotes the confidentiality message succinctly and clearly and can be displayed, together with details of specific practice policies and further reiterated within the practice leaflet and/or website.[6]

One of the most important factors in promoting confidentiality is ensuring that all staff are aware of the issues involved and are then able to demonstrate that efforts are being made to assure it. Common errors that create concern on the part of young people (and, indeed, all patients) include: staff discussion about patients within earshot of others; lists of names being visible inside reception; and overheard telephone calls, etc.

Box 3.4: The video *Trust* is a useful training aid

Trust is a 10-minute video that can be used for training general practices. It shows four interactions in a surgery and is designed to encourage discussion about confidentiality issues and how to improve primary care services for young people. It is available from the RCGP.[7]

The video *Trust* (*see* Box 3.4) and the *Confidentiality Toolkit* (*see* Box 3.5) are useful resources for training staff about the principles and practice of creating a confidential environment. Once this has been achieved, then it is appropriate to advertise and promote the approach taken.

Box 3.5: The *Confidentiality Toolkit*

This resource pack for training staff clearly explains the issues of confidentiality for teenagers. As well as information, it includes pages that can be copied onto overhead projection (OHP) slides for giving talks, sample confidentiality statements and policies for use in practice and a series of case scenarios to promote discussion. Copies of the *Confidentiality Toolkit* are available free from the DH.[8]

An informative environment

Although waiting should always be kept to a minimum, waiting is a fact of life and can be made more bearable in a number of ways. As well as ensuring that time is spent in some degree of comfort and is entertaining, it can be used constructively by providing appropriate health information. As a minimum, the waiting area can provide pictures of the primary healthcare team – parents can use this to potentially introduce children to the person they will be seeing, while young people can become familiar with other team members and the range of services provided.

Health promotion posters aimed at young people need to be designed for the specific age group. Young people ask for brightly coloured information with large interesting script in language that they can understand. Increasingly, televised, multimedia and web-based health information resources are available to facilitate learning, as in the touch-screen interactive resource described in Box 3.6 or the materials on the websites listed in Box 3.7. Health messages must be tailored to health needs whatever the media, be suitable in design and content and designed for maximum impact, while remaining sensitive to race, culture, gender and disability.

> **Box 3.6:** Barnsley Interactive Teenage Education
>
> This initiative has developed a simple interactive touch-screen computer with a sexual health programme to enable teenagers to make informed choices about risks from their sexual behaviours. It is available from www.medcal.co.uk. Young people were consulted about the content and design of the system, which can be sited in schools and GP surgeries.

Promoting choice: segregation or integration?

Children and teenagers have different environmental needs. It is possible – without any great resource implications – to organise the environment to be more user friendly to some groups without that being at the expense of the needs of others. For example, specific times can be set aside for young people, during which the music, posters and literature set out are geared towards them. (This, of course, does not address their expressed wish for rapid access to services on a drop-in basis at other times.) Another possibility is to have a specific section of the waiting area dedicated to children, young people and their parents.

There is an argument for making some degree of integration of the care of young people into that of older patients, while addressing their specific concerns, because part of the role of adolescence is to develop the abilities to deal with an adult environment. Thus, integrating them into the overall healthcare system, while facilitating their use of it, may be more appropriate in the longer term. For example, methods of facilitating access to primary care include a teenage entry card system, whereby if a young person arrives at reception with the card, then they are seen by the next available health professional and without necessarily having to give their name or any details.

> **Box 3.7:** Websites
>
> Health-related websites designed specifically for teenagers include: www.teenagehealthfreak.org and www.ruthinking.co.uk

Conclusion

Creating an environment suitable for the healthcare of children and young people need not be expensive or complicated, but requires a sensitivity to the needs of the age group, coupled with innovation and imagination. The checklist provided in Box 3.8 can be used as a framework for audit in this area.

Box 3.8: Audit checklist for general medical practices

- Are your setting and opening times accessible for parents of young children and for school-aged teenagers?
- Are your reception arrangements suitable for greeting patients of all ages in a confidential manner?
- Is your waiting area comfortable, well lit, warm and pleasantly decorated?
- Is the environment safe for young children?
- Are there toys, books and magazines in the waiting area suitable for children and young people of all ages?
- Have you a practice policy on confidentiality that specifically recognises the needs of young people?
- Have your staff received training on confidentiality issues and how to communicate with children and young people?
- Have you carried out a survey of parents of younger children, and of older children and young people themselves, about what they think about the surgery and your services?

References

1 Department of Health (2003) *Getting the Right Start: National Service Framework for Children. Standard for Hospital Services.* DH, London.
2 Churchill RD, Allen J, Denman S *et al.* (2000) Do the attitudes and beliefs of young teenagers towards general practice influence actual consultation behaviour? *Br J Gen Pract.* **50**: 953–7.
3 Hippisley-Cox J, Allen J, Pringle M *et al.* (2000) Association between teenage pregnancy rates and the age and sex of general practitioners: cross sectional survey in Trent 1994–7. *BMJ.* **320**: 842–5.
4 Davis M (2004) Workshop at Getting it Right for Teenagers: avoiding teenage pregnancy and promoting sexual health. Staffordshire University, Stoke-on-Trent.
5 McPherson A, Donovan C and Macfarlane A (2003) *Healthcare of Young People – promotion in primary care.* Radcliffe Medical Press, Oxford.
6 Brook (2002) *Here to Listen, Not to Tell.* Poster. Brook, London.
7 Royal College of General Practitioners (RCGP) Adolescent Task Group (2000) *Trust* video. RCGP, London.
8 Royal College of General Practitioners and Brook (2000) *Confidentiality and Young People – Improving Teenagers' Uptake of Sexual and Other Health Advice. A toolkit for general practice, primary care groups and trusts.* RCGP, London.

CHAPTER 4

Referring to others from primary care

Amanda Hampshire and Leon Polnay

Evidence about referrals from primary care

There is little research evidence concerning referral of children and young people from primary care to other services. One UK study found that 8.7% of children aged between 0 and 17 years were referred to consultant specialists each year.[1] This referral rate excluded referrals to accident and emergency departments or non-consultant-led services. The highest referral rates were for possible squints, hernias/hydrocoeles, pharyngitis/tonsillitis and hearing loss. These results illustrate the small proportion of children seen in primary care who are referred to secondary care services, as it is known that about 90% of children are taken to see their GP every year.[2]

A review of the research literature on GP referrals of patients of all ages found that variation in referral rates was largely unexplained.[3] There was no clear consensus on how to determine if referrals were appropriate and no clear link between referral rates and the quality of care in general practice.

Although published research evidence regarding referrals has mainly concentrated on referrals from GPs to hospital doctors, other members of the primary healthcare team, such as nurses and health visitors, also refer children. Children are also referred from primary care to many services other than specialists in secondary care. The principles and issues discussed in this chapter apply to all referrals of children and young people from primary care made by primary healthcare staff.

Principles

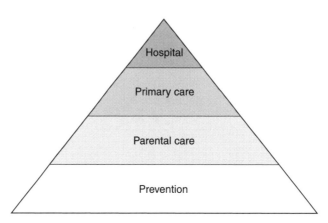

Figure 4.1: Triangle of healthcare

Figure 4.1 represents all children's and young people's illness as the area of a triangle. At the base are problems that are prevented or that parents manage themselves and at the apex are problems managed by secondary care services. In the middle are problems managed in primary care. The relative volumes of each sector will vary widely from practice to practice and are strongly dependent upon the nature of the population served, such as their social class, family structure and nature of support. In an ideal world, prevention is maximised, parents are competent at managing minor self-limiting illness and recognising serious illness and can access healthcare quickly and appropriately.

These principles are restatements of the themes that run through the work streams of the Children's NSF. Whether GPs manage 95% or 97% of paediatric consultations without referral would have little impact on the primary healthcare team, but the extra 2% of referrals would trigger a large impact on secondary care. Likewise, small variations in an individual parent's perceived need for professional advice may lead to large increases in workload for the primary healthcare team on a population basis. Social factors rather than medical necessity underlie these variations.[4–6]

Hospital specialists may have a restricted view of a child and his or her individual family and social circumstances. Their specialist knowledge will be greater and they will have access to resources not available to the primary healthcare team, but a holistic approach demands that there is dialogue between the two and to some extent negotiation of roles and responsibilities beyond the referral letter. GPs will often have had training in hospital paediatrics and hence experience of the specialist setting, but it is rare for specialists to have had experience of primary care, even where posts are part community and part hospital based. This needs to be borne in mind in any discussions around the needs of a family and how they may be met by the joint input of primary and secondary care health services and other agencies.

Managing the centre ground requires knowledge of the population environment and of the range of secondary care services with which the primary healthcare team can work in partnership. Population profiles compiled from routinely collected data[7] are an effective way of increasing such knowledge. Bringing about change is a slow process linked to individual health promotion and support and to national programmes such as the Surestart initiative.[8] Reducing the numbers of admissions deemed to be inappropriate requires agreed clinical guidelines between primary and secondary care, access to fast-track paediatric advice or provision of short-term support for parents at home.

Keeping services centred on the needs of the child or young person

Taking account of the child's views when making a referral

Children's views should be sought, recorded and taken into account when planning their healthcare or treatment, in a way that is appropriate to the age and stage of development of the child. This may not be current practice for many GPs and could require new skills. The younger the child, the greater the challenge may be to involve them in referral decisions. An objective of the Children's NSF is improving the patient's experience of healthcare by providing more information and more choice. Providing and explaining information about treatment and referral options in a way that children and young people can understand will also require new resources, skills and time.

Box 4.1: Scenario 1

An eight-year-old boy has had asthma for four years. He uses beclomethasone and salbutamol inhalers regularly and sees the asthma nurse at your asthma clinic. His inhaler technique seems to be good and you and the practice nurse think he is using his inhalers as prescribed. Over the past six months he has had several acute asthma attacks needing oral prednisolone and nebulisers. These attacks often occur at night and are frightening for him and his family. Increasing his regular dose of inhaled beclomethasone and using a spacer has not prevented further attacks. You are now considering referral to a hospital specialist.

---

vould discuss referral with the child in Scenario 1 in Box
ld's views may lead to difficulties where the child's and
ict such as in Scenario 2 (see Box 4.2). The primary care
ed in such a situation will need to negotiate carefully with
about whether or not to refer. The child's wishes should be
ere is a choice to be made (but see caveat in the following
9

Box 4.2: Scenario 2

A mother brings her 14-year-old daughter to see you. She had surgery in
the second year of her life and this has left her with a keloid scar on one
thigh. The mother wants a referral to hospital. Her daughter appears
content with her appearance, she is bright and confident and does not
want to be referred.

Consent

'Any young person, regardless of age, can independently seek medical advice
and give valid consent to medical treatment. The duty of confidentiality owed
to a person under 16 years is as great as that owed to any other person.'[10]

This statement followed the judgement of the Law Lords in *Gillick* v *West
Norfolk and Wisbech Area Health Authority.* It gave doctors discretion to act
according to their views of what is best in the interests of their young patients.
This concept, also known as *Gillick competence* or *Fraser guidelines*, is that a
child under 16 years old can give valid consent to treatment if they understand
its nature, purpose and hazards. This is a professional judgement for the doctor
to make.[10]

The situation is different where a competent child refuses treatment.
Parents may then give consent against a child's wishes,[11] for example where
a child is at risk of suffering grave and irreversible mental or physical harm
such as refusal of chemotherapy and where the benefits greatly outweigh the
risks. Over the age of 16 years, all children are competent to give or refuse
consent, unless they lack capacity using the same criteria as applied to adults.

Confidentiality

Information held in a child's medical records needs to be included in any
referral letter. Family medical and social history may also need to be shared.
Schools and social services may require medical information. Guidance taken
from codes of practice on confidentiality includes:[12,13]

- information provided in confidence should not be used or disclosed in a form that might identify the patient without his or her consent. This means patient information should be protected, patients informed in full about requests for information and given choices on restriction of disclosure
- medical information must be stored securely
- disclosure of medical information should be on a need-to-know basis.

In practice this means telling the patient, for example, 'I am referring you to Dr X at the hospital, who will need to know about the problems we have discussed today. Is it OK for me to put all this into the letter?'. It also means that requests for medical information from schools or other bodies should not be dealt with by photocopying letters that might contain information that the child or family do not wish to disclose. A new letter that only contains necessary information should be prepared and its content agreed with the child and family, as appropriate.

Children who attend unaccompanied by a parent (or adult with parental responsibility)

Young people may believe that they have to be over 16 years old to be able to see the GP or practice nurse alone, but the majority of GPs and practice nurses are willing to consult with unaccompanied under-16s.[14,15] A common reason for young people attending without a parent is for contraceptive advice and an example of when referral may be necessary would be someone under 16 requesting a termination of pregnancy. The Fraser guidelines regarding consent and confidentiality should be followed.[10] A young girl can be referred for termination without parental knowledge if the GP considers that she understands what is involved and the GP cannot persuade her to inform her parents or allow the GP to inform her parents of the referral.

Transfer of care to adult services

The Children's NSF highlights the importance of the transition from children's services to adult services, especially for young people with chronic medical conditions or mental health problems. This should be a coordinated process with the young person and family involved at all stages. Although secondary care services will change at this time, hopefully the primary healthcare team can provide valuable continuity of care. The GP should consider the needs of the young person and may have to be proactive in initiating transfer of care, by referring the young person to adult services.

Family-orientated care

Involving parents in the referral process

The Children's NSF recommends that parents' (and other carers') views are sought, recorded and taken into account when planning care, which includes referrals. Parents should have more information and more choice. To achieve this vision, primary care staff will need more information and information that is up to date about services that are available. The Children's NSF recognises that a supporting information strategy is key to its successful delivery and includes plans to provide information for children, parents and practitioners. With more information available to patients, e.g. via the Internet, parents may increasingly have knowledge about referral or treatment options that have not been provided by their primary healthcare team. A change of culture may be required within primary care and staff may need to learn new skills, in order to help increasingly well-informed parents make decisions about their children's care.[16]

Referral of families versus individual children

Both the Children's NSF and *Health for all Children*[17] recognise the impact of adult health (mental and physical) on child health.

General practitioners are ideally placed to see the whole picture represented by Tables 4.1 and 4.2, which show two complicated families. In Table 4.1, the parents' problems may be a large factor in the aetiology of the children's difficulties and may present significant barriers to solutions being found.

Table 4.1: A complicated family or a common problem? Example 1 – the G family

Primary healthcare team: GPs, health visitor, district nurse	
Mrs G Agoraphobia, pregnant	**Mr G** Schizophrenia, drinks, unemployed, debts, housing problems
Receiving help from: Obstetrician Midwife Social worker Psychiatrist Community psychiatric nurse Voluntary worker	Receiving help from: Psychiatrist Social worker Alcohol misuse worker Housing aid social worker Welfare rights

Jane, 3 years	**William, 6 years**	**Harry 10 years**	**Charlie 14 years**
Slow development	Enuresis	Slow progress? Attention deficit hyperactivity disorder	Slow progress, hearing problems, offending Secondary school
Family centre	Infant school	Junior school	Receiving help from: Education welfare staff
Receiving help from: Social worker Speech therapist Community paediatrician Child development centre staff	Receiving help from: Education welfare staff School nurse Community paediatrician	Receiving help from: Education welfare staff Educational psychologist Clinical psychologist Community paediatrician School nurse	Educational psychologist ENT surgeon Specialist teacher Hearing aid centre staff Youth offending team

In Table 4.2, the children's problems are biological rather than environmental, but limitations to the parents' parenting capacity will impact on management by the health service and other agencies. The size and complexity of the network are very large in both of these examples, making communication and coordination more difficult.

Table 4.2: A complicated family or a common problem? Example 2 – the *A* family

Primary healthcare team: GP, health visitor			
Mrs A		**Mr A**	
Deaf, speaks no English Severe arthritis, very limited mobility Receiving help from: Hospital rheumatologist Alternative therapies Obstetrician Midwife		A little English, works long hours, no transport	
Baby boy, 3 months	**Parveen, 6 years**	**Salina, 12 years**	**Razia, 15 years**
PKU	Quiet at school, poor English	No problems	Mild cerebral palsy Brachial plexus injury after road traffic accident
	Infant school	Mainstream secondary school	Special school
Receiving help from: Neonatologist Endocrinologist Dietitian Social worker	Receiving help from: School nurse Community paediatrician		Receiving help from: Educational psychologist Community paediatrician Speech therapist Physiotherapist Occupational therapist Connexions staff Alternative therapies

It is a useful exercise to construct diagrams like this for your own patients. How many additional contacts do you discover by doing so? Is everyone in primary care aware of the whole network? A complete professionals involved section is a very useful part of the clinical record and any referral letter. Carrying out this exercise for families or households rather than individuals may be most helpful. A glance at this might prevent children within one family coming under the care of different paediatricians in different hospitals. The gatekeeping role of referrers is as much to protect families from overload as it is to ensure that specialist services are not overwhelmed by referrals.

Adult specialists in secondary care are unlikely to go beyond the immediate clinical needs of their patient, whereas paediatricians, child psychiatrists and social workers may take a broader view which includes all the family. The challenge is that these services often become involved after harm has befallen the child. We should be moving from a management to a prevention culture. A realistic proposal is for adult specialists to work more closely with primary healthcare teams and children's services. Hospital and PCTs should consider together how care pathways for adults can proactively address the impact upon children.

Equitable and non-discriminatory care

Social factors

Tackling health inequalities is a key priority in the Children's NSF, because of the strong correlation between deprivation and indicators of child health, such as infant mortality and accidental deaths.[18] There is evidence that in primary care childhood consultation rates for illnesses increase from social classes 1–2 to social classes 4–5 and decrease for preventive activities.[4] There is also some evidence to suggest that variations in paediatric referral rates from primary care are associated with social class and practice deprivation scores.[5] Children who require referral should be referred appropriately whatever their social class.

Other social factors that are important to consider in the referral process include ethnicity and geography – where families live. If a family is likely to need an interpreter this should be stated in the referral letter. Families whose first language is not English may also need help in understanding letters about appointments, in order to be able to attend at the right time and in the right place. Where families live can influence their ability to attend appointments, especially in more rural areas if they do not have their own transport. Ask about transport when planning a referral.

Children in special circumstances

Children in a range of special circumstances share the common risk of poorer outcomes compared with their peers. Referrals for these groups of children can often be problematic. Frequent moves to different areas may lead to missing medical records and hospital appointments may arrive after a family has moved on to a new address. Housing moves also mean discontinuity of care and the lack of opportunity for families to form working relationships with professionals.

Children who have been the victims of abuse are more likely to be frightened of medical appointments and to have a strong preference for the gender of doctor that they see. They may want to see a doctor without their parent or carer being present, if they wish to discuss concerns related to parents or carers.

Consultations may be difficult, take extra time and some appointments may not be kept. However, failure to appreciate the underlying reasons for this and to take these into account in decisions about referrals can result in adverse effects on the health of these children and young people.

Hospital policies

Hospitals and primary healthcare teams frequently suffer from wasted capacity because of missed appointments. The inverse care law states that those who are least likely to attend are those with the greatest need.[19] The practice of offering a single first appointment to families and discharging them if they do not attend is now common in secondary care. A new referral would then need to be made and the young patient goes back to the bottom of the waiting list. This is not in the best interests of the children and young people most in need. Identifying barriers at the time of referral that will impede the parents or carers from taking the child or young person to the initial appointment can be helpful, e.g. illiteracy, poor personal organisation, many competing demands. Explaining to parents what will happen at the appointment and the absolute necessity to attend is essential. Practical help in getting to the appointment may be needed. On other occasions, direct negotiations with the hospital specialist may be required. Failure to attend appointments when all possible assistance has been given to the parent becomes a child protection or *child-in-need* issue.

High-quality and evidence-based care

One of the key themes of the Children's NSF is the importance of early identification and intervention. This means that when potential problems are identified, children should be referred without delay. The earlier a problem is identified, the greater the potential for preventing complications or disability. Long waiting lists for secondary care services should not act as a deterrent to referral.

Dictating a referral letter is not the end of the story regarding the primary healthcare team's responsibility to the child and family. The referrer should ensure that the referral is sent, copied to the family as appropriate and follow up the outcome. While a child is awaiting a secondary care appointment, primary care staff should continue to keep the child under review in case therapeutic interventions need to be started or conditions change before the family is seen in secondary care. The referrer can then ensure that the referral process does not break down, the family receives an appointment and is subsequently seen in secondary care.

Increasingly there are likely to be local or national guidelines on how referrals for certain conditions are to be made. These should be evidence based and regularly updated. Examples include guidance on referral for atopic eczema, glue ear and recurrent sore throat[20] and guidelines on diarrhoea and otitis media.[21] Keeping up to date with such guidance and having ready access to current information at the time of referral is a major challenge for NHS staff.

There is a risk that ensuring high-quality referrals and follow-up for children and families will not be an immediate priority for primary healthcare teams as the new GMS contract does not offer quality points for referrals.[22]

Integration with other services

Sharing information

While recognising the need to respect confidentiality, sharing information between services is recognised in the Children's NSF as essential to improving the care of children and many services and individuals may be involved in a child's or family's care. Primary care staff may have the most complete picture of the web of people involved. When making a referral, information about others involved in a child's care should be shared, but with consideration of the need for consent, as already discussed.

Communication back to primary care from others

Referral is not a one-way process from primary care to other services. Usually there is communication from those in secondary care back to the referrer about the referral or ongoing care. When the child is discharged back to primary care, hopefully a letter will also be sent outlining the care that has been received and any suggested plans for future management. Although the onus is on those working in secondary care to provide this information, the primary care team need to have an efficient system of ensuring that any communications are seen and acted upon by the most appropriate members of the team. Accurate information sharing between secondary and primary care about the use of medicines in children is especially important to avoid errors being made. GPs may be unfamiliar with particular drugs, their dosage or non-tablet formulations in relation to children and agreed shared protocols can be very helpful. Primary care trusts should work with hospitals to develop protocols that will facilitate the sharing or transfer of care and help to prevent medication errors.

Non-written communications

Telephone or face-to-face contacts can be very helpful when referring patients, especially if the referrer is uncertain about the appropriateness of the referral. Advice can be sought about whom the referral should be made to, the speed with which a child needs to be seen and if it would be beneficial to do any tests or start treatment in primary care. But being able to make contact at a time convenient to the referrer and the other health professionals involved is often not easy. Maintaining up-to-date records of whom to contact and their phone number can also be difficult when staff change or move. Increasingly, general paediatric outpatient work may be done in the community rather than in hospital and this makes face-to-face discussions easier.[23–25] This change in the delivery of care to children and young people could provide a more accessible service for patients and enable more rational and relevant clinical decision making by primary and secondary care staff.[26]

The future

There will be changes in healthcare that will influence the way referrals are made from primary care. It is possible to make electronic bookings of appointments for patients from general practice in some areas. This will become widespread. Full electronic patient records available to primary and secondary care are an objective of the government's information strategy for health.[27] The Children's NSF presents a vision of a more flexible workforce with appropriate training and skills to provide high-quality child-centred care. This may mean fewer referrals being made by doctors to doctors and more children being referred by and to other healthcare professionals.

References

1 Forrest C, Majeed A, Weiner J et al. (2003) Referral of children to specialists in the United States and the United Kingdom. *Arch Pediat Adolesc Med.* **157**: 279–85.
2 Office of Population Censuses and Surveys, Department of Health and Royal College of General Practitioners (1995) *Morbidity Statistics from General Practice 1991–1992.* HMSO, London.
3 O'Donnell C (2000) Variation in GP referral rates: what can we learn from the literature? *Fam Pract.* **17**: 462–71.
4 Saxeena S, Majeed A and Jones M (1999) Socioeconomic differences in childhood consultation rates in general practice in England and Wales: prospective cohort study. *BMJ.* **318**: 642–6.
5 Sturdy P, Pereira F, Hull S et al. (1997) Effect of deprivation on general practitioners' referral rates. Analyses should take age and sex into account. *BMJ.* **315**: 883–4.
6 Jarman B (1983) Identification of underprivileged areas. *BMJ.* **286**: 1705–9.
7 Polnay L (1995) *Health needs of School Age Children.* British Paediatric Association, London.
8 www.surestart.gov.uk
9 HM Government (1991) *The Children Act 1989, Guidance and Regulations.* HMSO, London.
10 British Medical Association, General Medical Services Committee, Health Education Authority et al. (1993) *Confidentiality and People Under 16.* British Medical Association, London.
11 Department of Health (2001) *Reference Guide to Consent for Examination or Treatment.* DH, London.
12 Royal College of General Practitioners and Brook (2000) *Confidentiality and Young People – Improving Teenagers' Uptake of Sexual and Other Health Advice. A toolkit for general practice, primary care groups and trusts.* RCGP, London.
13 Department of Health (2003) *Confidentiality: NHS Code of Practice.* DH, London.

14 Burrack R (2000) Young teenagers' attitudes towards general practitioners and their provision of sexual healthcare. *Br J Gen Pract.* **50**: 550–4.

15 Davies L (2003) Access by the unaccompanied under-16 year old adolescent to general practice without parental consent. *J Fam Plan Rep Health.* **29**: 205–7.

16 Jones R, Hampshire A, Tweddle S *et al.* (2001) The clinician's role in meeting patient information needs: suggested learning outcomes. *Med Educ.* **35**: 565–71.

17 Hall D and Elliman D (2003) *Health for all Children* (4e). Oxford University Press, Oxford.

18 Department of Health (2003) *Getting the Right Start: The National Service Framework for Children, Young People and Maternity Services. Emerging findings.* DH, London.

19 Hart J (1971) The inverse care law. *Lancet.* **1 (7696)**: 405–12.

20 www.nice.org.uk

21 www.rcpch.ac.uk

22 General Practitioners Committee/NHS Confederation (2003) *New GMS Contract. Investing in general practice.* British Medical Association, London.

23 Didcock E and Polnay L (2001) Pioneers, paediatricians and public health: the evolution of community child health services, Clifton, Nottingham 1983–1999. *Public Health.* **115**: 412–17.

24 Royal College of Paediatrics and Child Health (2002) *The Next Ten Years: educating paediatricians for new roles in the 21st century.* RCPCH, London.

25 Royal College of Paediatrics and Child Health (1998) *Ambulatory Paediatric Services in the UK.* Report of a Working Party. RCPCH, London.

26 Spencer N (1993) Consultant paediatric outreach clinics – a practical step to integration. *Arch Dis Child.* **68**: 496–500.

27 Department of Health (2004) *Delivering 21st Century IT Support for the NHS.* National Strategic Programme. DH, London. www.dh.gov.uk/assetRoot/04/07/16/84/04071684.pdf

CHAPTER 5

Working with parents

Mary Crowley

The quality of parenting that children receive has an enormous effect on their lives. We know that: 'The most important influence on a person's level of self-esteem is their parents. Once parents have had their say, little else in life will be able to modify the opinion of self thus formed'.[1]

Poor parenting creates health problems

A Canadian survey interviewed parents of 23 000 children aged under 11 years and concluded that poor parenting practices are strongly associated with relationship and behavioural problems in children.[2] The statistics showed that children who were exposed to hostile or ineffective parenting were nine times more likely to show behavioural problems. Parenting style, much more than income, determines children's behaviour and their academic success in school. Negatively parented children are twice as likely to show delayed development of motor and social skills and three times as likely to be slow in acquiring vocabulary.[2] This was echoed in UK work: 'Parental involvement in the form of interest in the child and manifest in the home as parent–child discussions can have a significant positive effect on children's behaviour and achievement even when the influence of background factors such as social class or family size have been factored out'.[3]

Others have found links between poor parenting and increased frequency of physical disease: 'There is a link between levels of parental caring in childhood and the incidence of major disease such as cancer, heart disease and diabetes in adulthood. Of those who reported high levels of caring in childhood from father and mother, only 25% suffered from a major illness at age 55 years, compared to 87% of those reporting low caring from father and mother'.[4]

The Mental Health Foundation reports a strong link between poor parenting and mental illness,[5] while others link maternal depression in infancy and children's behaviour problems.[6] Authoritarian or neglectful parenting during the preschool period can adversely affect social competence and peer inter-action.[7] A lack of parental discipline, supervision and warmth during early adolescence can lead to antisocial behaviour, delinquency and crime in later adolescence.[8]

What can those working in primary care do?

You should consider the nature of the interaction between health staff and parents and the type of interventions that can be offered to help parents to parent as well as they can.

Parents are the main service providers for children. They are inevitably involved to a greater or lesser extent in all medical interventions, services and information provided to children. Your relationship with parents can have a considerable effect on outcomes for children. If parents are worried about their child, it is harder for them to take in information or think through problems. So make sure that their concerns are addressed and that they understand and support interventions for their children.

Difficulties in accessing NHS services

Parents may not know where to turn for help. It is hard to find good information and advice if you do not speak or read English or are feeling confused or exhausted by a child who has not been well. Parents turn to the family doctor, health visitor, school nurse or reception staff at their doctor's surgery, because they know and trust them. Health staff, who are used to knowing the answers to health problems, can find they are expected to solve parenting issues too. So you need up-to-date knowledge of what parenting help and support is available locally and how to refer parents to it. Parents are more likely to take up such opportunities when suggested by a professional who is known to them. Make sure that the parent knows how to locate the place they are being referred to and, if possible, give them a name to ask for.

Some parents, often from the most vulnerable groups, say that they do not feel listened to. A national study of 1754 parents in poor environments looked at health issues.[9] Half the sample had no one in paid work in the household and the median income was £7000 per annum. Fifty per cent said they were worried about money almost continually. These parents were in considerably worse health than adults in the wider population. Two in five had long-term health problems; two in five were caring for a child with a long-term health problem. Half said they often wished for help. Only one-third had wished for no help or support since they became parents. The main barriers they identified to their use of services were lack of awareness of what is available and lack of access to services. The researchers asked about health centre-based and home visiting services as well as local play and childcare provision and they concluded that 'services don't meet parents' self-defined needs'. In general, they are offered what services providers think they want or should want, rather than what would really be of use. One parent said, 'If health visitors talked to you properly rather than telling me, it would be better'. Services can make parents feel undermined rather than supported. 'They think you don't know anything – that you're stupid.'

NHS staff need to remember that the vast majority of parents, no matter what difficulties they are experiencing, feel the same about their children as staff feel about their own children.[10]

A partnership model is a way of recognising parents as the experts in relation to their own children, working alongside experienced professionals offering them a range of help, when the parents themselves identify what is useful to them.[11] As one survey found: 'Parents want to feel in control; they want input into defining their needs, a sense of agency. . . If you ask for parenting education from professionals, they will start to take over. . . The parents in the survey did not feel confident of confidentiality. . . . "There is nobody you can talk to without feeling they will check you over.". . . Parents said they want services when they need them, that meet their self-defined needs rather than being professionally defined. . . Parents want to be respected, not talked down to or belittled'.[9]

Some groups of parents may find it particularly difficult to access help when they need it. They may be reluctant to draw attention to themselves in case they are perceived as not coping and they fear having their children taken into public care. Children can share these fears and conceal problems to protect their families from outside interference. The worry about the family being separated outweighs the problems they are coping with. Parents at risk of not taking up services can include lone parents, very young parents, parents with mental health problems, gay and lesbian parents or a parent who is in a violent relationship with their partner.

Catering for a mix of parents

The definition of parent is wider than biological parent and includes anyone taking responsibility for bringing up a child: step-parent, foster parent and those working with looked after children for a local authority. All cope with similar challenges and all are keen to do the best job they can for the child in their care.

Any publicity material should use text and pictures that make it clear that services are for all parents. Staff should be careful not to make assumptions about partners or domestic arrangements. Gay and lesbian parents say that they sometimes feel a little tired of advice from well-meaning professionals about the importance of ensuring the children have contact with adults of both sexes, as though they themselves had somehow failed to notice that one sex was absent from their domestic arrangements!

It is admirable that some services now ask mothers whether they have any problems with domestic violence and know where to refer them for help. But if you start such a conversation take care it is private and that the mother's partner is not listening in on the other side of a thin partition.

Step-parents face particular challenges because their role is unscripted by tradition and has to be negotiated with the children. Children can feel that the attention that is devoted to the step-parent by their biological parent rightly belongs to themselves and they may resent the step-parent as a result. The issue of authority can also be difficult in the case of older children. There is sometimes a perception by a step-parent that if they contribute financially, this confers on them the authority of a parent over any children of the household. This assumption can lead to resentment and poor relationships. The biological parent can feel pressure from both sides, be anxious to please everyone and guilty because whatever they do seems likely to upset somebody. Access to local parenting groups for reforming families can be useful in helping to sort out the power dynamics of the joined-up household and in thinking through how to ensure that the child or children develop or maintain positive relationships with all the significant people in their lives. A short cartoon video 'Joined-up families' gives a wise and entertaining look at the issues (www.leedsanimation.demon.co.uk).

The Parenting Education and Support Forum has identified the following qualities as necessary for those who work with parents: antidiscriminatory (including antisectarian), creative, empathetic, enthusiastic, humble, non-judgemental, reflective, respectful and valuing others, self-aware and self-confident, supportive.[12]

Providing parenting support

Despite the overwhelming evidence of the importance of good parenting, most parents receive no training and little support. Health and education providers are sometimes reluctant to offer parenting classes, support groups or other interventions, because they think knowing how to parent should be something that comes naturally. But this is not the case for many parents. For many people, themselves from small families, the first baby they ever hold will be their own. Not everyone is born a good parent. 'What comes naturally reflects the way parents were themselves raised, as well as what is truly natural. So unhelpful parenting practices that have developed over time tend to get handed down from one generation to the next . . . a growing body of research shows that our familiar assumptions about bringing up children are not always correct.'[13]

The range of help that should routinely be available to parents includes: a free 24-hour telephone helpline, home-based one-to-one visits by professionals or trained volunteer befrienders, local drop-in centres, leaflets and videos, parenting groups or classes and web-based sources of help. It is difficult to prescribe who the providers of this help should be because the picture varies so much across the country. In one area, mental health services take the lead; in another, the strategic health authority or local authority adult education service may be the prime provider. This underlines the importance of the multiagency planning proposed in the Green Paper *Every Child Matters* to enable providers and those referring parents at local level to know what is available and where there are gaps in services.[14] There are 62 local parenting forums throughout England, set up to enable those involved in this work to plan and exchange information.

Box 5.1: Local befrienders for parents

Home Start and the Thurrock Community Mothers Programme offer effective help from local volunteer befrienders who are trained to offer help to isolated or hard-pressed mothers of children under five years old.

Tel: 0800 686368; www.home-start.org.uk

Tel: 01375 858512; email: communitymothers@thurrockcouncil100. fsnet.co.uk

---

The 20% most disadvantaged wards in England will have access to Children's Centre services, which are planned and managed by local authorities. The Children's Centre programme is based on the concept that providing integrated education, care, family support and health services is a key factor in determining good outcomes for children and their parents. They offer drop-in centres that can provide information, advice and referral to further local sources of help, without there being a stigma attached to using them. In areas where they are not available, health centres – where expectant parents go for preparation for parenthood – could continue to offer drop-in support to parents of growing children.

Provision of parenting classes falls to different agencies and often struggles to identify secure continuing funding. Some PCTs have committed funding and staff. Tameside and Glossop PCT, for instance, convinced of the value of parenting support, ensures that at least 10 or 12 parenting programmes are available at any one time in their area. These are provided by a variety of agencies in various locations for different target groups.

Box 5.2: Examples of health service investment in parenting initiatives

Cheshire and Merseyside Workforce Confederation has developed three strands of work via the regional parenting education development officer by: creating a model parenting resource; providing training for practitioners; working with local universities to develop accreditation for training to work with parents (nina.taylor@stockport-tr.nwest.nhs.uk).

North East Derby PCT provides 'Living with Children' and 'Living with Teenagers' programmes for the parents in their area (cath.bedford@ nederbypct.nhs.uk).

Surrey Children's Service set out its long-standing commitment to provision of free parenting education in its parenting support strategy. It works in partnership with the local college of further education to organise training for practitioners. It is currently developing a quality framework (www.surrey-camhs.org.uk).

In Cheshire the lead agency in provision for parents is the LEA adult education service. It links the provision of parenting courses to its extensive programme of family learning, where parents and children learn together and provides a route into continuing education and training for parents.

In Cornwall, provision for parents of all ages of children is led by a voluntary organisation, Promoting Effective Parenting (www.pep-uk.org), which offers one-day workshops in schools throughout the county followed by longer courses. Like all voluntary sector organisations, there is uncertain funding and a struggle to survive.

The five different models of provision described in Box 5.2 have the advantage that they are offered to all parents and there is no suggestion that bad or inadequate parents are being targeted.

There is often a feeling on the part of practitioners that parents do not want this kind of help. This assumption is false. In 1999, a survey was carried out by the Department of Public Health of the University of Oxford, which mailed 1155 families from three general practices in Oxford with children from an age range of 2–8 years old.[15] There was a 70% response rate. Fifty-six per cent of parents said that they were interested in, or might be interested in, attending parenting education programmes. Those who were most interested in attending had children who scored high on the behaviour concern scale. Seventy-two per cent in the clinical concern range expressed an interest in attending. There was no social class difference in those interested or not interested in attending. It is well worth offering this type of education. Where parents of young offenders have been sentenced to attend parenting classes as part of a parenting order, in practically all cases they say 'Why did I not get these classes before? I have been asking for help for years'. Over 90% would recommend classes to their friends.

The earlier parents can access help and support, the better. A good time to offer help is during pregnancy. There is a greater readiness on the part of parents, both fathers and mothers-to-be, to receive guidance. It is an opportunity to normalise parenting support for both parents-to-be. It should include preparation for the emotional aspects of parenthood and for the potential effect of a child on the couple's relationship, as well as the preparation for labour and parentcraft which is normally offered. It is best to separate fathers from mothers for some of the meetings so that fathers can express their worries in an all-fathers' group, in case their female partners feel that they are being unsupportive. PIPPIN (Parents in Partnership: Parent Infant Network), a small national voluntary organisation that works with expectant and new parents and their partners, provides excellent training for work with parents during this transition to parenthood (www.pippin.org.uk).

The father can sometimes feel that he is the forgotten parent, although he really wants to be involved. When health visitors in Andover carried out a small study with fathers, they found deep dissatisfaction with antenatal and postnatal provision.[16] Sixty-seven per cent of fathers said that they would like to improve their parenting skills. The barriers they identified were hours of employment and tiredness. Parenting classes were being held when at least half were unlikely to be able to attend.

There is a lot of work to be done in meeting the needs of parents from minority ethnic communities and those who do not speak English well or at all. Local strategic partnerships could make it a priority to draw up and implement a plan for parenting support that meets the needs of their own local population.

Further opportunities for parenting education need to be provided as children grow up. These should include the targeting of parents of children at specific ages. Normalise provision by linking it to key transition points such as when children start nursery and primary schools and at the transfer to, and end of, secondary school. School nurses could be trained to provide parenting groups, as well as advice and support to parents on health matters concerning their children, including mental health and sex and relationships education issues.

Even where health providers are convinced of the value of parenting classes, they sometimes hesitate to provide them because they do not feel confident that they have the necessary skills and knowledge. Their reluctance is well-founded. It can be quite alarming to take on this task without appropriate training. The Parenting Education & Support Forum core curriculum for the training of staff for work with parents describes the Forum's view of what training is needed (*see* Box 5.3). Practitioners should insist on appropriate training before embarking on this demanding work. The effectiveness of any parenting education will depend upon the quality of the trainers delivering the programme.

Box 5.3: Core curriculum for training people who work with parents as devised by the Parenting Education & Support Forum (www.parenting-forum.org.uk)

- To understand that how we work with and relate to parents is as important as what we do when working with them.
- To be aware of the growth, stability and change in human behaviour between birth and old age.
- To understand the implications of the general, personal, sociocultural, economic and psychological influences that affect both the experience and process of parenting.
- To understand how the relationship between parents and children evolves and to incorporate this understanding appropriately in work with parents.

- To understand the changes in the developmental needs of children and parents that influence the relationship that develops between them from pregnancy and birth, through infancy, toddlerhood, early childhood and middle childhood and to incorporate this understanding appropriately in work with parents.
- To explore ways of enabling parents to feel confident in handling the range of behaviours and activities that contribute to everyday life with children and with pre-adolescents and adolescents and to develop the confidence and skills to apply these in practice.
- To have the awareness, confidence and skills to develop and make the most effective use of group work with parents and to undertake the administrative tasks involved in providing parenting programmes.
- To be aware of the factors that contribute to the effective facilitation of parenting groups and to be able to demonstrate these in the practice of parenting group facilitation.

Work has now started on the development of National Occupational Standards for work with parents. Further information can be obtained from the Parenting Education & Support Forum.

References

1 Emler N (2001) *Self-Esteem: the costs and causes of low self-worth.* Joseph Rowntree Foundation, London.
2 Sheridan M (1998) *National Longitudinal Survey of Children and Youth Cycle 2, 1996–97.* Statistics Canada, Special Surveys Division. www.statcan.ca/Daily/English/981028/d981028.htm
3 Russek LG and Schwartz GE (1997) Perceptions of parental caring predict health status in midlife: a 35-year follow-up of the Harvard Mastery of Stress Study. *Psychosom Med.* **59 (2)**: 144–9.
4 Desforges C and Abouchaar A (2003) *The Impact of Parental Involvement, Parental Support and Family Education on Pupil Achievement and Adjustment: a literature review.* DfES, London.
5 Mental Health Foundation (1999) *Bright Futures: promoting children and young people's mental health.* Mental Health Foundation, London.
6 Murray L, Sinclair D, Cooper P *et al.* (1999) The socioemotional development of 5-year-old children of postnatally depressed mothers. *J Child Psychol Psychiat.* **40 (8)**: 1259–71.
7 Baumrind D (1991) The influence of parenting style on adolescent competence and substance use. *J Early Adolesc.* **11 (1)**: 56–95.
8 Larzelere RE and Patterson GR (1990) Parental management: mediator of the effect of socioeconomic status on early delinquency. *Criminology.* **28 (2)**: 301–23.
9 Ghate D and Hazell N (2002) *Parenting in Poor Environments: stress, support and coping.* Jessica Kingsley Publishers, London.

10 Braun D (2003) Parentline (unpublished personal communication).

11 Davis H, Day C and Bidmead C (2002) *Working in Partnership with Parents: the parent adviser model.* The Psychological Corporation, London.

12 Pye Tait for Parenting Education & Support Forum (2001) *An Occupational and Functional Map of the UK Parenting Education and Support Sector.* National Training Organisation for Community-based Learning and Development, for the Parenting Education & Support Forum, London.

13 Royal College of Paediatrics and Child Health (2002) *Helpful Parenting: report of a joint working party.* RCPCH, London.

14 Cm 5860 (2003) *Every Child Matters.* The Stationery Office, London.

15 Patterson J, Mockford C, Barlow J *et al.* (2000) Need and demand for parenting programmes in general practice. *Arch Dis Child.* **87**: 468–71.

16 Fisher M (2004) Unpublished dissertation. Andover, Hants.

CHAPTER 6

Supporting parenting – the evidence

Kirsty Licence

Introduction

The evidence presented in this section relates to parenting support in the form of information giving or education, provided individually or in groups. Comprehensive support for parenting is much wider than this and encompasses a wide range of social, fiscal and other policies that create a supporting and enabling environment for parents and families, in which the parental role is respected.[1,2] That includes:

- addressing child poverty
- ensuring that families are housed in suitable accommodation, which is not damp or mouldy, provides space for play and for privacy, is safe and allows families access to education, leisure and other community facilities
- supporting parents to take up work and education. Unemployment and poverty are associated with poor housing, homelessness and lack of community facilities and all of these place great strain on parents and families. Provision of good work and employment opportunities for parents with pre-school and other childcare facilities allows them to break out of the poverty trap. In order to support optimal social and emotional development of children, non-parental childcare should provide learning opportunities within secure boundaries and with the opportunity for the child to form attachments
- child-friendly policies in the workplace. Policies for maternal and paternal leave and workplace policies that allow families to spend time together have an important role in improving the quality of parenting that can be provided. This is a particular issue for fathers in Britain, who work the longest hours in Europe.

Background

The impact of parenting style

The quality of the relationship between parent and child is one of the most important determinants of health and development. The effects on a child of parenting style can be positive or negative, either promoting resilience against possible adverse outcomes of a poor social and economic environment or increasing susceptibility to a range of health and social problems.[3] These effects may persist well into adulthood. Most of the available evidence relates to the impact of parenting on mental health, but there is also evidence that a positive parent–child relationship can influence physical health.[1,4–6] Features of positive and negative parenting styles are shown in Box 6.1.

Box 6.1: Features of positive and negative parenting styles[1,3]

Positive parenting style

Warmth
Sensitivity
Attunement
Clear, consistent, age-appropriate
   boundaries
Taking interest in child and their
   activities

Negative parenting style

Intrusiveness
Harsh or inconsistent discipline
Frank abuse or neglect

Parents are one of the most significant influences on a child's self-esteem, which in turn influences the likelihood of a range of psychosocial outcomes, including teenage pregnancy, eating disorders, suicide attempts and employment prospects.[7] Parent–child relationships also appear to predict the way that children relate to others in later life, influencing their ability to form supportive intimate relationships and to contribute to or benefit from social capital.[4,5] Parenting style is partly determined by the way that parents themselves were raised, so that unhelpful parenting practices tend to be passed on from generation to generation.[1]

Access to parenting education and support

The National Family and Parenting Institute (NFPI) has mapped the availability of family services are available in England and Wales.[8] This showed the diversity of services and providers available and revealed a lack of services for certain groups, including:

- families with children over five years of age
- fathers
- ethnic minority groups
- families who refer themselves (open access rather than targeted services)
- families living in rural areas.

A range of parenting support services exist within the statutory and voluntary sectors (*see* Box 6.2). Surveys of parents suggest that many of these services have a low public profile, apart from the mainstream provision of, for example, parentcraft or antenatal classes.[9]

Box 6.2: Examples of currently available services to support parenting

- Antenatal and parentcraft classes for expectant parents
- Homestart services
- Sure Start
- Health visitors
- Early years development and childcare partnerships
- Social services
- Child and adolescent mental health services

Effectiveness of interventions to support parenting

What sort of support do parents want?

Surveys show that parents value family support services and that many would welcome additional support in specific areas.[9-11] Parents from all social backgrounds have been found to be interested in attending parenting groups.[11] The age of the oldest child and existing behaviour problems may be better determinants of the level of interest than social background.[11]

Key issues for parents in the design of support services include:

- the need for universal services that are non-stigmatising and that do not limit access only to parents of children with identified problems[9]
- the need for support services to be empowering and respectful and to enable parents to regain control of family situations[12]
- the need for issues such as childcare and transport to be considered in planning services[9]
- the desirability of involving male parents and how this can be achieved[9,13]
- the value of the support offered by other parents within a group or from a group leader who is also a parent (*see* Box 6.3).[9,12,13]

Box 6.3: A role for non-professionals in supporting parents – the Community Mothers Programme[14,15]

The Community Mothers Programme uses experienced volunteer mothers to support first-time parents in disadvantaged areas. In a randomised controlled trial of a Community Mothers Programme in Ireland, community mothers were identified by a public health nurse. Each of these volunteer experienced mothers offered support to between five and 15 first-time parents in disadvantaged areas through monthly visits until the child reached the age of one. Assessment and training were carried out by a family development nurse. The programme focused on general child development issues, nutrition and healthcare and was designed to develop the skills of parents and improve their self-esteem through:

- drawing out the potential of the parents rather than giving advice or direction
- using a behavioural approach in which parents agree to undertake various tasks
- using cartoon sequences to illustrate different ways of dealing with various child-rearing problems.

The trial found that intervention group children scored better than control group children in terms of immunisation status, cognitive stimulation and nutrition. Intervention group mothers scored better in terms of nutrition and morale. Seventy-six of the original group of 232 families were re-assessed seven years after the end of the programme. The main findings were:

- there were no significant differences between the groups in terms of immunisation status, but a tendency for subsequent children of intervention group parents to be more fully vaccinated than subsequent children of control parents
- intervention group children and mothers tended to have more appropriate intake of all food groups, including fruit and vegetables
- only around one-third of all the parents read to their children. Intervention group children were significantly more likely than controls to visit the library weekly
- intervention group mothers were significantly more likely than controls to check children's homework nightly
- intervention group mothers were significantly more likely than controls to disagree with the statement that 'children should be smacked for persistently bad behaviour'
- when asked what they had learnt from their experience with their first child which would be helpful with subsequent children, intervention group mothers were significantly more likely than controls to mention ways of relating to their child, such as how to play with their child and how to respond to the child's behaviour

- intervention group mothers were more likely than controls to have never suffered from tiredness, headaches, feeling miserable or not wanting to go out
- intervention group mothers were significantly more positive about their role as a mother than were controls
- children in the intervention group were less likely than controls to have attended hospital following an injury, although more likely to have been admitted to hospital due to illness (latter finding probably due to chance).

Conclusions were that:

- the intervention improved several aspects of the parenting provided in the first year of life
- there were benefits to the intervention group children and to their mothers and also for subsequent children
- some benefits of the programme were sustained several years later.

Information needs vary, with some parents saying that they have sufficient information.[16,17] Where information was desired, topics of interest included:

- more information about normal behaviour
- what to expect at different ages
- how to deal with problems with behaviour
- education and schools
- pros and cons of different ways of disciplining
- parenting teenagers.

Much of the research into parenting support has focused on young children, especially the under-fives and this age group has also been the focus of government initiatives such as Sure Start. Surveys of the views of parents show that the first five years are perceived as a difficult time by many parents, but that the adolescent and teenage years are equally, if not more, challenging.[16] In the survey carried out by the NFPI, 14% of parents felt that they needed more information to help them to understand the behaviour of their teenage children and so offer them support through the teenage years, compared with 7% for children between the ages of one and five years.[14]

The model of parenting support developed by the NFPI has received broad support through consultation (see Figure 6.1).[18] It meets most of the needs expressed by parents, such as a range of services allowing support to be tailored to the individual, with universal access to some programmes. Those delivering programmes should receive proper training and parents should be involved in the definition of local need and in the design of programmes.

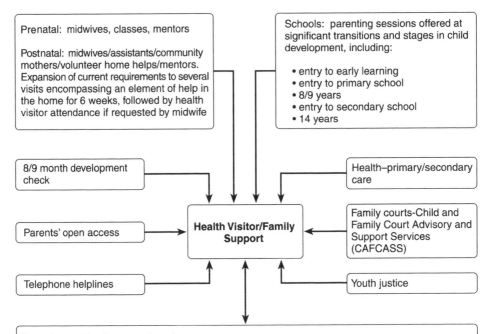

Figure 6.1: Universally available preliminary support to be available to all parents[18]

Acceptability and effectiveness of parenting support programmes

Parents who have taken part in parenting groups report positive outcomes in terms of:[12,13]

*   providing peer support, reassurance and confidence
*   increasing respect for children
*   increased empathy with children and better understanding of what motivates children to behave in certain ways

- regaining a sense of control, through having the opportunity to reflect on parenting issues and being given new tools with which to handle difficult situations.

Several recent studies and systematic reviews have shown that parenting programmes can be effective across a range of outcome measures in different groups.

- In a systematic review of antenatal education classes for childbirth and parenthood, Gagnon[19] identified a single study examining the impact of education on frequency of caesarean delivery and five studies examining more general outcomes. All of the trials examining general outcomes were small (having between 10 and 67 participants) and the interventions, participants and outcomes measured were variable. One trial that included 16 women showed positive outcomes of antenatal education for maternal role preparation and one trial (n = 10) showed greater frequency of maternal attachment behaviours when antenatal classes included a specific element of maternal attachment preparation. Overall, the size, quality and heterogeneity of the studies meant that no firm conclusions could be drawn.
- A systematic review of randomised controlled trials showed that group-based parenting programmes can reduce levels of maternal depression and anxiety/stress, raise maternal self-esteem and improve relationships with a partner in the short term.[20] There was no evidence that the intervention improved mothers' social support networks. The majority of the included studies involved mothers of children with identified behavioural problems or learning difficulties, including attention deficit hyperactivity disorder (ADHD), conduct disorder and Down's syndrome.
- A systematic review of five randomised or quasi-randomised controlled trials showed a positive short-term impact of group-based parenting programmes on the mental health of 0–3 year olds.[21] Outcomes measured related to emotional and behavioural adjustment (four trials) and sleep patterns (one trial). The generalisability of the findings is uncertain as participants were self-selected or the intervention was targeted to at-risk families or families with children meeting criteria for behavioural problems. All the intervention programmes were behavioural or cognitive-behavioural (including Webster-Stratton[22] and STAR-Stop, Think, Ask, Respond).
- A systematic review of 21 studies, including 18 randomised controlled trials, of training for parents of children aged 3–10 years whose primary problem was conduct disorder showed positive results in terms of the behaviour of the children and parents' perceptions of their children's behaviour.[23] Community-based group parent training programmes were more effective than individual clinic-based programmes for improving behaviour, as well as being more cost-effective and more acceptable to parents. Programmes using a behavioural approach were more effective than other approaches.

- A systematic review of parenting interventions targeting teenage parents found positive results on a range of maternal and child measures.[24] Four randomised controlled trials were included, all of relatively small size (31–127 participants) and with some methodological problems. Statistically significant outcomes were reported for measures of parental knowledge and attitudes, mealtime communication, maternal confidence and identity and mother–child interaction. Large but statistically non-significant benefits were apparent for infant language development. Three of the four interventions were one-to-one education programmes.
- A multicentre controlled trial of a Webster-Stratton based[22] group parenting programme found significant improvements in parenting skills and in child behaviour when provided for parents of children referred to child and adolescent mental health services with antisocial behaviour.[25]
- A randomised controlled trial of a parenting programme delivered by health visitors in a primary care setting found a positive impact on some aspects of child mental health, in particular conduct problems, at immediate and six months follow-up. Participants were selected following a postal survey that included the Eyberg Child Behaviour Inventory. Parents whose children scored above the median for survey respondents on this scale were invited to participate. The benefits were not sustained at 12 months follow-up, possibly because of a need for reinforcement of the skills learned.[26]
- Positive outcomes for parenting style were reported from a systematic review of the effectiveness of home visiting.[27] Almost all the included studies were targeted at disadvantaged families or at families with children identified as being at risk or with known developmental difficulties. The interventions to support parents were varied:
  - education and advice about interacting with the child and about child development
  - education and advice about childcare
  - advice about how best to manage child behaviour problems
  - trying to improve the social support networks of the mothers
  - providing help in the home.

About half the studies reviewed used the HOME (Home Observation for Measurement of the Environment) Inventory as an outcome measure to assess the quality of parenting.[27] This uses six subscales:
  - emotional and verbal responsiveness of the mother
  - avoidance of restriction and punishment
  - organisation of the environment
  - provision of appropriate play materials
  - maternal involvement with the child
  - opportunities for variety in daily routine.

The reviewers combined the results of 10 randomised controlled trials that reported changes in the HOME Inventory scores in a meta-analysis. This showed a highly statistically significant positive effect of the home visiting programmes on the quality of the home environment and on mother–child interactions.

Cost-effectiveness of parenting programmes

A number of American economic studies have shown that parenting support can be highly cost-effective when targeted at disadvantaged families or at the parents of children with special needs. The nature of the parenting support in these evaluations is variable:

- provision of preschool education and home visits by teachers[28,29]
- home visiting to provide guidance on childcare, followed by day-care provision[30]
- training for parents and family therapy where young children have shown aggressive behaviour or begun to act out[30]
- training programmes for disruptive children, their parents and teachers[31]
- prenatal and early infancy support through home visiting by nurses trained in parent education and preschool education for children.[32]

It is difficult to extrapolate from the findings of US studies to the situation in the UK, where health, education and social services provision are different.

Scott *et al.* showed that parenting support groups using the Webster-Stratton programme can be effective in the short term for improving parenting style and reducing antisocial behaviour in selected children in the UK.[25] The programme cost £571 per child to deliver. The same investigators used longitudinal data to analyse the cumulative costs to UK public services of children with antisocial behaviours as they grow into adulthood.[33] By the age of 28 years, those diagnosed with antisocial behaviour disorder at age 10 had incurred public service costs that were 10 times higher than those with no problems at age 10 years and 3.5 times higher than those with conduct disorders.

For less targeted approaches, total costs in research studies outweigh quantifiable benefits, but long-term benefits are often excluded, as are those that are difficult to quantify, such as increased social capital. Hence, it is difficult to comment on the true cost-effectiveness of more universally available parenting support programmes.

Improving access: reaching the hard to reach

Studies have identified a number of techniques for reaching *hard-to-reach* parents, including fathers (*see* Box 6.4), low-income families, those who find educational institutions intimidating, those with access problems and those accommodated in, for example, hostels and prisons.[34] These include:

- establishing strong links in the community and a sustained presence through long-term funding and ongoing recruitment
- consultation with local groups to establish needs and gaps in provision, while avoiding duplication

- using a range of methods to deliver the support programme, e.g. mobile services, distance learning using phone or web, one-to-one help, drop-in facilities, evening provision
- ensuring the availability of transport and childcare
- wide distribution of culturally appropriate information in a variety of formats and languages
- ensuring recruitment materials are readily available and highly visible
- involving the target audience and participants as much as possible, including in the development and delivery of the programme
- contacting those who express an interest in the programme
- evaluation including feedback from participants.

Box 6.4: Engaging with hard-to-reach parents

WILD Young Parents Project

This project runs in Sure Start areas in Cornwall. It provides opportunities for fathers aged 16–25 years to meet and participate in activities such as father and toddler swimming sessions and trips to indoor play areas. The project runs play sessions for fathers and their children, supporting the father–child relationship and improving fathers' knowledge of child development. As well as weekly group sessions, one-to-one support is offered and the worker can act as an advocate for young fathers, if requested. Creche facilities and travel expenses are provided and evening sessions for young fathers-to-be. The project is supported by Health Action Zone grants.

http://www.haznet.org.uk/hazs/hazmap/h_cornwall.asp

What primary care teams can do

The service model proposed by the NFPI[18] puts clear responsibilities on health, education and social services to ensure that a comprehensive range of services is in place. This will require services to work together to assess local needs and to ensure that these needs are met, while avoiding unnecessary duplication. Consideration needs to be given to who should provide support at different stages, for different groups and in what settings. Making parents and professionals aware of available services is also critical to providing a comprehensive and accessible parenting support service.

The Medway Positive Parenting Network aims to achieve these goals and links the parenting support providers with those caring for vulnerable children, providing a joined-up service that will contribute to the 'identification, referral and tracking' procedures for the most vulnerable children and young people (*see* Box 6.5).

To contribute to the development of comprehensive local services, primary care teams can:

- assess the current need for and local provision of, parenting support
- review their provision of antenatal care and parentcraft classes, to ensure that parenting style and ways of coping with common early problems, such as crying and poor sleep patterns, are covered
- ensure that parents are provided with information on available parenting support services at appropriate stages
- evaluate the use of current services by different sectors of their population and use the methods described above to ensure that services are advertised and made accessible to hard-to-reach groups
- ensure that they make training available for staff who wish to develop skills in parenting support
- work with other sectors, for example schools, to provide open-access parenting support at key stages in the lives of children and young people, such as transition to primary and secondary schools and in adolescence
- use their knowledge of events within families that may make additional support desirable, such as illness (including mental illness) or bereavement. Teams may develop ways of providing information to parents and liaising with other relevant agencies which may be able to offer specialist support at such times.

Box 6.5: Medway Positive Parenting Network (Medway PPN)

This Internet-based system brings together local information from a wide range of agencies that can provide support for parents. Statutory and voluntary agencies are represented, including those concerned with health, disability, education, counselling, behaviour, bereavement, careers and recreation. This allows the network to develop values and principles that address parenting across a range of domains, including the home, the community, workplace, etc.

The system provides a database of locally available services and the facility for those accessing the site to ask questions of the professionals represented on the site. Groups represented on the site each update their own information and may use the system for file storage and sharing, polling and survey services and display of pictures and documents. A bookshelf is available for groups, which provides a network-wide parenting library. Groups can select the suite of facilities that best meets their requirements for promotion of their organisation, provision of services and networking with other agencies.

The PPN is designed for use by professionals, as well as by parents themselves. Alongside the public access elements, the PPN project incorporated Medway's integrated children's system for shared client record keeping for children in need. Having assessed a family's needs and completed relevant records with the project software, practitioners in the community can use the network to find information and identify local resources and services to meet the needs. The PPN system provides a second level of professional networking facilities that allows childcare workers to keep in touch, develop services and share files. Registered staff can access confidential areas of the site, which promotes interagency collaboration on casework. This joined-up approach aims to 'connect the parenting community with the practice community' and should help to facilitate identification, referral and tracking of children in need.

Medway PPN was designed as a model for use across the UK. It was supported by a Treasury grant under the 'Invest to Save' initiative. Free Internet access is provided throughout Medway, in local libraries, schools, clinics and other community centres. Medway PPN has proved successful as a pilot model. Every local authority will now be required to have an equivalent information-sharing service that links practitioners with local resources by the end of the year.

www.medwayppn.org

(Additional information has been provided by Harry Harrison, Medway PPN)

Areas for further research

The benefits of parenting support have been widely studied. Because parenting support can be provided in many different ways, involving different groups of participants and using a variety of theoretical approaches, there is a need for further research, in order to refine our understanding, so that we can use it most effectively. Particular areas for further research include:

- comparisons of different approaches to parenting education to determine the most appropriate and effective approaches in different situations and with different groups of parents
- the effectiveness of universal, untargeted parenting support programmes
- the effectiveness of parenting support offered at points of change or transition in a child's life and the best way of delivering such support
- ways of improving access to parenting support, in particular for hard-to-reach groups
- establishing the most effective and desired elements of antenatal education, examining outcomes that include preparation for parenthood, postnatal experiences, including depression and parenting skills.

References

1 Joint Working Party initiated and hosted by the Royal College of Paedia-   P
   trics and Child Health (2002) *Helpful Parenting.* RCPCH, London.

2 Harker L and Kendall L (2003) *An Equal Start – Improving Support During*   D
   Pregnancy and the First Twelve Months. Institute for Public Policy
   Research, London.
   www.ippr.org.uk/research/files/team24/project10/literature%20 review.doc

3 Buchanan A (1999) *What Works for Troubled Children?* Barnardos   D
   Publications, Basildon.

4 Stewart Brown S, Shaw R, Morgan L *et al.* (2002) *The Roots of Social*   A2
   Capital: a systematic review of longitudinal studies linking relationships
   in the home with health and disease. Health Services Research Unit,
   University of Oxford, Oxford.

5 Stewart Brown S, Fletcher L, Wadsworth M *et al.* (2002) *The Roots of Social*   B3
   Capital II. The impact of parent-child relationships on mental and
   physical health in later life: an analysis of data collected in the three
   British national birth cohort studies. Health Services Research Unit,
   University of Oxford, Oxford.

6 Jellinek M, Patel BP and Froehle MC (eds) (2003) *Bright Futures in Practice:*   P
   mental health – volume 1. Practice guide. National Center for Education
   in Maternal and Child Health, Arlington, VA.
   www.brightfutures.org/mentalhealth/index.html

7 Emler N (2001) *The Costs and Causes of Low Self-Esteem.* Joseph   D
   Rowntree Foundation, London.

8 Henricson C, Katz I, Mesie J *et al.* (2001) *National Mapping of Family*   C1
   Services in England and Wales – a consultation document. National
   Family and Parenting Institute, London.

9 Grimshaw R and McGuire C (1998) *Evaluating Parenting Programmes: a*   C1
   study of stakeholders' views. Joseph Rowntree Foundation and National
   Children's Bureau, London.

10 MacDonald G and Williamson E (2002) *An Evaluation of Child and Family*   C2
   Support Services. Joseph Rowntree Foundation, London.

11 Paterson J, Mockford C, Barlow J *et al.* (2002) Need and demand for   C1
   parenting programmes in general practice. *Arch Dis Child.* **87 (6)**: 468–71.

12 Barlow J and Stewart Brown S (2001) Understanding parenting pro-   C1
   grammes: parents' views. *Primary Health Care Res Develop.* **2**: 117–30.

13 Plugge E and Stewart Brown S (2002) *Parents' views of parenting pro-*   C1
   grammes: the family caring trust in South Buckinghamshire. Unpublished.

14 Johnson Z, Howell F and Molly B (1993) Community Mothers Programme: B1
   randomised controlled trial of non-professional intervention in parenting.
   BMJ. **306**: 1449–52.

15 Johnson Z, Molloy B, Scallan E *et al.* (2000) Community Mothers Pro-   B1
   gramme – seven year follow-up of a randomised controlled trial of non-
   professional intervention in parenting. *J Public Health Med.* **22 (3)**: 337–42.

16 National Family and Parenting Institute (2001) *Listening to Parents. Their*   C1
   worries, their solutions. NFPI, London.

17 National Family and Parenting Institute (2001) *Listening to Minority*   C1
   Ethnic Parents. Their worries, their solutions. NFPI, London.

18 Henricson C (2002) *The Future for Family Services in England and Wales:*   U2/P
   consultation responses to the mapping report. NFPI, London.

19 Gagnon AJ (2004) Individual or group-based antenatal education for child-   **A1**
    birth/parenthood. Cochrane review. In: *The Cochrane Library*. Issue 1.
    John Wiley & Sons Ltd, Chichester.

20 Barlow J and Coren E (2004) Parent-training programmes for improving   **A1**
    maternal psychosocial health. Cochrane Review. In: *The Cochrane
    Library*. Issue 1. John Wiley & Sons Ltd, Chichester.

21 Barlow J and Parsons J (2004) Group based parent-training programmes for   **A1**
    improving emotional and behavioural adjustment in 0–3 year old children.
    Cochrane Review in: *The Cochrane Library*. Issue 1. John Wiley & Sons
    Ltd, Chichester.

22 Webster-Stratton C and Hancock L (1998) Training for parents of young   **P**
    children with conduct problems: content, methods and therapeutic pro-
    cesses. In: JM Briesmeister and CE Schaefer (eds) *Handbook of Parent
    Training* (2e). Wiley, New York.

23 Barlow J (1997) *Systematic Review of the Effectiveness of Parent-Training*   **A1**
    Programmes in Improving Behaviour Problems in Children aged 3–10
    Years: a review of the literature on parent-training programmes and child
    behaviour outcome measures. Health Services Research Unit, University
    of Oxford, Oxford.

24 Coren E and Barlow J (2004) Individual and group-based parenting pro-   **A1**
    grammes for improving psychosocial outcomes for teenage parents and
    their children. Cochrane Review. In: *The Cochrane Library*. Issue 1. John
    Wiley & Sons Ltd, Chichester.

25 Scott S, Spender Q, Doolan M *et al.* (2001) Multicentre controlled trial of   **B2**
    parenting groups for antisocial behaviour in clinical practice. *BMJ*. **323**:
    194–9.

26 Stewart Brown S, Patterson J, Mockford C *et al.* (2004) Impact of a general   **B1**
    practice based group parenting programme: quantitative and qualitative
    results from a controlled trial at 12 months. *Arch Dis Child*. **89**: 519–25.

27 Elkan R, Kendrick D, Hewitt M *et al.* (2000) The effectiveness of   **A1**
    domiciliary health visiting: a systematic review of international studies
    and a selective review of the British literature. *Health Technol Assess*. **4**
    (13): 1–339.

28 Schweinhart LJ and Weikart DP (1980) *Young Children Grow Up: the*   **C1**
    effects of the Perry Pre-school Project on youths through age 19. High/
    Scope Educational Research Foundation, Ypsilanti, MI.

29 Barnett WS (1993) Benefit-cost analysis of pre-school education: findings   **CE**
    from a 25 year follow-up. *Am J Orthopsychiat*. **63 (4)**: 500–8.

30 Greenwood PW, Model KE, Rydell CP *et al.* (1998) *Diverting Children*   **D/CE**
    from a Life of Crime. RAND Organisation, Santa Monica, CA.
    www.rand.org/Abstracts

31 Aos S, Phipps P, Barnoski R *et al.* (2001) *The Comparative Costs and*   **CE**
    Benefits of Programmes to Reduce Crime (4e). Washington State Institute
    for Public Policy, Washington.

32 Karoly LA, Greenwood PW, Everingham SS *et al.* (1998) *Investing in Our*   **D/CE**
    Children: what we know and what we don't know about the costs and
    benefits of early childhood interventions. RAND Organisation, Santa
    Monica, CA. www.rand. org/Abstracts

33 Scott S, Knapp M, Henderson J *et al.* (2001) Financial cost of social   **C1**
    exclusion: follow up study of antisocial children into adulthood. *BMJ*.
    323: 191–5.

34 Parenting Education and Support Forum (2002) *Reaching 'Hard to Reach'*   **P**
    Parents. PESF, London.

CHAPTER 7

Linking health with education priorities through the National Healthy School Standard (NHSS)

Marilyn Toft

About the NHSS

The National Healthy School Standard (NHSS) has three strategic aims:

1   to reduce health inequalities
2   to promote social inclusion
3   to raise levels of pupil achievement through school improvement.

The NHSS in England is sponsored by the DfES and the DH and is based at the Health Development Agency (HDA). Strategies to support similar work exist in Wales, Scotland and Northern Ireland.

The programme was launched in England in 1999, after extensive consultation with a wide range of stakeholders, from national strategic leaders through to local practitioners in LEAs and health services, as well as school staff, parents and pupils. Outcomes of the consultation influenced the content of the Healthy School Standard and contributed to consensus, ownership and authority, as well as support for its national implementation. For example, all 150 LEAs and health authorities signed up to achieving the requirements of the NHSS in 1999.[1] The requirements of the NHSS are set out in Box 7.1.

By April 2002, the programme had met its government target, with all LEAs and health partners meeting the requirements of the Standard and achieving national accreditation.[2] The main purpose of the accreditation is to ensure:

• programmes are based in sustainable education and health partnerships
• participation of schools and young people

We are grateful to Colin Noble, national adviser, NHSS and Babs Young, PSHE CPD programme coordinator for community nurses, NHSS who advised on the contents of this chapter.

- quality management of local healthy schools programmes
- programmes are responsive to schools' and local needs, as well as national priorities
- evidence is gathered to demonstrate effectiveness.

Since 1999, funding has been devolved to LEAs through the Standards Fund. This allows them to support the maintenance and development of partnerships between LEAs and PCTs and their delivery of healthy schools programmes within their local communities.

Box 7.1: Requirements of the NHSS

The local healthy schools programme must demonstrate:

Partnership working: at a strategic and operational level

Management: ensure that systems are established to deliver effective services to schools

Work with schools: offering challenge and support while contributing to the whole school education and health improvement.

These requirements are exemplified through sets of standards, which are broken down into components under each section.

School engagement in the programme

School involvement in the programme has been steadily increasing since its inception. In 2003, the NHSS reported that 14 000 schools were participating in a local programme through centrally organised training or related activity that adhered to the principles and practices of the NHSS. Of these schools, 8000 were working at an intensive level, a third of which were schools serving the most disadvantaged communities.[2] These schools and local communities have been identified using free school meal eligibility (FSME) as an indicator. Schools are deemed to be serving highly disadvantaged communities if 20% or more of pupils in the school qualify for free school meals.[3]

Impact of school engagement

Nationally, intensive level has been described as level three. To achieve level three status, schools must demonstrate evidence of impact (*see* Box 7.2) by carrying out supported self-review or audit to reveal strengths, achievements and areas for improvement and development. Reviews usually involve members of the whole school community ranging from the headteacher and senior management team, including governors, through to school staff, pupils and parents/carers. Action planning then follows, highlighting targets, success indicators and sources of support, as well as lead responsibilities and milestones.

Box 7.2: Achieving level three status

Local programmes report that a school has reached level three status when there is a range of evidence of impact under the following criteria:

- social inclusion and health inequalities inform the development and implementation of activities
- the impact of continuing professional development (CPD) on the success of healthy school activities is regularly evaluated and informs programme development
- the school is delivering the requirements of the national curriculum, particularly in relation to sex and relationships education and drug education (including alcohol and tobacco) in line with statutory requirements, non-statutory guidance and NHSS criteria
- pupils' views are reflected in school activities, including those at most risk of being disaffected
- the whole school community is invited to take part in policy development, physical, social and cultural activity and support each others' learning
- the school provides a culture and environment to support the taught PSHE and citizenship curriculum.

Having established nationally accredited local education and health partnerships with a remit to support schools through local healthy schools programmes, the challenge now is to ensure that activities are achieving sufficient impact in schools and their local communities, as well as making a contribution to the three strategic aims of the NHSS. The example given in Box 7.3 could serve as a model of good practice to other areas.

Box 7.3: Making an impact in a primary school

A good example of the impact of the NHSS can be found in the Barnet healthy schools programme. There, targeted work was put into place for primary school-age children experiencing physical coordination difficulties. The intervention was funded by the LEA, the PCT and the Saracens Foundation. It was led by a multiagency working party, including representatives from the education psychology team and Barnet consultant paediatricians and physiotherapy teams. A motor skills programme was developed and targeted at children with specific needs, which promoted physically active lifestyles at home and school.

Current government targets

In 2002–03, new national targets were agreed for the NHSS programme.

- To ensure that all schools serving highly disadvantaged communities (as defined by FSME – a total of approximately 7500 schools) achieve NHSS level three status by March 2006, while retaining the universality of the programme.
- To have a teacher in every secondary school who has successfully achieved PSHE certification, by March 2006.
- To ensure that every secondary school serving a highly disadvantaged community, targeted by the NHSS (approximately 1000 schools in England) and its local communities have access to the knowledge and skills of a community nurse who has successfully achieved PSHE certification, by March 2006.

To achieve school targets, stepped targets have been agreed with all LEAs and PCTs up to March 2006, signed off by the directors of education and public health. Local partnerships are encouraged to identify these targets in their strategic planning – LEAs in their Education Development Plans under the headings of school improvement, inclusion and behaviour and PCTs in Local Delivery Plans under health inequalities and children and young people.[4]

Policy into practice development

The programme is directed at national level through a DH, DfES and HDA sponsorship group. The national team responsible for implementation is the 'Schools and young people's health' team based at the HDA. A team of national advisers, led by the NHSS coordinator, provides support services to local healthy schools programme coordinators, as well as CPD opportunities for teachers and community nurses.

Regional coordinators aligned to government office region (GOR) boundaries provide professional networks for local colleagues, as well as developing strategic partnerships with teenage pregnancy and drug teams, together with public health children's leads, among others.

Since the early stages of its development, the programme has used a tried and tested delivery mechanism that has the potential to provide a package of support to schools and local communities on a range of government priorities and health-related matters.[5]

Given the potential of the NHSS as a delivery mechanism that provides a national framework for local action, the Standard has often been described as the programme of choice to introduce and develop work on health-related matters. These include sex and relationships education (SRE) and drug education, through to healthy eating and physical activity in schools (*see* Box 7.4).

The Standard enables schools to define the starting point based on supported self-review within the context of local needs and circumstances. Local programmes will often draw on the resources of PCTs to define local health needs. For example, knowledge of a relatively high incidence of dental caries among primary schoolchildren in a locality, high levels of childhood obesity or high levels of smoking among teenage girls may be used to inform planning. Data held by the LEA may be used, such as the underachievement of boys at GCSE and poor levels of attendance.[6]

It is important that schools are included in health needs assessments undertaken by primary care professionals and when planning health promotion campaigns and service delivery.

Box 7.4: Specific themes of the NHSS

Each programme supports schools to work on specific themes including:

- personal, social and health education
- citizenship
- sex and relationships education
- drug education including alcohol and tobacco (DATE)
- physical activity
- healthy eating
- safety
- emotional health and wellbeing (including bullying)
- local priorities such as reducing levels of obesity
- school priorities such as raising levels of achievement among boys.

Local healthy schools programme teams manage the interface between government priorities and the development of effective practice in schools with staff, pupils and parents, through the adoption of a holistic whole school approach (*see* Box 7.5). In this important context, the national team ensures that evidence about what works is realised in local practice and schools and that experience from practice informs future activity.

Based on school improvement and what is known about effectiveness in relation to the management of change, schools are encouraged to develop a whole school approach to working effectively on the specific themes.

An example of how one of the specific themes of the NHSS might be addressed through a whole school approach is given in Figure 7.1 on page 71.

Box 7.5: Whole school approach recommended by the NHSS

Elements of this approach include:

- leadership, management and managing change
- policy development, for example in sex and relationships education, drug education
- curriculum planning and resourcing including working with external agencies
- teaching and learning
- school culture and environment
- giving pupils a voice
- provision of pupils' support services
- staff professional development needs, health and welfare
- partnerships with parents/carers and local communities
- assessing, recording and reporting pupils' achievements.

The central aim is to develop a supportive school ethos and a sense of whole school responsibility. The NHSS presents a whole systems approach in the school setting and supports collaborative organisational development, a key factor in achieving school improvement that is sustainable over time.[7]

NHSS support materials include those on staff health and wellbeing, drug education (including alcohol and tobacco), reducing health inequalities and promoting social inclusion. A toolkit for local coordinators assists with school recruitment and retention and encourages local programmes to share good practice and focus on the aims of the NHSS.

To support practice development, partnerships are in place at local level across education and health services through LEAs and PCTs. There are broader professional relationships too, with those working in related government programmes, including:

- teenage pregnancy coordinators
- substance misuse education workers
- neighbourhood renewal leads
- school sport coordinators
- five a day coordinators
- school travel coordinators
- childhood and adolescent mental health teams
- youth offending teams
- Connexions and Sure Start advisers.

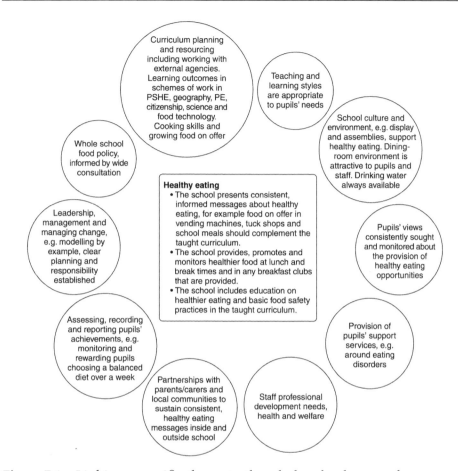

Figure 7.1: Linking a specific theme to the whole school approach

Emerging findings from monitoring and evaluation

There are different types of evidence to show that the NHSS is having an impact and making progress in relation to its strategic objectives of contributing to raising achievement, promoting social inclusion and reducing health inequalities.

The evidence

1   The NHSS has helped LEAs and PCTs to work better together:[8]

'In all the LEAs who are involved with NHSS, it has had a significant and beneficial impact by

- improving co-operative working between LEAs and Health Authorities or health promotion teams
- helping to develop key policies such as drug education, SRE, health, etc.'

2 The NHSS is addressing issues of social inclusion by targeting schools serving more deprived areas:[8,9]

'Recruitment of schools is positively related to eligibility for free school meals, showing that the NHSS is meeting its objective of encouraging schools in deprived communities to participate.'

3 The NHSS is helping to raise achievement:[8]
- 'There are a number of key areas where the NHSS primary and secondary schools are making improvements at a rate faster than schools nationally:

   (i)   behaviour of the pupils
   (ii) standards of work in the classroom
   (iii) quality of PSHE programmes
   (iv) management and support of the pupils.'

- 'Schools working at level three of the Standard (7000 of them) have better results for all Key Stage 1 assessments and Key Stage 2 Science compared with other schools.'[9]
- The headteacher of the most improving school in the country, Blackwell primary school in Derbyshire, emphasised the crucial use of the NHSS whole school approach in the school's work to raise self-esteem and promote the emotional health and wellbeing of the pupils, which in turn has led to better academic standards.

   'You can see the difference if you walk around the school. Children who were once sullen and withdrawn are now engaged, polite and eager to succeed. Introducing circle time, peer buddying and playground improvement, in the whole school fashion advocated by the NHSS, has had a real impact.'[7]

4 The NHSS is effective in addressing health inequalities. A catalogue of case studies (www.wiredforhealth.gov.uk) shows how thousands of schools are putting systems into place that enhance the healthy lifestyles of pupils. One example describes how the Blake High School in Somerset has introduced a very successful project to:

- further develop health education in school
- provide a strategy to improve attendance
- support work already undertaken to reduce pupil exclusion
- have a framework in which to assess the school's progress in health education.

5 The NHSS is effective in introducing and enhancing continuous profes-
   sional development.
   – The PSHE (includes sex and relationships education and drug educa-
     tion) CPD programme for teachers attracted 730 participants from up to
     50 LEAs in 2003–04. Hopefully there will be a teacher who has
     successfully completed the programme in every secondary school by
     March 2006.
   – The PSHE CPD programme for community nurses was piloted in
     2003–04. The national target is for a specialist community nurse to be
     available to every NHSS target secondary school by March 2006.
   – The Diploma in Managing a Healthy Schools Programme, established
     by the University of London, has been taken up by local healthy schools
     programme teams.
6 The NHSS is helping to increase participation. Research undertaken by the
   National Children's Bureau (NCB) has reported increased pupil participation as a result of NHSS involvement. Examples include schools with
   FSME >40%, indicating that the NHSS is effectively addressing social
   inclusion.[10]

Other evidence demonstrates that local healthy schools programmes are
being used to deliver priorities identified in local teenage pregnancy strategies, local substance misuse plans, Neighbourhood Renewal, single regeneration programmes and the Children's Fund through effective partnership
working. The NHSS is being identified as key to delivering priorities within
government strategy documents such as the updated National Drugs Strategy (2002),[11] Health and Neighbourhood Renewal Guidance Document
(2002),[12] Health Inequalities Strategy (2002),[13] National Service Framework
for Children: emerging findings (2003)[14] and the Green Paper *Every Child
Matters* (2003).[15]

The NHSS has provided an effective infrastructure on which to build. The
combination of health professionals working alongside educational experts
bodes well for the future, in terms of securing good physical and emotional
health for children and young people.

What the primary care team can do to support the NHSS

Health professionals have a specific contribution to make to the NHSS. The
emphasis is on empowering children and young people to take responsibility
for their own health. General practitioners and practice nurses, for example,
link into schools by providing support to pupils experiencing particular health
conditions such as asthma, enabling self-management, as well as advising on
use of medicines. Some schools arrange pupil drop-in sessions at local GP
surgeries and visits to sexual health clinics.

Community nurse support is evident through local CAMHS where, as part of a multidisciplinary team, outreach advice and support is offered to children and families in need. Community nurses lead smoking cessation groups for young people and provide babysitting training, as well as sessions on parenting skills.

The NHSS provides the coordinated framework for local action and facilitates access to schools for the school health team in a health education or clinical support role (*see* Box 7.6). Local healthy schools programme coordinators encourage school health teams to be represented on the healthy schools task groups, ensuring that those schools are linked to community and primary care health services.

Box 7.6: Encouraging health links between primary schools and primary care

In Middlesbrough, families were alerted to the dangers of children accessing medicines and dangerous substances in the home, through the primary school/primary care health links project. This encouraged communication about drugs between parent and child at an early age and built confidence and trust in the school nurses involved, alongside primary care health services.

The work was facilitated by the local healthy schools programme, which funded the activity and drew together professional networks by providing joint training for teachers and school nurses, leading parent information sessions and arranging parent/carer and child workshops. An unexpected benefit was the improved involvement of parents and carers in the life of the school generally.

Links are already being developed and strengthened with the Office for Standards in Education (Ofsted), National College for School Leadership, National Primary Strategy, Key Stage Three Strategy, extended schools, PSHE and citizenship and the London Challenge, to maximise strategic influence at all levels.

What PCTs can offer

Primary care trusts bring child health expertise. Health professionals can support schools in the development of PSHE programmes and aid their overall approach to emotional health and wellbeing. They are in a key position to influence the health of the whole school community with a captive audience, able and willing to receive health information and advice. Generally, teachers welcome health professionals working alongside them in the classroom and/or, in some cases, offering more tailored support to groups and individuals – to pupils and their families. On-site health services are now being developed in some schools to respond to community needs, through the government's extended school programme.[16]

Box 7.7: Supporting pregnant teenagers via a local healthy schools programme

Hull has one of the highest rates of unwanted teenage conception in the country. In Kingston upon Hull, the local healthy schools programme involved a schoolgirl mums unit in activities. Involvement in the programme brought about changes in the curriculum offered, evidence of improved self-confidence among the young women and better links with community nurses, including health visitors. All activities were informed by the views of young women themselves. Specific changes that were implemented included: more physical activity, first-aid course, peer education working with pupils in mainstream schools and a well-supported creche.

Many secondary schools and colleges are working more closely with PCTs in developing closer links between school and primary care services, as the example in Box 7.7 shows. The benefits include a teenage-friendly service for young people wanting health advice, as well as education about the NHS and what it has to offer.

Future of the NHSS

External evaluation is being undertaken on the impact of the NHSS. Consultation is also under way on key performance indicators relating to the NHSS level three schools and drug education (including alcohol and tobacco), as well as on the NHSS and engagement of pupil referral units.

The DfES and DH are working together on the development of a healthy school/healthy living action plan. This will focus on taking forward the recommendations of the recent Wanless Report[17] and mainstreaming activities relating to healthy eating, physical activity and sport and travel to school.

References

1 Rivers J, Aggleton O, Chase E *et al.* (2000) *Setting the Standard: research linked to the development of the National Healthy School Standard.* DH/Department for Education and Employment (DfEE), London.
2 Department for Education and Employment (2001) *NHSS Guidance.* DfEE, London.
3 National Healthy School Standard (2003) *NHSS Confirming Healthy School Achievement.* HDA, London.
4 National Healthy School Standard (2002) *Making the Best Use of the NHSS – a guide for PCTs.* HDA, London.
5 National Healthy School Standard (2002) *Reviewing Past Achievements, Sharing Future Plans.* HDA, London.
6 National Healthy School Standard (2003) *Using the NHSS to Raise Boys' Achievement.* HDA, London.
7 National Healthy School Standard (2003) *How the NHSS Contributes to School Improvement.* HDA, London.
8 Office for Standards in Education (Ofsted) (2001) *Her Majesty's Inspectorate (HMI) Review of Local Education Authorities (LEAs) and School Inspection Reports 2000–2001.* Ofsted, London.
9 Scottish Council for Research in Education (2002) *DfES Research Briefing RBX07–02.* DfES, London.
10 Madge N, Franklin A and Willmott N (2003) *NHSS and Participation.* National Children's Bureau, London. Unpublished.
11 Home Office (2002) *National Drugs Strategy.* Home Office, London.
12 Department of Health (2002) *Health and Neighbourhood Renewal Guidance Document.* DH, London.
13 Department of Health (2003) *Tackling Health Inequalities. A programme for action.* DH, London.
14 Department of Health (2003) *National Service Framework for Children: emerging findings.* DH, London.
15 Cm 5860 (2003) *Every Child Matters.* The Stationery Office, London.
16 Thistle S (2003) *Secondary Schools and Sexual Health Services Forging the Links.* PSHE and Citizenship Spotlight series. Sex Education Forum, National Children's Bureau, London.
17 Wanless D (2003) *Securing Good Health for the Whole Population.* Population Health Trends, HMSO, London.

CHAPTER 8

Promoting a healthy diet and physical activity for children and young people – the evidence

Kirsty Licence

Trends in children's diet and levels of physical activity

It is important that children develop healthy attitudes and practices in relation to diet and exercise early in life. This will help them to avoid ill health in childhood and increase the likelihood that these habits will be carried through into adulthood. Unfortunately, there is evidence that children are becoming increasingly sedentary and are consuming a less healthy diet than in the past.[1,2] Although total energy intake in food is falling, people in developed countries and those from richer sectors in less developed countries are consuming more energy-dense, refined carbohydrate foods and drinks, more fatty foods and less fruit and vegetables than in the recent past.[1,3,4]

Recent surveys show that 5–15 year olds currently consume only 12% of the recommended five portions of fruit or vegetables per day.[5] Children in the lowest income households are most likely to consume an unhealthy diet that fails to meet their nutritional needs for healthy growth and develo~~pment~~.[?] Between social classes 1–2 and 4–5 there is a steady r~~ed~~~~uction~~ ~~in~~ fruit and vegetables and an increase in the a~~mount~~ consumed by children aged 2–15 years old. Th~~is~~ a range of factors, including the accessibilit~~y~~ relative cost of healthy food against less he~~althy~~ carbohydrate foods.

The current expert recommendation is that y~~oung~~ in at least one hour of moderate-intensity activi~~ty~~ from a range of activities, including organised ~~sport,~~ cycling and physical education (PE) in school. ~~However, time~~ spent on PE in schools has fallen in recent yea~~rs~~

England provide the lowest level of PE of all European countries. The provision of PE in primary schools has also fallen substantially since the mid-1990s.[7] In addition to formal PE, children's participation in physical activity at break times and after school has decreased and substantially fewer children than 20 years ago now walk or cycle to school, removing any regular daily physical activity from the lives of many youngsters.[7] Children now spend more of their leisure time watching television and playing computer games. Survey data from the United States show that up to a quarter of children aged 8–16 years watch more than four hours of TV each day.[8] Environmental and societal factors that contribute to lower levels of physical activity in childhood include fears about children being injured when walking or cycling or abducted while playing out of doors, combined with poor access to space for active play.

The obesogenic environment in which many young people now live may be epitomised by the fast-food drive-through, where 'a maximum of energy can be obtained with a minimum of exertion'.[9]

Health effects of poor diet and a sedentary lifestyle

A healthy diet and regular physical activity reduce the risk of a range of health problems in children and adults. These include coronary heart disease, certain cancers, hypertension, diabetes, dental caries and gum disease. The effects of poor diet and lack of physical activity are being seen especially in the rapidly rising prevalence of childhood overweight and obesity.

Between 1984 and 1994, the prevalence of overweight among primary schoolboys in the United Kingdom increased from 5.6% to 9.0% and among girls from 9.3% to 13.5%.[10] Over the same time period, obesity in this age group increased in prevalence to 1.7% for boys and 2.6% for girls. The prevalence of obesity increases through childhood. A survey published in 1999 found that, at age 15 years, 31% of children in the UK were overweight and 17% obese.[11]

The prevalence of obesity also rises with increased socioeconomic deprivation.[12] This probably reflects both the poorer diet of these children and the lack of space and facilities for active play in poorer communities. Epidemiological studies in the US have also shown ethnic variations in the prevalence of obesity.[8] This is especially significant when considered alongside the already well-recognised predisposition of some ethnic minority groups towards diabetes, hypertension and coronary heart disease. Genetic factors probably contribute a small amount to the growing international epidemic of childhood obesity.[1,9]

Being overweight or obese puts children at risk of a range of complications, including:[9,12]

- development of risk factors for cardiovascular disease, hypertension, adverse profiles, adverse changes in left ventricular mass, coagulopathy and

hyperinsulinaemia. Type 2 diabetes, with its associated micro- and macro-vascular complications, is being seen increasingly in obese adolescents and older children
- respiratory conditions such as asthma and obstructive sleep apnoea
- musculoskeletal complications
- psychosocial consequences, including poor self-esteem, bullying, depression and disordered eating patterns.

There is debate over the significance of childhood overweight and obesity as a predictor of adult obesity and the associated health risks in adulthood.[13] However, a poor diet and sedentary lifestyle are the main risk factors for adult overweight, so instilling good habits early in life can only be beneficial in terms of adult outcomes.

The consumption of high sugar foods, especially sugary carbonated drinks, is a major risk factor for the development of dental caries and periodontal disease.[14,15] Although oral health has improved over the past few decades, preventable morbidity still persists and there are marked social class inequalities in the experience of dental disease, especially for young children.[16] The National Diet and Nutrition Survey[14] found that, overall, 53% of young people aged 4–18 years had evidence of dental caries (tooth decay) and over one-third of the sample had unhealthy gums. Prevalence of caries was higher in Scotland (66%) and among young people living in the most socioeconomically deprived households.

The majority of young people attend the dentist for regular check-ups and the age at which children first visit the dentist has decreased over the past 10 years.[14] A substantial minority of 4–18 year olds, however, still brush their teeth less than twice per day.[14] This is more common among young people living in households headed by a manual worker, where the parents are in receipt of benefits or where the mother has no formal educational qualifications.

Poor teeth are often considered to be unattractive and may therefore contribute to low self-esteem. Tooth decay may cause pain and sepsis, resulting in antibiotic use, disruption to daily life, time off school and time away from work for parents. In more severe cases and in the long term, poor oral health may lead to social problems through eating restrictions and communication difficulties.

Effectiveness of interventions for improving children's diet and levels of physical activity

General dietary interventions

It is never too early to begin to establish healthy eating patterns. The benefits of breast-feeding are well established and the World Health Organization (WHO) now recommends breast-feeding as the sole source of nutrition for infants up to six months of age.[17] The early introduction of solid foods may lead to inadequate iron intake and the consumption of non-milk extrinsic sugars.[18,19] Children who are breast-fed have a reduced risk of obesity at age 5–6 years, relative to children fed wholly or partially with infant formula.[20] Breast-feeding can be supported through informal discussion groups and peer support programmes, as well as by wider measures to improve breast-feeding facilities in public places and to normalise breast-feeding in the media.[21]

Knowledge about a healthy diet and dietary intentions can be improved for pre-school children through educational programmes. These are most effective when parents are involved as well as children.[22] Behavioural modification programmes that encourage children to try novel healthier foods can be successful when food tasting forms part of the programme. The 'Fun with Food' project incorporates several of these features (*see* Box 8.1).

Box 8.1: Sure Start Dover 'Fun with Food' project[23,24]

'Fun with Food' was a project developed from a 'healthy eating on a budget' model. Eight adults attended each course and it was facilitated by a Sure Start health promotion worker. The core of the project was an eight-week course of two-hour sessions, involving preparation of a meal and then sharing the food among those attending, their children, childcare workers and the facilitator. Other important features of the project were:

- provision of transport for those who needed it
- free creche for those who needed it
- the group planned the menu and the order and division of tasks between themselves
- ingredients were purchased by one participant and the facilitator each week, from a local supermarket used by participants
- leftover ingredients were shared out for participants to take home
- people who participated in the first course were given the opportunity to facilitate a future course
- a reunion was held several weeks after completion of the course. After the first course, participants and their families were invited to a picnic, each bringing food on the theme of 'healthy eating on a budget'.

During the preparation and consumption of the meal, discussion was facilitated around the menu, healthier or cheaper food options and budgeting. Health promotion resources, including information leaflets covering a variety of topics, were distributed during the sessions. At the end of the eight sessions, participants were given a recipe book.

An evaluation of the first and second courses has been carried out by a Sure Start community health development worker. All but one participant in the first two courses felt that they had learnt new cooking skills. Most participants felt that they had learnt a lot about healthy eating and nutrition. Eight out of 13 respondents felt that their knowledge of eating healthily on a budget was improved through the sessions. At the reunions, all participants reported having recreated some of the dishes prepared on the course, at home. Other benefits mentioned by participants included:

- the opportunity to make new friends
- improved confidence with cooking
- parents and children eating together socially
- ideas on how to introduce new foods to children
- the opportunity to learn about other Sure Start services.

Suggested changes to the course included: improved information on budgeting, use of a range of local supermarkets, capitalising on special offers and attempting to increase participation of men.

For older children, there is some evidence that school-based health promotion programmes can be effective in improving diet and levels of physical activity.[25] Within 'Health Promoting Schools' programmes, a range of projects aimed at improving cardiovascular health and oral health have included interventions to improve diet and encourage physical activity (*see* Box 8.2). These programmes usually involve changes in the school ethos and environment, a taught component within the school curriculum. They involve families and the wider community, as well as targeting individual behaviour such as school lunch and snack choices.

Box 8.2: Examples of school-based projects to improve children's diet and physical activity

- Displaying grades on school lunch items, indicating how *healthy* each dish is. Red, amber, green traffic light grading is simple and easy to understand.
- Carrying the healthy eating theme across the curriculum, for example in reading about food in novels and children's stories and learning about what happens to food during its preparation in science lessons.
- Healthy tuck shops and vending machines.
- Increasing the time spent in vigorous activity during PE lessons.

The American Heart Association has issued guidance for health professionals for improving the cardiovascular health of children.[26] This includes advice on ways of improving levels of physical activity and diet and emphasises the importance of addressing these issues in routine health surveillance contacts with children and young people. Although the UK does not have programmes of routine health surveillance for older children and adolescents, a recent study showed some success with a health promotion clinic for adolescents run by a practice nurse (*see* Box 8.3).[27]

Box 8.3: Nurse-run health promotion clinic for adolescents[27]

In a randomised controlled trial of health promotion for teenagers, young people aged 14 or 15 years were invited to attend a 20-minute appointment with a practice nurse. The nurses were trained in consultation skills for the promotion of self-efficacy for behaviour change. The intervention was informed by the views of local teenagers, elicited from surveys and focus groups. Participants in the control and intervention groups were asked to complete a baseline questionnaire. Two-thirds of those who completed the questionnaire felt that they ate unhealthily and 39% took little exercise. Forty-one per cent of those invited for a consultation attended. Three-quarters of these young people indicated at least one health behaviour that they would like to work on – most commonly this was diet (50%) or exercise (36%).

The intervention was successful in encouraging young people to think more positively about improving their diet and level of physical activity at three months after the consultation (positive movement through the stages of change), although the difference was not sustained at 12 months. There were no statistically significant differences between the groups in terms of actual behaviour change, but the intervention group showed more positive change in behaviour patterns in respect of their diet and levels of exercise than the control group did.

The media are important in shaping children's attitudes to diet, exercise and body image. A systematic review of the effects of food promotion to children was commissioned by the Food Standards Agency.[28] It seems that food promotion does have an impact on children's food choices in several ways. The review concluded that:

- there is substantial promotion of food to children, focusing especially on sugary breakfast cereals, soft drinks, confectionery, savoury snacks and fast-food outlets
- the diet depicted in food promotion aimed at children differs markedly from the recommendations for a healthy diet. The healthy diet receives very little promotion
- children enjoy food advertisements
- food advertisements influence children's food preferences, such as snack choices and purchasing behaviour, for example from vending machines
- in some contexts, food promotion affects children's knowledge of the nutritional value of foods, appearing to confuse them about what constitutes healthy products

- in relation to investigating any link between food promotion and obesity, there are confounding factors in most of the research, which make it difficult to draw conclusions.

There is still debate over the best way to reduce the harmful effects of food advertising and use the media to promote a healthier diet.

Interventions for improving the oral health of children and young people

Given the well-recognised association between dietary sugar and dental caries, it is surprising that there have been few good studies evaluating the effectiveness of interventions that aim to reduce dietary sugar intake. Published studies are of limited validity as they have used only behavioural intentions and self-reported behaviour as outcome measures.[16] Dietary recommendations for preschool children have been extrapolated from knowledge of the process of caries development (*see* Box 8.4).[15]

Box 8.4: Improving children's oral health–dietary recommendations for pre-school children[15]

- Avoid frequent consumption of sugar-containing drinks, especially from bottles or sipper cups.
- Children should not sleep with a bottle.
- Offer non-sugary snacks.
- Limit sugary foods to mealtimes.
- Sugary snacks and sweets that are retained in the mouth for long periods are especially harmful and should be restricted, e.g. hard sweets, lollipops.
- Clean sugars from the mouth as soon as possible, preferably by tooth-brushing.

The most effective dietary intervention for improving oral health is the use of fluoride, either in toothpaste[29] or in water.[30] Fluoride supplements used in schools or at home have not proved effective.[31] School-based educational programmes that have included daily brushing with fluoride toothpaste have not been effective.[16] Water fluoridation is the most effective way of delivering the benefits of fluoride to the most deprived children, who are most at risk of tooth decay.

Interventions for reducing childhood obesity

There have been several recent reviews of interventions for the prevention and management of childhood obesity.[12,32–34] All of these comment on the lack of high-quality evidence for the effectiveness of interventions. Particular methodological problems that arise repeatedly are:

- small numbers of participants, leaving studies inadequately powered
- unclear allocation concealment
- blinding of outcome assessments inadequately reported
- inadequate consideration of the potential for contamination between control and intervention groups.

The bulk of the published research has been carried out in the United States and may not be generalisable to UK settings. Most of the interventions studied have been school or family based. In trials of treatment, most participants have been recruited from specialist hospital obesity clinics.[34]

Bearing in mind these weaknesses, several broad conclusions emerge from these reviews.

- Dietary education alone has mixed results in the prevention of obesity.[32]
- Interventions that involve school-based physical activity programmes alone have proved unsuccessful in obesity prevention.[32]
- School-based preventive programmes involving dietary education and a physical activity programme have been more successful, either in improving body mass and adiposity indices or in improving diet.[32]
- Treatment programmes are more successful when physical activity is increased through lifestyle exercise (such as walking, climbing stairs) or reducing sedentary behaviours (especially TV viewing) than when specific exercise programmes are provided.[34]
- Behavioural therapy and relaxation therapy are also effective in treatment programmes.[34]
- Parenting practices, such as close parental monitoring of food intake, restraint or attentiveness to non-eating, can reduce children's ability to self-regulate their eating.[8] Behavioural therapy that involves parents as the agents of change may be more effective than if the child is targeted as the key agent of change. Such programmes may include parent training in child management skills and communication.[33]

Drug treatment of childhood obesity is not considered in any of the published reviews and no drug for the treatment of obesity is currently licensed for use by children in the UK.

The National Audit Office (NAO) review of obesity management in England[1] found that GPs were unsure about the most effective approaches to managing obesity. It concluded that further information was required to guide primary care staff. Similarly, in a review of the management of child and adolescent obesity in the US, the American Academy of Pediatrics found that many health professionals did not feel proficient in some aspects of the management of obese children.[35] In particular, doctors, nurses and dietitians felt that they lacked skills in behavioural counselling and motivational interviewing. Training was also needed in recognising some of the causes and complications of childhood obesity.

A Cochrane review has examined interventions aimed at improving the management of obesity by health professionals.[36] Although many of the studies included in the review had methodological problems, interventions that showed promise included:

- the use of reminder systems to prompt dietary or other advice
- training interventions for professionals to improve the quality of behavioural advice given to obese patients
- shared care between GP and hospital
- inpatient care
- dietitian-led management.

While giving appropriate publicity and priority to the problem of childhood overweight and obesity, extreme dieting behaviour and other eating disorders should not be forgotten. The international prevalence of anorexia nervosa among women in late adolescence and young adulthood is 0.5% to 1% and the prevalence of bulimia nervosa in this population is 1% to 3%.[37] In an Australian study, up to one-third of subjects had used some extreme form of weight control at some time in their lives.[38] Although no adverse effects in terms of the prevalence of eating disorders have been reported from trials of interventions to prevent or treat obesity, the evaluation of such interventions should include an assessment of their impact on dieting behaviour and, where appropriate, on the prevalence of eating disorders. Programmes for the treatment and prevention of obesity and those that focus on eating disorders should be complementary and give consistent messages about healthy diet and levels of physical activity.

What primary care teams can do

While there is a need for further research into individual and population-based interventions for childhood obesity, any such intervention is likely to meet with limited success unless steps are taken to reduce the environmental factors that promote poor diet and a sedentary lifestyle and that limit the opportunities for regular physical activity.

A broad holistic approach is required to achieve substantial and lasting changes in the diet and activity patterns of children and young people. The National Heart Forum has set out a range of desirable actions, from public policy measures, through action in schools and communities, to individual changes in its project 'Young at Heart'.[39]

Primary care teams can contribute through a combination of direct actions, supporting the efforts of other agencies and lobbying for effective policy changes at a national level.

Direct actions

- Training should be provided for health professionals to enable them to deliver family-based interventions for the prevention and management of obesity, including parenting interventions.
- In routine consultations or where there is cause for concern about an individual child or family, health professionals should encourage parents to limit the time children and young people spend in sedentary activities such as TV viewing and computer use. Children and young people should be encouraged and supported to incorporate regular sustainable physical activity into their daily routines, for example through walking, cycling, climbing stairs, helping with chores in the home and out of doors.
- Health professionals' interventions with individual children should follow expert guidance (*see* Box 8.5). Particular attention should be given to:
  - measurement of body mass index (BMI) and plotting on appropriate BMI charts
  - family history, food intake, levels of physical activity and time spent in sedentary activities
  - physical examination and any investigations if a congenital syndrome, endocrine disorder or other cause is suspected
  - physical examination for obesity-related morbidity (using suitable cuff size if blood pressure is to be measured)
  - any psychological factors leading to the onset of obesity and psycho-social impact of obesity
  - management should usually aim for weight maintenance to allow natural growth to bring the BMI out of the obese/overweight range. Slow weight loss may be appropriate in older and more severely affected children and adolescents.[40]
- Environmental approaches that have been successful in schools should be tried in other settings, such as clinics and practice waiting rooms. Water and healthy snacks should be provided in health service settings in place of machines vending sweets and fizzy drinks.

Box 8.5: Online guidance for primary care professionals

- An approach to weight management in children and adolescents (2–18 years) in primary care[40] www.rcpch.ac.uk/publications/recent_publications/Approach_2PAGES_TOGETHER.pdf
- Management of obesity in children and young people[12] www.sign.ac.uk
- Evidence-based management of childhood obesity[41] www.bmj.com
- Cardiovascular health in childhood[26] www.circulationaha.org

---

Supporting the efforts of other agencies

- Healthy schools programmes that take a whole environment approach to improving the nutrition of children and young people should be supported. Such approaches could include:
  - action on school meals and availability of healthy drinks, especially water and healthy snacks
  - input to the curriculum, for example through personal, social and health education, physical education and food technology teaching
  - action on travel to school
  - considering the health aspects in commercial school sponsorship schemes
  - activities within the wider community outside the school itself.

- Support for initiatives that promote and normalise breast-feeding and that enable women to breast-feed for as long as they wish.

Lobbying for effective policy changes at a national level

- National and local government action is needed to improve the safety of our environment for child pedestrians and cyclists.
- National and local initiatives should be used to increase the availability and reduce the relative cost of healthier foodstuffs such as fruit and vegetables.
- Advertisements of unhealthy food products during peak TV viewing times for children should be controlled. The media should promote healthy body images to children and young people and in turn children and young people should be encouraged to view the images presented in the media critically.
- Schools should be required to provide the minimum level of two hours of physical education each week for all pupils. Activities should be tailored to the age and gender of participants and offer alternatives to competitive team sports.
- Guidelines for the nutritional quality of school meals should be enforced to ensure that they offer a good range of fruit and vegetables and avoid an excess of foods high in fat, sugar or salt.

Areas for further research

The current body of evidence provides some indicators towards effective interventions for improving nutrition and levels of physical activity in children and young people. In many areas, however, the conclusions that can be drawn are limited by the relatively poor quality of the available evidence. Priority areas for further research include:

- more good-quality research into the prevention and treatment of overweight and obesity in childhood and adolescence
- the training requirements of healthcare professionals to enable them to recognise and effectively manage children and families affected by overweight and obesity
- updated and ongoing epidemiological research into the impact of the current trends in childhood overweight and obesity on adult obesity and associated mortality and morbidity.

References

1 National Audit Office (2001) *Tackling Obesity in England. Report by the Comptroller and Auditor General.* The Stationery Office, London.   **D**

2 Office for National Statistics (2000) *National Diet and Nutrition Survey: young people aged 4 to 18 years. Volume 1: report of the diet and nutrition survey.* The Stationery Office, London.   **B3**

3 Department for Environment, Food and Rural Affairs (2001) *National Food Survey 2000: annual report on food expenditure, consumption and nutrient intakes.* The Stationery Office, London.   **B3**

4 World Health Organization (1997) *Obesity, Preventing and Managing the Global Epidemic: report of the WHO consultation on obesity.* World Health Organization, Geneva.   **D**

5 Department of Health (2003) *Health Survey for England: the health of children and young people.* The Stationery Office, London.   **B3**

6 Health Development Agency www.hda-online.org.uk/html/improving/physicalactivity.html   **P**

7 British Heart Foundation (2000) *Couch Kids – the growing epidemic.* British Heart Foundation, London.   **D**

8 American Academy of Pediatrics (2003) Prevention of pediatric overweight and obesity. Policy statement. *Pediatrics.* **112 (2)**: 424–30. http://aappolicy.aappublications.org   **D**

9 Ebbeling CB, Pawlak DB and Ludwig DS (2002) Childhood obesity: public-health crisis, common sense cure. *Lancet.* **360**: 473–82.   **D**

10 Chinn S and Rona RR (2002) Prevalence and trends in overweight and obesity in three cross-sectional studies of British children 1974–1994. *BMJ.* **322**: 24–6.   **B3**

11 Reilly JJ, Dorosty AR and Emmett PM (1999) Prevalence of overweight and obesity in British children: cohort study. *BMJ.* **319**: 1039.   **B3**

12 Scottish Intercollegiate Guidelines Network (2003) *Management of Obesity in Children and Young People. A national clinical guideline. Number 69.* Scottish Intercollegiate Guidelines Network, Edinburgh. www.sign.ac.uk   **A1**

13 Wright CM, Parker L, Lamont D *et al.* (2001) Implications of childhood obesity for adult health: findings from thousand families cohort study. *BMJ.* **323**: 1280–4.   **B3**

14 Office for National Statistics (1998) *National Diet and Nutrition Survey* **B3**
*1997: young people aged 4–18 years. Volume 2: report of the oral health
survey.* The Stationery Office, London.

15 Tinanoff N and Palmer CA (2000) Dietary determinants of dental caries **D**
and dietary recommendations for preschool children. *J Public Health
Dentist.* **60 (3)**: 197–206.

16 Watt R and Stillman-Lowe C (2001) *Assessing the Evidence-Base for Oral* **A2**
Health Promotion: a review. HDA, London.

17 World Health Organization (2003) *Global Strategy for Infant and Young* **P**
Child Feeding. World Health Organization, Geneva.
www.who.int/nut/documents/gs_infant_feeding_text_eng.pdf

18 Tedstone A, Dunce N, Aviles M *et al.* (1998) *Effectiveness of Interventions* **A1**
to Promote Healthy Feeding in Infants under One Year of Age: a review.
Health Promotion Effectiveness Reviews 9. Health Education Authority,
London.

19 World Health Organization (2002) *Report of the Expert Consultation on* **A2**
the Optimal Duration of Exclusive Breast-feeding. World Health
Organization, Geneva.
www.who.int/nut/documents/optimal_duration_of_exc_bfeeding_
report_eng.pdf

20 Von Kries R, Koletzko B, Sauerveld T *et al.* (1999) Breast-feeding and **B3**
obesity: cross sectional study. *BMJ.* **319**: 147–50.

21 NHS Centre for Reviews and Dissemination (2000) Promoting the initia- **A1**
tion of breast-feeding. *Effective Health Care.* **6 (2)**: 1–12.

22 Tedstone A, Aviles M, Shetty P *et al.* (1998) *Effectiveness of Interventions* **A1**
*to Promote Healthy Eating in Pre-school Children aged 1 to 5 Years: a
review.* Health Promotion Effectiveness Reviews 10. Health Education
Authority, London.

23 Lister-Sharp D, Chapman S, Stewart-Brown *et al.* (1999) Health promoting **A1**
schools and health promotion in schools: two systematic reviews. *Health
Technol Assess.* **3 (22)**: 1–207.

24 Watson J (2003) *Fun with Food. Course one evaluation summary* (August **C1**
2002) *Course two evaluation* (January 2003). Sure Start, Dover.

25 Phipps L (2003) *Annual Report 2002/2003.* Sure Start, Dover. **Data/
activity
report**

26 Williams CL, Hayman LL, Daniels SR *et al.* American Heart Association **P**
(2002) Cardiovascular health in childhood. A statement from the committee on atherosclerosis, hypertension and obesity in the young (AHOY) of the
council on cardiovascular disease in the young. *Circulation.* **106**: 143–60.
www.circulationaha.org

27 Walker Z, Townsend J, Oakley L *et al.* (2002) Health promotion for **B1**
adolescents in primary care: randomised controlled trial. *BMJ.* **325**:524–7.

28 Hastings G, Stead M, McDermott L *et al.* (2003) Review of research on the **A1**
effects of food promotion to children. Centre for Social Marketing, London.
www.food.gov.uk/healthiereating/promotion/readreview

29 Marinho VC, Higgins JP, Sheiham A *et al.* (2003) Fluoride toothpaste for **A1**
preventing dental caries in children and adolescents. Cochrane Review. In:
The Cochrane Library. Issue 4. John Wiley & Sons Ltd, Chichester.

30 NHS Centre for Reviews and Dissemination (2000) *Fluoridation of* **A1**
Drinking Water: a systematic review of its efficacy and safety. Report
number 18. University of York, York.

31 Sprod AJ, Anderson R and Treasure ET (1996) Effective oral health promotion: literature review. Technical report 20. Dental Public Health Unit, Health Promotion Wales, Cardiff.   **A1**

32 Campbell K, Waters E, O'Meara S *et al.* (2003) Interventions for preventing obesity in children. Cochrane Review. In: *The Cochrane Library*. Issue 4. John Wiley & Sons Ltd, Chichester.   **A1**

33 NHS Centre for Reviews and Dissemination (2002) The prevention and treatment of childhood obesity. *Effective Health Care*. **7** (**6**): 1–12.   **A1**

34 Summerbell CD, Ashton V, Campbell KJ *et al.* (2003) Interventions for treating obesity in children. Cochrane Review. In: *The Cochrane Library*. Issue 4. John Wiley & Sons Ltd, Chichester.   **A1**

35 Barlow SE and Dietz W (2002) Management of child and adolescent obesity: summary and recommendations based on reports from paediatricians, paediatric nurse practitioners and registered dieticians. *Pediatrics*. **110** (1-Supplement): 236–8.   **C1**

36 Harvey EL, Glenny A-M, Kirk SFL *et al.* (2003) Improving health professionals' management and the organisation of care for overweight and obese people. Cochrane Review. In: *The Cochrane Library*. Issue 4. John Wiley & Sons Ltd, Chichester.   **A1**

37 American Psychiatric Association (1994) *Diagnostic and Statistical Manual of Mental Disorders (DSM-IV)* (4e). American Psychiatric Association, Washington.   **C1**

38 Wade T, Heath AC, Abraham S *et al.* (1996) Assessing the prevalence of eating disorder in an Australian twin population. *Aust New Zealand J Psychiat*. **30** (**6**): 845–51.   **B3**

39 National Heart Forum (2002) *Towards a Generation Free from Coronary Heart Disease. Policy action for children's and young people's health and wellbeing*. National Heart Forum, London.   **P**

40 Gibson P, Edmunds L, Haslam DW *et al.* (2003) *An Approach to Weight Management in Children and Adolescents (2–18 Years) in Primary Care*. Produced for the Royal College of Paediatrics and Child Health and National Obesity Forum. Royal College of Paediatrics and Child Health, London.   **P**
www.rcpch.ac.uk/publications/recent_publications/Approach_2PAGES_TOGETHER.pdf

41 Edmunds L, Waters E and Elliott EJ (2001) Evidence based management of childhood obesity. *BMJ*. **323**: 916–9.   **D**

CHAPTER 9

Promoting good mental health and positive self-esteem – the evidence

Kirsty Licence

Background

Mental health and wellbeing are difficult to define. As with physical aspects of health, they are more than just the absence of recognisable disease. Characteristics of a mentally healthy individual have been defined by the UK Mental Health Foundation as in Box 9.1.[1]

Box 9.1: Features of mental wellbeing in children and young people[1]

Children and young people who are mentally healthy will have the ability to:

- develop psychologically, emotionally, creatively, intellectually and spiritually
- initiate, develop and sustain mutually satisfying personal relationships
- face problems, resolve them and learn from them
- be confident and assertive
- be aware of others and empathise with them
- use and enjoy solitude
- play and learn
- develop a sense of right and wrong.

Mental health problems range from short-term behavioural or emotional difficulties, possibly associated with stressful life events, to long-term conditions that meet strict diagnostic criteria for a mental disorder. Findings from the *Health Survey for England*[2] suggest that 12% of boys aged 4–15 years old and 8% of girls in this age group may be experiencing behavioural, emotional or relationship difficulties at any time. A survey in 1999 found that overall, 10%

of 5–15-year olds had a mental disorder (based on strict diagnostic criteria and ICD-10 diagnostic categories) with impairment.[3] Half of these children met criteria for conduct disorder, 4% were suffering from an emotional disorder and 1% were assessed as being hyperactive. There is good epidemiological evidence that mental health problems in children and young people have been increasing in prevalence in recent years.

Children with emotional and behavioural problems are prone to mental health problems in later life and are at increased risk of school exclusion, offending, antisocial behaviour, marital breakdown, drug misuse and alcoholism.[4]

The determinants of good mental health are complex, but certain personal and social factors can be protective against the potential negative psychological impact of adverse events, including:[1,4]

- individual emotional resilience
- confidence in one's own sense of personal value
- supportive relationships within the family and in the wider community
- social inclusion
- a healthy social and economic environment.

More specifically, the existence of at least one good parent–child relationship and of affection within the family, parental supervision and authoritative discipline are associated with mental resilience in children.[1] Promoting positive mental health in childhood is, therefore, closely bound up with the promotion of positive parenting.

Self-esteem or positive self-concept is an important determinant of mental health and of other health, behavioural and social outcomes. Longitudinal studies suggest that relatively low self-esteem in childhood is a risk factor for teenage pregnancy, eating disorders, self-harm, suicide attempts and suicidal thoughts.[5,6] In boys and young men, low self-esteem also seems to be associated with lower earnings and unemployment in young adulthood.[5] In contrast, high self-esteem also seems to predispose young people to certain behaviours, including crime and delinquency, racial prejudice, teenage smoking and child maltreatment. Other risk-taking behaviours such as driving too fast or being under the influence of alcohol have also been linked to high self-esteem. But self-esteem is only one of a number of risk factors for any of these behaviours or outcomes and may, in itself, have a relatively small impact.

Parental approval and acceptance are key qualities contributing to the development of positive self-esteem.[5] Abuse, family conflict and breakdown are among the most damaging factors to a child's self-esteem. Other factors influencing a child's level of self-esteem include race, gender and socioeconomic position.

A range of biological and social factors increase the risk of poor mental health, especially poverty, combined with the impact of adverse events, including bereavement, parental separation and divorce and abuse in childhood.[1,2,7] Children and young people with chronic illnesses are also at increased risk of mental health problems and this should be considered in planning services for these children.[1]

There are significant associations between parental mental health and the mental health and happiness of their children. In the survey by Meltzer *et al.*[3] parents with a high (neurotic) score on the general health questionnaire (GHQ) were more likely to have children with mental disorders than those parents with lower GHQ scores (18% of children versus 8% respectively). It is difficult to differentiate between cause and effect in cross-sectional surveys. However, even if a parent's mental health problems are not a causal factor for mental disorder in children, such problems are likely to impact on the parents' ability to cope with their child's mental health problems and to parent in a positive style.[8]

Universal (population-based) programmes for prevention are especially suited to the field of mental health because:

- there is a high lifetime prevalence of mental health problems
- mental wellbeing and mental illness lie on a continuum of experience with a unimodal distribution of prevalence against severity.[4]

Hence, effective universal primary prevention programmes that increase the emotional resilience and coping skills of the population as a whole have the potential to benefit large numbers of people. In terms of reducing inequalities in health, it is important to focus on children in deprived communities who are at greater risk of mental health problems and children experiencing adverse life events, such as parental separation or divorce.

Primary preventive programmes and early identification and intervention may be aimed at the general population (universal programmes) or targeted towards groups who could be considered to be at high risk due to social or individual characteristics. The interventions described below focus on the role of Tier 1 services, which include primary care, educational and social services[9] (illustrated in Figure 9.1).

Tier 1-a primary level, which includes interventions by:

• GPs • health visitors • residential social workers • juvenile justice workers • school nurses • teachers	These non-specialist staff: • identify mental health problems early in their development • offer general advice and, in certain cases, treatment for less severe mental health problems • Pursue opportunities for promoting mental health and preventing mental health problems

Tier 2 – a level of service provided by professionals working on their own, who relate to others through a network rather than within a team

• clinical child psychologists • educational psychologists • paediatricians – especially community • community child psychiatric nurses or nurse specialists • child psychiatrists	These CAMHS professionals offer: • training and consultation to other professionals, including those in Tier 1 • consultation for professionals and families • outreach to identify severe or complex needs where children or families are unwilling to use specialist services • assessment which may trigger treatment at this level or in a different tier

Tier 3 – a specialist service for the more severe, complex and persistent disorders, usually a multidisciplinary team or service working in a community child mental health clinic or child psychiatry outpatient service

• social workers • clinical psychologists • community psychiatric nurses • child and adolescent psychiatrists • art, music and drama therapists • child psychotherapists • occupational therapists	This tier of service offers: • assessment and treatment of child mental health disorders • assessment for referrals to Tier 4 • contributions to the services, consultations and training at Tiers 1 and 2 • participation in research and development projects

Tier 4 – infrequently used but essential tertiary services such as day units, highly specialised outpatient teams and inpatient units for older children and adolescents who are severely mentally ill or at suicidal risk

Figure 9.1: Key components, professionals and functions of tiered Child and Adolescent Mental Health Services (CAMHS)[10]

(Source: *Children in Mind.* The Audit Commission[10])

Effectiveness of interventions aimed at promoting good mental health and positive self-esteem

The Mental Health Foundation advocates a public health approach to the promotion of mental wellbeing in children and young people.[1] This requires intervention at different levels, to improve the economic and social circumstances that adversely affect the mental health of children and young people, as well as school, community and family-based interventions. Interventions may be implemented by PCTs, schools and local communities. Health and social care professionals have a role in advocating for wider public health interventions, including those that improve the financial and housing conditions of children and young people.

Population-based interventions for mental health promotion

There have been several reviews of population-based primary prevention programmes for promoting positive mental health in children and young people aged under 19 years.[4,11–14] Many of the interventions studied have been entirely or mainly school based. Most of these reviews have found that school-based mental health promotion programmes can be successful at improving aspects of mental wellbeing and emotional resilience. Positive outcomes have been found for improvements in self-esteem and self-efficacy, negotiating and problem-solving strategies and for reducing bullying.[4,13] Although most of the studies included in these reviews were carried out in the US, mental health promotion initiatives have also been successfully implemented in the UK, for example within 'Health Promoting Schools' projects.[13]

The research suggests the following findings.

- School-based mental health promotion projects tend to be most successful if they take a whole school approach, including environmental and cultural change within the school. Projects should aim to involve staff as well as pupils and to promote a supportive, trusting and participatory environment in the school.[4,12] However, even purely classroom-based interventions can have a positive impact on outcomes relevant to mental wellbeing.[14]
- Implementing preventive programmes over prolonged periods of time (more than one year) seems to improve the outcomes.[4]
- Universal programmes that help young people to develop generic coping skills are likely to be effective in helping them to negotiate potentially stressful events within the school curriculum and transitions such as the move from primary to secondary school.[9] Educational programmes that

focus on stress management can improve students' self-esteem and levels of anxiety and improve anger management.[14]

- Promotion of positive mental health seems to be more readily achieved than prevention of particular problems, such as aggressive behaviour or suicide. Direct comparisons are difficult, however, because of the different outcome measures used to assess these different aspects of mental health.[4,12]

- The outcomes of universal suicide prevention programmes have been mixed.[4,14] Although programmes have shown improvements in suicide-related knowledge and attitudes and improvements in self-esteem, some interventions have shown adverse effects on subgroups of participants. Boys were more at risk of being negatively affected by suicide prevention programmes than girls.

- There has been a recent systematic review and meta-analysis of trials of interventions aimed at preventing depression in children and young people.[15] This considered educational (defined as information giving) and psychological (attempting to teach skills to reduce depression, such as stress management, problem solving) interventions separately. Some interventions were provided on a population basis; others were targeted. Targeted groups included young people whose parents were depressed, those with elevated (but non-clinical) depression scores or elevated depression symptoms, those reporting poor family relationships and those failing at school or who had dropped out of school. Based on one study, purely educational interventions were not effective. Meta-analysis of 13 studies showed a significant short-term reduction in depression scores for targeted psychological interventions, but not for universal interventions of this type. Depressive episodes were significantly reduced immediately after both universal and targeted psychological interventions. For all psychological interventions, the number needed to treat was 10 to prevent one diagnosis of depression. Trials that reported longer term follow-up showed mixed results. Trial quality was rated as poor for many of the 21 included studies. Only two studies compared the active intervention with a *placebo*, defined as a control condition that resembled the test intervention but which lacked the elements thought to be active in prevention of depression. All other trials used a waiting list or no intervention comparison group. The trials that attempted to use a placebo showed no effect, although both had significant methodological problems that made a negative result more likely.

- Some school-based initiatives have been found to be effective for improving self-esteem. There is, however, little evidence about the effectiveness of such programmes for improving the potential adverse long-term outcomes of poor self-esteem. In some cases, such as teenage pregnancy, efforts to raise self-esteem may be less effective than improvements in health education and provision of contraception, although ideally, efforts should be made to improve a range of determinants. Improving parenting skills and reducing the risk of child abuse are most likely to have a positive impact on children's self-esteem.[5]

- Ekeland *et al.* have carried out a systematic review of 23 trials of exercise-based interventions aiming to improve self-esteem in children and young people.[16] Included trials were generally small and had at least a moderate risk of bias. Participants included healthy children, children with learning disability, children with emotional disturbance, young offenders, children with low self-image and children with deficits in gross motor skills. Some interventions were purely physical exercise, while others were more complex, including counselling, skills training and social activities alongside an exercise programme. Twelve studies were included in meta-analyses, eight in which the intervention was purely exercise and four in which the intervention was more complex. In both groups, the meta-analysis showed significant short-term benefits for improving self-esteem. The size of the effect was similar for exercise-only and complex interventions, but the reviewers noted that the trials of exercise-only interventions were more heterogeneous, so combining them in a meta-analysis may not be appropriate. The reviewers conclude that there is some evidence that exercise can contribute to short-term improvements in self-esteem in children and young people.
- There has been some positive research into outdoor pursuits programmes as a means of developing self-esteem.[11]

Targeted interventions

Targeted school-based primary preventive programmes have been found to be effective in helping children cope with a range of adverse life events, including parental separation and divorce and bereavement.[7,11]

For children showing behavioural problems, school-based interventions and group parent training programmes can improve the child's conduct and mental wellbeing.[7] Teaching parents and teachers behavioural techniques to manage preschool age children with aggressive and disruptive behaviour has shown some success.[17] The size and quality of studies in this area, however, limit the conclusions that can be drawn.

A review of psychological interventions for children with chronic medical illness concluded that such interventions are effective for improving disease-related and emotional/behavioural problems. The methodology used in the review was, however, criticised by reviewers from the NHS Centre for Reviews and Dissemination, who themselves concluded that the review provided weak evidence for the effectiveness of such interventions.[18]

The findings of targeted depression prevention programmes have been discussed above.[15]

Support for parents

Support for parents is essential for promoting the mental health and self-esteem of children. A range of approaches can be used, including:[7,19,20]

- universal parenting support programmes
- support targeted at vulnerable families
- primary prevention programmes for common behavioural problems
- programmes that offer early support for parents whose children have been identified as suffering from behavioural or emotional problems.

Healthcare services

The model of CAMHS proposed by the NHS Health Advisory Service envisages a role for primary community mental health workers, who can support and advise on Tier 1 services, offering early intervention and onward referral to specialist CAMHS where necessary (see Box 9.2).

Box 9.2: Role of primary mental health workers – Hull and East Riding Inter-agency Link team, Hull and East Riding Health Action Zone

This project was funded jointly by the Health Action Zone, CAMHS, the NHS Modernisation Fund and Mental Health Specific Grant monies. The project employs a multidisciplinary team of health visitors, paediatricians, community medical officers, family support workers, community nurses and education officers. The Inter-Agency Link team takes referrals from GPs, social services and others and aims to:

- support primary care services in meeting the needs of children, young people and families where behavioural, emotional or mental health difficulties exist
- identify and advise on appropriate services to meet needs
- aid young people and families to access specialist services.

The team received 263 referrals in the first three months of 2001. Around one-third of referrals were directed to the CAMHS team, but 23% were closed or discharged following intervention from the link team. The provision of early intervention by the link team has contributed to a substantial reduction in the waiting list for local specialist CAMHS.

Source: www.haznet.org.uk/hazs/hazmap/hull_upstream-cyp.pdf

One approach to training such primary mental health workers is the parent adviser model, used by the Centre for Parent and Child Support as described in Box 9.3. It has been shown that community child mental health workers trained using this model can be successful at improving child behavioural and emotional problems, improving parenting skills and the home environment, improving maternal self-esteem and reducing anxiety and depression in mothers.[21,22] Although the reported studies have been non-randomised quasi-experimental studies without blind assessment, the findings merit further research into this approach.

Box 9.3: Centre for Parent and Child Support (CPCS)

This is a national centre based at Guy's Hospital, London. The work of the centre aims to promote family psychosocial wellbeing through improved support for children and parents. The CPCS has three main roles:

1 *training* in the parent adviser model is available to any practitioners working with children. This model aims to improve the confidence and expertise of practitioners in working with parents and children at risk of, or suffering from, psychosocial difficulties. Training programmes for practitioners wishing to use this approach consist of up to 16 sessions, each of 3½ hours duration, with assignments between sessions
2 *consultation* for service development and evaluation of community-based parent and family support workers
3 *research* into the application and impact of the parent adviser approach.

Source: www.cpcs.org.uk

What primary care teams can do

Mental health promotion for children should begin early, with good support for expectant mothers and in the immediate postnatal period, better recognition and management of postnatal depression and ongoing support for parents, especially for those in socioeconomically deprived circumstances.

Primary healthcare staff have a key role to play within Tier 1 of a comprehensive child and adolescent mental health service.[9] The main functions of staff at this level are:[1]

- early recognition and identification of problems
- early intervention
- liaison with Tier 2 and more specialised services
- signposting families to other services, such as those in the educational, social care and voluntary sectors, for both primary prevention and early intervention
- health needs assessment and the identification of those at high risk for targeted interventions
- supporting schools and communities in the delivery of preventive services.

In order to deliver these elements of primary prevention and early recognition and intervention, primary care staff need to be trained in *everyday* child mental health and in the recognition and assessment of other risk factors within the family and community. This includes parental mental health problems and drug and alcohol misuse within the family.

Primary care teams can work with other sectors of the health service, other agencies and lay groups to investigate the most appropriate way of delivering community child mental health services locally.

Areas for further research

The rising prevalence of mental health problems in children and young people means that we need to give higher priority to prevention and early recognition of such problems. Further research is required into the effectiveness of specific mental health promotion interventions and into the support required for parents in order to promote positive mental health and self-esteem in children. In terms of specific interventions to promote mental health, areas for further research include:

- the impact on mental wellbeing, physical health and self-esteem of physical activity and of outdoor pursuit programmes
- the effectiveness of health promotion interventions in the prevention of internalising disorders (anxiety, depression, eating disorders) in young people. A health technology assessment carried out in New Zealand noted that most research to date has focused on the more publicly disruptive externalising disorders, including substance misuse and conduct disorder.[13]

References

1 Mental Health Foundation (1999) *Bright Futures. Promoting children and young people's mental health*. Mental Health Foundation, London. **P**

2 Department of Health (1998) *Health Survey for England: the health of young people '95–'97*. The Stationery Office, London. www.archive.official-documents.co.uk/document/doh/survey97/hse95.htm **B3**

3 Meltzer H, Gatward R, Goodman R *et al.* (2000) *Mental Health of Children and Adolescents in Great Britain*. The Stationery Office, London. **B3**

4 Wells J, Barlow J and Stewart-Brown S (2001) *A Systematic Review of Universal Approaches to Mental Health Promotion in Schools*. Health Services Research Unit, University of Oxford, Oxford. **A1**

5 Emler N (2001) *The Costs and Causes of Low Self-Esteem*. Joseph Rowntree Foundation, London. **D**

6 Hawton K, Rodham K, Evans E *et al.* (2002) Deliberate self-harm in adolescents: self report survey in schools in England. *BMJ*. **325**: 1207–11. **B3**

7   NHS Centre for Reviews and Dissemination (1997) Mental health   A1
    promotion in high risk groups. *Effective Health Care.* **3 (3)**: 1–12.

8   Falkov A (2002) Addressing family needs when a parent is mentally ill. In: D
    H Ward and W Rose (eds) *Approaches to Needs Assessment in Children's
    Services.* Jessica Kingsley Publishers, London.

9   NHS Health Advisory Service (1995) *Together We Stand. The commission-*   P
    ing role and management of child and adolescent mental health services.
    HMSO, London.

10 The Audit Commission (1999) *Children in Mind.* The Audit Commission,   P
    London.

11 Tilford S, Delaney F and Vogels M (1997) *Effectiveness of Mental Health*   A1
    Promotion Interventions: a review. Health Education Authority, London.

12 Durlak JA and Wells AM (1997) Primary prevention mental health   A2
    programmes for children and adolescents: a meta-analytic review. *Am J
    Community Psychol.* **25 (2)**: 115–52.

13 Nicholas B and Broadstock M (1999) *Effectiveness of Early Interventions*   A1
    *for Preventing Mental Illness in Young People: a critical appraisal of the
    literature.* New Zealand Health Technology Assessment, Christchurch.

14 Lister-Sharp D, Chapman S, Stewart-Brown S *et al.* (1999) Health promot-   A1
    ing schools and health promotion in schools: two systematic reviews.
    Health Technol Assess. **3 (22)**: 1–207.

15 Merry S, McDowell H, Hetrick S *et al.* (2004) Psychological and/or   A1
    educational interventions for the prevention of depression in children
    and adolescents. Cochrane Review. In: *The Cochrane Library.* Issue 1.
    John Wiley & Sons Ltd, Chichester.

16 Ekeland E, Heian F, Hagen KB *et al.* (2004) Exercise to improve self-esteem   A1
    in children and young people. Cochrane Review. In: *The Cochrane Library.*
    Issue 1. John Wiley & Sons Ltd, Chichester.

17 Bryant D, Vizzard LH, Willoughby M *et al.* (1999) A review of interventions   D
    for preschoolers with aggressive and disruptive behaviour. *Early Education
    and Development.* **10 (1)**: 47–68.

18 Kibby MY, Tyc VL and Mulhern RK (1998) Effectiveness of psychological   D
    interventions for children and adolescents with chronic medical illness: a
    meta-analysis. *Clin Psychol Rev.* **18 (1)**: 103–17.

19 Ciliska D, Mastrilli P, Ploeg J *et al.* (1999) *The Effectiveness of Home*   A1
    *Visiting as a Delivery Strategy for Public Health Nursing Interventions to
    Clients in Prenatal and Postnatal Period: a systematic review.* Effective
    Public Health Practice Project for the Public Health Branch, Ontario
    Ministry of Health, Ontario.
    www.hamilton.ca/PHCS/EPHPP/Research/Full-Reviews/98–99/Prenatal-&-
    Postnatal-Home-Visiting- review.pdf

20 Barlow J and Parsons J (2004) Group based parent-training programmes for   A1
    improving emotional and behavioural adjustment in 0–3-year old children.
    Cochrane Review. In: *The Cochrane Library.* Issue 1. John Wiley & Sons
    Ltd, Chichester.

21 Davis H, Spurr P, Cox A *et al.* (1997) A description and evaluation of a   B2
    community child mental health service. *Clin Child Psychol Psychiat.* **2 (2)**:
    221–38.

22 Davis H and Spurr P (1998) Parent counselling: an evaluation of a   B2
    community child mental health service. *J Child Psychol Psychiat.* **39 (3)**:
    365–79.

CHAPTER 10

Implementing good mental health in primary care settings

Caroline Lindsey

The recommendations of the group reporting on Child and Adolescent Mental Health and Psychological Wellbeing within the Children's NSF highlighted children's mental health as being 'everyone's business', to convey its central importance for all providers of health and social care, as well as education. It is challenging for professionals who meet children, young people and their families in their day-to-day work to feel that they have an opportunity and a responsibility to assess and, if necessary, intervene to promote and address their mental health needs. Many feel daunted by addressing these issues because of their lack of knowledge and fear of making matters worse, particularly with children with whom they may feel they do not know how to communicate. It will require a significant investment in their training and skills development for primary care workers to do this work effectively and safely and investment in child and adolescent mental health services (CAMHS) resources to support, consult and liaise with them.

Primary care and CAMHS teams working together

For many years GPs and nurses as well as practice counsellors and mental health professionals from local CAMHS have been engaged in working collaboratively in relation to mental health issues, in many primary healthcare settings. In a significant number of primary care settings, there has been regular input from psychologists and family therapists from CAMHS and child and adolescent primary mental heath workers or their equivalent, sometimes known as parent advisers.[1] These professionals have offered a range of interventions, such as direct work with patients, joint sessions with healthcare professionals and their patients, consultation and training.

But it has been frustrating that the provision of these support, training, consultation and face-to-face services to primary care professionals (Tier 1) and their patients is patchily distributed around the country, since not all CAMHS are sufficiently well resourced to provide them. Research has shown that it is those CAMHS that are better staffed and able to provide specialist services which are also providing services to primary care.[2] So, there should be expansion of CAMHS.

The development of Sure Start for families with children under five years old has also contributed to early intervention, providing parenting support and the recognition of children's developmental and emotional needs. Voluntary organisations, such as Newpin and Homestart, have contributed to the support of mothers with young children too. The professionals who worked on the CAMHS component of the NSF recommended that there should be specific specialist child mental health teams within CAMHS to work with primary care health services, Sure Start and other agencies in touch with families of children under five years old, to provide early intervention for serious or complex cases.

Addressing mental health problems in children and young people

Mental health problems in children and young people, for example ADHD and depression, are generally poorly recognised in primary care. Parents rather than GPs are the prime instigators of referral to child mental health services. Brief focused training on the recognition of child mental health disorders and early intervention in primary care has been successfully developed.[3]

Gledhill and colleagues have developed training in therapeutic identification of depression in young people, for primary care practitioners.[4] They have shown improved recognition and management of adolescent depression by GPs.

Child psychiatrists have developed and piloted brief interventions for parents of children with emotional disorders (who are frequent practice attendees), which may be adapted for use by primary care professionals.[5] Long waiting lists in some areas have also meant that once the needs of children and young people with more serious problems have been recognised, they have not always been dealt with expeditiously, leading in turn to poor take-up of services when they are eventually offered.

Implementation of the initial recommendations made by the CAMHS NSF group[6] for future improvements has been facilitated by an increase in the CAMHS grant to local authorities to be spent in collaboration with the health sector over the period 2003–06 and by an increase in baseline budgets to PCTs for 2004–06. This constituted a total of £250 million extra funding for CAMHS. An explicit expectation by the DH[7] that each area will acquire several CAMHS primary care workers by 2004[8] means that this development has been supported all over the country, with an investment in training for these workers also becoming available in 2004. A survey of CAMHS has documented the increase in primary mental health worker posts who provide a liaison service between primary care and specialist CAMHS.[2] This hopefully means that, in future, it should be easier for primary healthcare services to obtain help from these workers to meet the presenting mental health needs of the children, young people and families in their practices.

Prevalence of mental health problems in children and young people

Research has repeatedly shown that one in four of the child population attending primary care services suffers from mental health problems[9] and recently, others have shown that 10% of 5–15 year olds have a diagnosable mental health disorder.[10] This suggests that some 1.1 million children and young people under 19 years old would benefit from access to specialist services. Forty-five per cent of looked after children aged 5–17 years have a mental disorder.[11] Among children and young people with significant learning disabilities, prevalence rates for mental disorder are 3–4 times those for other children and young people, with rates for those with severe learning disabilities higher still.[12-14] Since many of these children and young people and their parents present first to primary care settings, it is essential to improve the recognition of their difficulties. In addition, many families will never agree to go to specialist services, despite the complexity of their problems. It is also clear from these statistics that there will never be enough specialist services available to meet all the need, which is why it is important to improve preventive and early intervention services in the community.

Providing interventions in primary care

Chapter 9 reviewed a range of mental health promotion and early interventions that are currently available. Many of these are delivered in schools. Professionals working in primary healthcare settings are potentially in a position to intervene effectively with parents, infants and young children as well as young people. General practice offers the opportunity to see families briefly, but repeatedly, over time and sometimes over generations, because of its relatively good access.

Patients who are refugees or from ethnic minorities, who may not traditionally access mental health services, can have their mental health needs identified in primary care because of its universal accessibility, recognising that this implies the availability of competent interpreting services. For many families, the GP, practice nurse and health visitor as well as the community pharmacist are trusted and familiar professionals who do not carry the stigma commonly attached to mental health workers. Counsellors and CAMHS practitioners working in primary care are often more acceptable to patients because they are seen in the local health centre. Patients, parents or their children, present with a range of problems that can be understood in both physical and psychological terms, allowing the GP or nurse to take a mental health focus for a consultation as seems appropriate.

The primary care setting offers the opportunity to advise and support pregnant mothers, to identify those who may be at risk of postnatal psychiatric disorders, including most prevalently (10%) postnatal depression.[15] This ensures that those who have been disturbed following previous pregnancies or who are currently unwell are identified to the maternity services. It also enables recognition of those who are dependent on alcohol and other substances or who are victims of domestic violence and those mothers who because of their own histories may be at risk of offering poor parenting to their children.

Untreated postnatal depression may prevent the secure attachment of the infant to the mother as well as having adverse cognitive and social developmental effects.[16] Brief psychological interventions by health visitors with postnatally depressed mothers have been shown to be effective.[17,18] Visiting by health visitors or other trained primary healthcare professionals to facilitate the mother's sensitive responsiveness to the baby over the first six months may enhance the development of secure attachment and should be available to high-risk groups of patients. Emotional and practical skills-based support in child rearing may increase parental competence and self-esteem and prevent the onset of emotional and behavioural problems. The early recognition of children with developmental delay and the provision of coordinated multidisciplinary care reduce secondary disadvantage and the demoralisation experienced by parents who often cannot obtain the assessments and services they need.

Child protection issues often first become apparent in primary care settings when children are brought, for example, with unexplained failure to thrive, recurrent urinary infections and psychosomatic complaints. The need to respond appropriately to such concerns is now very topical following the Victoria Climbie Inquiry by Lord Laming,[19] but this is probably one of the most difficult areas for any professional to address and for which training is required. General practitioners and nurses are among the first to know when a family is facing a bereavement or terminal illness or when parents separate and divorce. Offering families the chance for counselling or support at these times has been shown to have positive effects on emotional wellbeing for those who are able to make use of such services.

Increasing familiarity with the range of common child psychiatric disorders and available treatments, including for example ADHD, depression, anxiety and panic and behavioural disorders, as well as developmental problems, feeding and sleeping difficulties and autistic spectrum disorders in early childhood and the more serious but rarer disorders such as eating disorders and early-onset mental illness in young people, may facilitate the early recognition of difficulties and intervention in primary care and referral to more specialist services, where appropriate. The hope is that closer collaboration between primary and specialist services, through joint training and provision of mental health services in primary care, will enhance the care received by children and their families and promote and improve their mental health and emotional wellbeing.

References

1 Davis H, Spurr P, Cox A *et al.* (1997) A description and evaluation of a community child mental health service. *Clin Child Psychol Psychiat.* **2 (2)**: 221–38.
2 Bradley S, Kramer T, Garralda EM *et al.* (2003) Child and adolescent mental health interface with primary services: a survey of NHS Provider trusts. *Child Adolesc Mental Health.* **8**: 4170–6.
3 Day C, Davis H and Hind R (1998) The development of community child and family mental health services. *Child: Care, Health Develop.* **24**: 487–500.
4 Gledhill J, Kramer T, Iliffe S *et al.* (2003) Brief report. Training general practitioners in the identification and management of adolescent depression within the consultation: a feasibility study. *J Adolesc.* **26**: 245–50.
5 Coverley CM, Garralda MR and Bowman FM (1995) Psychiatric intervention in mothers whose children have psychiatric disorder. *Br J Gen Pract.* **45**: 235–7.
6 Department of Health (2003) *Getting the Right Start: The National Service Framework for Children, Young People and Maternity Services – emerging findings.* DH, London.
7 Department of Health (2003) *Child and Adolescent Mental Health Service (CAMHS) Guidance 2003/04.* DH, London.
8 Gale F and Vostanis P (2003) The primary mental health worker role within child and adolescent mental health services. *Clin Child Psychol Psychiat.* **8 (2)**: 227–41.
9 Garralda ME and Bailey D (1986) Children with psychiatric disorders in primary care. *J Child Psychol Psychiat.* **27**: 611–24.
10 Meltzer H, Gatward R, Goodman R *et al.* (2000) *Mental Health of Children and Adolescents in Great Britain.* HMSO, London.
11 Meltzer H, Corbin T, Gatward R *et al.* (2003) *The Mental Health of Young People Looked After by Local Authorities in England.* HMSO, London.
12 Rutter M, Tizard J and Woodward (1970) *Education, Health and Behaviour.* Longmans, London.
13 Einfeld SL and Tonge BL (1996) Population prevalence of psychopathology in children and adolescents with intellectual disability. II Epidemiological findings. *J Intellec Disability Res.* **40**: 99–109.
14 Dykens EM (2000) Psychopathology in children with intellectual disability. *J Child Psychol Psychiat.* **41**: 407–17.
15 O'Hara MW (1997) The nature of postpartum disorders. In: L Murray and PJ Cooper (eds) *Postpartum Depression and Child Development.* Guilford, New York.
16 Murray L (1992) The impact of postnatal depression on infant development. *J Child Psychol Psychiat.* **35**: 29–72.

17 Holden JM, Sagowsky R and Cox JL (1989) Counselling in a general practice setting: controlled study of health visitor intervention in treatment of postnatal depression. *BMJ.* **298**: 223–6.

18 Cooper PJ and Murray L (1997) The impact of psychological treatments of postpartum depression on maternal mood and infant development. In: L Murray and PJ Cooper (eds) *Postpartum Depression and Child Development.* Guilford, New York.

19 Department of Health (2003) *Keeping Children Safe – The Government's Response to the Victoria Climbie Inquiry Report and Joint Chief Inspectors' Report Safeguarding Children.* The Stationery Office, London.

CHAPTER 11

Effective care for pregnant teenagers

Meryl Thomas and Heather Mellows

Introduction

Teenage pregnancy is a topical issue at the heart of the government agenda for improving public health. Publication of the Children's NSF is an opportunity for PCTs to initiate change in the organisation of services and develop a strategy of care, focusing on the needs of pregnant teenagers.

In 1997, there were 90 000 known teenage conceptions, resulting in 56 000 births, with the remainder ending in abortion.[1] There are 87 000 children in England who have a teenage mother. The four countries of the UK have the highest teenage pregnancy rates in Europe. The Teenage Pregnancy Unit was established to tackle the issue. The goals were to reduce the rate of conception in under-18 year olds by 15% by 2004 and by 50% by 2010. In addition, there is a goal to increase the proportion of teenage parents continuing in education, training or employment by 60% and by doing so, reduce their longer term risk of social exclusion and deprivation.

This chapter focuses on what action can be taken by individuals and groups of professionals, working in and with PCTs, to further develop services that are appropriate and effective for the care of teenagers in pregnancy and birth. These services should provide them with the support they need in order to establish their parenting role.

The importance of effective maternity care

Some groups in society are more vulnerable because of their cultural background or language. These groups include members of travelling communities, those living in social isolation, abusers of drugs or alcohol and people who fear disclosing issues such as domestic violence and teenage pregnancy. The Maternity Care Working Party[2] urged the government to ensure that maternity care is not just a delivery service but also a key intervention, offering the physical, emotional and social support that is needed at the very start of life.

Pregnant teenagers are vulnerable because of their young age, both for child bearing and for assuming the responsibilities that come with being a parent.

While teenage pregnancy occurs across all social groups, it is more common in those from deprived backgrounds, those with low self-esteem and emotional or mental health problems and those with unstable family relationships. Even when a teenager is in good physical and mental health these factors present a public health challenge.[1]

There are increased risks associated with teenage births. Premature onset of labour, low birth weight and perinatal and early infant death are more common, as is the incidence of postnatal depression in the mother. Providing care for pregnant teenagers within traditional maternity services does not meet their needs. There is evidence that a comprehensive programme of care for pregnant teenagers is associated with improved pregnancy outcomes.[3]

Planners in PCTs should identify local needs relating to teenage pregnancy. Data on teenage pregnancy and areas of most need will enable the PCT to develop appropriate local action plans to reduce teenage pregnancy rates and establish teenage pregnancy support services (TPSS). The short-term gains of TPSS will be to increase early uptake and attendance for pregnancy care, enable early identification of needs and planning the most appropriate care or intervention, with the teenager.[4] In the longer term, investment in a TPSS will improve healthcare outcomes, public health and wellbeing.

There are a number of established TPSSs whose work is commendable, some within Sure Start initiatives while others have been instigated through joint initiatives between PCTs and maternity services in response to local needs.[5] Such good practices reflected in the standards in the NSF will be levers for facilitating change in primary care settings.

Action for change

An effective TPSS requires joined-up thinking, a shared philosophy of care and effective collaborative networks between the services and professionals. The project should be led by one professional or by a small group of professionals, accountable to the PCT and hospital trust. Planning and development should be based on a local needs profile. As with any change and development of services, there should be a system of ongoing monitoring and review by the PCT, ensuring clear lines of accountability, reporting and resource management.

The strategy for a TPSS should be informed by the views of local user groups, the views of teenagers who have experienced the local maternity care services and the views of related voluntary agencies. The literature and evidence on TPSS initiatives and the Teenage Pregnancy Unit website relate good practice that is already tried and tested in England and which may be used as a model for local development. Good practice includes development of a teenage pregnancy care pathway (TPCP) to form the basis of a framework for care and development of services to meet local needs.

A midwife with special responsibility for pregnant teenagers may take on the role of lead professional. She or he works in partnership with local GPs, school health services, health visitors, local authority services including social care, education and housing services, family planning and contraceptive services and, importantly, an obstetrician with a special interest in and responsibility for care of, pregnant teenagers. There should also be input to the strategy from psychiatric and paediatric services, to ensure that referral and advisory systems are comprehensive and fully linked in.

Joint multiprofessional training and regular update briefings should be arranged for all the staff whose work will involve the care of pregnant teenagers.

Developing the service

Confidentiality and a culture of trust are paramount to the development of a teenage pregnancy service. Information emphasising the one-to-one basis of maternity care and the privacy and nature of TPSS may be advertised through the local media, schools and colleges, youth centres, contraceptive services and in other social venues frequented by teenagers. Information through word of mouth and learning from the experiences of their teenage peers is likely to be effective as the service develops.[6]

Early acknowledgement and confirmation of pregnancy is essential and must be encouraged and made easy, so that pregnant teenagers access services as soon as possible following conception. The first point of contact may be through traditional routes such as the GP or sexual health services (including family planning or genito-urinary medicine clinics), but may also be facilitated through other agencies, such as substance misuse services. Barriers to access may be the timing or location of clinics. Local agreements on access, for example the provision of designated out-of-hours services, drop-in family planning or midwife sessions in non-traditional venues, or direct self-referral to a midwife are helpful in achieving this. Whatever is developed locally should focus on helping teenagers to access services as early as possible, preferably within the first eight weeks of pregnancy.

Early confirmation of pregnancy allows full and informed discussion to take place with the teenager. Written information, specifically designed for teenagers on the choices about pregnancy and the care and support services available, should be available to assist the dialogue. An early follow-up appointment should be made to enable further discussion about her specific needs, choices and decisions about the pregnancy and to agree the action to be taken. Where the teenager has a partner whom she wishes to be involved in decisions about the pregnancy, it is important that he too is made to feel significant. He can play an important role in supporting her to make important decisions about the pregnancy.

If a teenager decides she wishes to seek termination of her pregnancy, the local strategy should ensure speedy referral to the termination services, whether this is by her GP, the midwife or through the contraceptive services.

It is vital that appropriate and accessible counselling and support services are available before and following termination. This should include effective contraceptive advice and prescription and where a partner is involved, it should also include advice for him.

Continuing care for pregnancy and preparing for parenting

When a teenager and, when involved, her partner choose to continue with the pregnancy, there are a number of important considerations which should inform the care pathway and the delivery of care. Trust and open discussion between the pregnant teenager and the professionals who care for her is more easily achieved when there is:

- choice regarding the lead carer
- continuity of care by as few professionals as possible for safe care
- consistent advice from all those she encounters.

Usually a teenager chooses her midwife as lead professional. Alternatively, she may choose her GP or the obstetrician based within the maternity unit. Whoever leads her care, there will need to be effective liaison to ensure that the girl is given information about local activities for teenage pregnancy advice, birth and preparation for parenthood.

All women should have individualised and high-quality maternity care. Teenagers often have particular needs, which go beyond those of the majority of child-bearing women. The lead professional may be required to act as an advocate for the teenager at some point in the pregnancy or birth. This may be in relation to telling her family she is pregnant and in gaining parental support for her decisions about the pregnancy, whether her choice is to terminate or to continue. There is usually a teenage father who may or may not wish to be involved or supportive. Some girls may have had a casual sexual encounter leading to pregnancy or may be in a relationship with an older man. There should be help and advice from the TPSS to support her in making decisions about informing those whose support she would wish to have for child bearing and parenthood.

Whatever the situation, the framework of care should allow for flexible services to provide appropriate support to the girl in making decisions and choices. All involved in care and advice for teenagers under 16 years old should be aware of the legal implications relating to under-age sex, consent to treatment of minors, termination of pregnancy and contraception as well as the rights of parents, guardians and the father of the baby. Knowledge and skills in dealing with these issues and with any challenging or angry behaviour are important in those providing care within the TPSS. There is a need to avoid stress for the girl or her family, but also to avoid the major complaints about services when such issues are badly handled. Those dealing with very young pregnant girls must remain aware of the issues of child abuse and coercion. Where there is a need, sensitive, informed and skilful handling of these issues, by members of the TPSS who have the necessary knowledge and training, is essential for successful outcomes. Effective communication within the TPSS can help to avoid the pitfalls of making wrong assumptions and mishandling sensitive situations.

Subjects such as drug abuse, alcohol indulgence, sexually transmitted diseases, smoking and physical or sexual abuse are all difficult, but important to tackle in managing teenage pregnancy. There are some excellent examples within some Sure Start initiatives of group work relating to healthy living, sexual health, nutrition and making lifestyle choices. These aspects of care are particularly important in the care pathway for pregnant teenagers and, where possible, their partners. Many young people have increased health risks because of poor diet and lifestyle choices and there is a known link between foetal and neonatal under-nutrition and coronary heart disease in later life. Teenage girls are more likely to have growth-retarded and low-birthweight babies unless systems are in place to help them to improve their lifestyle. Systems should be in place for links between the TPSS and smoking cessation services, public health nurses and others involved in health promotion activities. Consistent and sound information, advice and support should be available to tackle these public health issues during pregnancy.

Preparing for birth and parenting

Some teenagers who are in stable relationships with partners who are involved and supportive to them may choose to attend mainstream parent preparation sessions. Most pregnant teenagers, particularly the very young, find these classes inappropriate and embarrassing and feel stigmatised and disadvantaged by them. Easily accessed, local and designated birth and parenting sessions should be available for teenagers. Teenage pregnancy and parenthood support groups are known to be successful and valued by young people. They provide a source of mutual interest and peer support, often leading to social contacts and friendships for girls who are otherwise isolated. These are most beneficial when continued throughout and beyond pregnancy and birth, with the mid-wives, health visitors and doctors from the TPSS keeping in contact to provide a venue and give support and advice. Non-participants or non-attenders can be noted and discreetly followed up to offer advice or instigate care if there are problems. In the maternity services at Blackburn, initiatives to provide effective services for pregnant teenagers and their partners have been effect-ively developed to tackle local needs. Preparation classes and support groups that involve teenage mothers who have experienced the service and who are caring for their babies have proved to be effective. Giving peer advice and providing role modelling in this way can also raise the morale and esteem of the group and the confidence of individuals in facing their birth experience and becoming parents.[6]

Every pregnant woman, including teenagers, should be given a choice about the place of birth and options relating to her care in labour and delivery. She should have unbiased and evidence-based information about risk factors and the type of facilities available to her should be made clear using language that she understands. Ideally, the teenager should be able to choose between midwifery-led and consultant-led care, but she should be helped to understand the higher risks associated with teenage pregnancy and birth and the possible need for prompt availability of consultant obstetric help.

Post-birth depression is more common in unmarried young mothers.[7] Changes in the mental wellbeing of the girl should be monitored and where necessary, the opinion of the community psychiatric services should inform actions. Any girl with a history of psychiatric problems, or who is emotionally unstable to the extent that she is raising professional concern, should be reviewed by the psychiatric services. The TPCP should include and enable prompt and uncomplicated referral and ongoing support.

It is known that there is a lower uptake of breast-feeding by teenage mothers. Pre-birth advice should include education and support in promoting her confidence, ability and desire to breast-feed. Where the father of the baby is involved and participates in the parenting, it is important to include him in promoting breast-feeding. Where the mother is not supported by the father, there may be another member of her family or a trusted friend who can provide support and encouragement and they too can benefit from the preparatory sessions. The support, consistency of advice and the care given by midwives and health visitors is crucial in successful establishment of breast-feeding. The use of breast-feeding support workers has been effective in some services and can be particularly helpful for teenage mothers and their babies.[8]

Breast-feeding will not be the preferred option for many teenagers. Where the baby is to have formula feeds, it is crucial that the mother is supported in establishing effective feeding and understands the principles and correct techniques for making formula feeds.

Teenage fathers

Where a teenage couple are married or in a stable relationship, the problems are fewer, even where the pregnancy was not planned. They are still vulnerable because of their age or lifestyle choices and there are often financial pressures. The teenage father should not feel alienated or disempowered by the system of care. The TPSS should focus on a father friendly approach, including preparing them for parenting. The fears, sensitivities and aspirations of teenage fathers differ from those of older fathers, as much as those of mothers of different ages.

Younger teenage fathers are less likely to be established in a steady relationship with the mother. They may drink heavily, use illicit drugs and respond aggressively to authority, especially in challenging situations. The TPSS strategy and inter-agency liaison should focus on promoting the confidence of these young men, helping them to cope with responsibility and avoid situations that lead them into crime or unemployment and social deprivation.[1] Open classes for teenage fathers to drop in, which are well publicised, can be a means of engaging this group.

Liaison and networks across services

Links and networks between and across services are important for reducing the incidence of teenage conception and this should be part of the TPSS. Support for teenagers to continue their education in school or college should be central to any teenage pregnancy strategy. Appropriate local provision of education, which continues during pregnancy and after birth and is coupled with appropriate, affordable childcare facilities during studies, should be included in the local action plan in a way that meets locally identified needs. Information on local employment and training opportunities requires links with the employment services. This can assist in reducing the discrimination against teenage mothers and increase employer support to them in retaining their employed position and their rights to maternity care and maternity leave.

The Maternity Alliance produces up-to-date publications specifically for pregnant teenagers, which make the complex system of benefits and rights as simple as possible to access.[9] Primary care trusts and local maternity services should use these in their work with teenagers to supplement a locally produced and regularly updated teenage pregnancy advisory and information booklet.

The local authority housing department should be included in the TPSS network and partnership. Social workers working within the team are able to act as advocates for teenagers who may need accommodation. It could also fall on the teenage pregnancy midwife, GP or health visitor to arrange accommodation when a girl is forced to leave the family home or if she seeks refuge from threatening or violent behaviour. Close liaison, information exchange and guidelines for emergency action by members of the teenage pregnancy service enable appropriate action to be quickly implemented and positive support for teenagers to be provided at a time when they are most vulnerable.

Conclusions

This NSF identifies standards relating to meeting the needs of vulnerable groups and improving the quality and standards of care for those whom the service has often failed, until now. Action by PCTs with maternity services to establish or further develop teenage pregnancy care is an important and pressing issue if public health is to improve now and for the future.

References

1 Social Exclusion Unit (1999) *Teenage Pregnancy: a report*. HMSO, London.
2 Maternity Care Working Party (2000) *The Case for a National Service Framework for Maternity Care*. HMSO, London.
3 Davies J and Evans F (1991) The Newcastle Community Midwifery Care Project. In: S Robinson and A Thompson (eds) *Midwives, Research and Childbirth*. Vol 2. Chapman and Hall, London.
4 Burden B, Worth D, Saville S *et al.* (2002) Changing the way we care for young mothers. *Midwives J*. **5 (5)**: 170–3.
5 Cheema K (2002) Supporting pregnant teenagers. *MIDIRS*. **12**, supplement 1: S26–9.
6 East Lancashire Hospitals NHS Trust (2003) *Information For Young People*. Queen's Park Hospital, Blackburn.
7 Rozette C, Houghton-Clemmy R and Sullivan K (2000) A profile of teenage pregnancy: young women's perceptions of the maternity services. *Practising Midwife*. **3 (10)**: 23–5.
8 World Health Organization and UNICEF (1989) *Protecting, Promoting and Supporting Breast-feeding: the Special Role of Maternity Services. A Joint Statement*. WHO, Geneva.
9 Maternity Alliance (2003) *Rights for Pregnant Teenagers and Young Mothers 2003*. Maternity Alliance, London.

CHAPTER 12

Reducing unintentional injury in children and young people – the evidence

Kirsty Licence

Background

Injury is still the leading cause of death in children aged 0–14 years old in the UK and is also a major cause of ill health and disability amongst children and young people. It has been estimated that for each death due to injury, there are a further 45 hospital episodes, 630 doctor consultations and 5000–6000 minor injuries.[1]

Overall, 46% of child deaths due to injury are the result of road traffic crashes.[2] One-quarter of all injury deaths of children aged 0–14 years old are child pedestrian injuries. Suffocation accounts for 18% of deaths due to injury in 0–14 year olds, fire and drowning for 9% each and poisoning for 4%.

Child deaths due to injury are a major area of socioeconomic inequality in the UK, with the death rate from fires for children in the lowest socioeconomic groups being 15 times higher than that of children in the highest groups. For child pedestrian deaths, the mortality rate in social class 5 is five times that in social class 1.[2]

In international comparisons, the UK compares well with other developed countries in terms of the overall child mortality rate from injury.[3] For child pedestrian injuries, the UK compares less favourably with other countries of the Organisation for Economic Co-operation and Development.[4]

Government targets for reducing childhood injury deaths have existed since 1991 and the mortality rate from injury has been falling throughout the 1990s. *Saving Lives – Our Healthier Nation (1999)* set new targets for reducing injury-related mortality and morbidity in England.[5] These new targets, to be achieved by 2010, aim for a 20% reduction in the overall death rate due to injury and a 10% fall in the rate of serious injury.

Effectiveness of interventions to reduce unintentional injury to children

Road traffic injuries

Pedestrians and cyclists

Child pedestrians and cyclists are among the most vulnerable road users, yet children need to be able to use the streets to access play spaces, to socialise and to learn independence. Fear of road traffic injury is a major reason for parents not allowing children to walk or cycle to school or to play outside. This contributes to low levels of physical activity among children and environmental degradation through the use of cars for very short journeys. Promoting safe walking and cycling can therefore have a wider impact on the health of children and young people than simply the prevention of injury-related death and disability.

It is often not possible to identify particular accident blackspots for child pedestrians. Instead, it is the general road environment, especially in the areas where children live, that predicts child pedestrian injury.[2] Factors that predict higher rates of injury to child pedestrians are shown in Box 12.1. All these features are more common in the most deprived urban areas.[6]

Box 12.1: Factors associated with higher rates of child pedestrian injury

- High vehicle speeds
- High traffic volume
- High levels of on-street parking
- Lack of safe play spaces in residential areas
- Children having to cross many roads to reach play areas, schools or other facilities

---

Area road safety schemes have been shown to be effective in reducing injuries to child pedestrians and cyclists. These include traffic restrictions, speed restrictions with effective enforcement, pedestrian priority areas, provision of safe crossings and home zones.[6,7] A recent Cochrane review found a significant reduction in the number of fatal road crashes following the introduction of area road safety measures (combined rate ratio of 0.63, 95% confidence interval 0.14 to 2.59).[8] Such schemes were also associated with a significant reduction in the number of crashes leading to injury (combined rate ratio 0.89, 95% confidence interval 0.8 to 1.0).

Reducing dependence on cars through land-use planning policies and public transport strategies is also important for protecting pedestrians from injury, as well as improving the environment. These sorts of interventions usually require support from across communities in order to be implemented successfully. Information provided by those working in education, social and healthcare may also be useful in identifying the need for such measures.

It is difficult to draw conclusions about the effectiveness of formal programmes of pedestrian skills training for children. Children's knowledge of safe pedestrian behaviour and their reported behaviours and behaviour in simulated traffic situations can be improved by training delivered by lay people or in school. The most effective programmes involve some element of practical experience in real traffic situations. However, improvements in knowledge fall off rapidly over time[7,9] and there is little evidence that proxy measures such as knowledge or reported behaviour predict the likelihood of child pedestrian injury.[9] A recent systematic review found no randomised controlled trials that evaluated the impact of pedestrian skills training using actual injury rates as an outcome measure.[9] One non-randomised Swedish study of the impact of traffic clubs showed an increased injury rate in the intervention group and one UK study showed some reduction in casualties, but these studies are open to bias because of their non-randomised design.[7] The injury minimisation programmes for schools initiative (*see* Box 12.2) demonstrates the importance of combining practical skills training with classroom teaching in education about injury prevention.[10]

Box 12.2: Injury minimisation programme for schools (IMPS)

(*See*: www.impsweb.co.uk)

The IMPS[10] was developed in Oxford by a group of healthcare professionals in response to injury reduction targets set out in *Health of the Nation* (DH 1992).[11]

It started in 1994 and the programme now runs in 11 areas across the UK. The programme is aimed at Year 6 pupils and focuses on road safety, the potential for injuries in the home, fire, electricity, poisons and water hazards. The programme involves the school and local hospitals. Teachers are provided with resource packs and the material covers national curriculum subjects; for example, statistics on injuries are provided that can be used in maths teaching. Pupils attend local hospitals to receive first aid and basic life support training and they are given a tour of the accident and emergency (A&E) department. This element of the programme aims to desensitise children from the fear they may experience when faced with an injury, as well as improving general life-skills.

IMPS was evaluated in a prospective, non-randomised matched control study. Altogether, 1200 10 and 11 year olds took part in the study, 600 of whom received the IMPS intervention and 600 of whom received no intervention. Five months after completion of the programme, children who received the intervention:

- demonstrated significantly greater knowledge than control children in first aid for burns and for choking and in the correct procedure for making a 999 call
- were significantly better than control children in almost all areas of basic life support and were more willing to undertake life-saving procedures
- were significantly better than controls at identifying subtle hazards and were more likely to tell others to stop doing something dangerous.

There is some evidence that cycling skills training can improve safe cycling behaviour.[5] On-road training is a core feature of successful programmes. As with pedestrians, there is no good evidence of associated reductions in injury to child cyclists. More research is needed using injury rates as an outcome measure.

Visibility aids, including fluorescent garments, flashing lights and reflective materials (especially if positioned at major joints), improve detection and recognition of pedestrians and cyclists by drivers, but a recent review found no studies evaluating the impact of these aids on injury risk.[12]

Cycle helmet use has been shown to reduce head and facial injuries in collisions and falls.[13] Measures to increase uptake include education and promotion campaigns, discount purchase schemes and legislation.[6,7] Legislation has been used in several countries and although head injury rates have fallen, the impact on overall injury rates is less clear and there is some evidence that the level of cycling among the affected population has fallen. Legislation may be more effective if it follows campaigns that make cycle helmet wearing more acceptable so that cycling uptake does not diminish.

Education and promotional campaigns have been successful in increasing purchase and reported use of helmets in a variety of settings, especially if combined with discount purchase schemes. The increase in use of helmets appears to be highest in younger age groups, among girls and among higher income groups.[7] Evidence from a programme in which cycle safety advice was provided when children attended accident and emergency departments with a cycling injury was inconclusive, showing a small but statistically insignificant rise in cycle helmet use.[7]

Car occupants

Child car seat restraints, used properly, reduce occupant injuries in collisions.[4,5] There is reasonable evidence that loan schemes, which include education and demonstration of correct fitting, do increase the proper use of child car seats,[7] although none of the studies in this review included children over two years old. These loan schemes were all either hospital or primary care based. There is also some evidence that educational interventions can be effective and this evidence extends to older children. The behaviour of teenagers in respect of wearing of seatbelts was least amenable to change. Reward schemes were effective whilst in operation.[7]

Alcohol and drug intoxication remain significant factors in causing road crashes and in other unintentional injuries and deaths, such as drowning. Children and young people are injured by intoxicated adult drivers, as well as being responsible for road crashes through their own risk-taking behaviour. The passing and enforcement of laws relating to drink-driving has proved effective and pilot projects are in place to enforce the laws relating to driving while impaired through drugs. Young drivers are especially at risk of being involved in crashes while under the influence of illicit drugs and educational interventions need to address this growing risk factor. For young people starting to drive, graduated licensing schemes, minimum learner driver periods and logbooks do help. A driver training logbook scheme has been proposed for the UK.

Burn injuries and scalds

A number of social factors have been identified that are associated with child deaths in house fires: [2]

- living in poor council housing
- living in temporary accommodation
- living in a single parent household.

Ownership of a functioning smoke alarm is associated with a reduced risk of death in house fires.[14] Households least likely to own a smoke alarm include those:

- that contain one adult residing alone
- in privately rented accommodation
- in a purpose-built flat
- in which somebody smokes
- in affluent urban areas
- with residents who have got into financial difficulties
- in properties built before 1984
- in which the respondent (to the survey) has no educational qualifications
- in which the respondent to the survey is Asian
- in properties in poor physical condition.[2]

The factors listed above may help in the identification of households most likely to benefit from interventions.

A systematic review of controlled trials of interventions to promote smoke alarm ownership found that general educational programmes had little effect on smoke alarm ownership.[14] However, advice about fire prevention and use of smoke alarms delivered in the context of child health surveillance visits was effective for increasing smoke alarm ownership and function. Several non-randomised trials showed beneficial effects of the free distribution of smoke alarms, but these trials may be subject to bias. Free distribution in combination with fitting of the alarm was most beneficial,[14] while in higher risk households, free distribution alone appears to be ineffective in reducing injury and deaths.[15] The type of alarm fitted and provision of regular maintenance are also important factors in determining if smoke alarms will be functioning and therefore effective.[16,17]

There is little evidence that distribution of water temperature control devices has any prolonged impact on home hot water temperature or reduces injuries from scalds.[7]

Injury in the home

A systematic review from the US of trials of counselling in primary care about the prevention of childhood unintentional injuries reported positive effects in 18 out of 20 studies.[18] Results of trials involving home visiting and provision of injury prevention advice at baby clinics in the UK have been mixed. Home visits with assessment of hazards, often combined with provision of free or low-cost safety equipment, have been successful in some studies at improving knowledge and the safety of the home environment.[7] A systematic review of eight trials of home visiting, seven of which focused on disadvantaged families, found a significant reduction in injury rates for children in visited families.[19] A recent Cochrane review of environmental interventions that aimed to reduce injuries in the home found few good-quality research studies.[20] In particular, most studies identified were too small to detect possibly significant effects. This review covered educational interventions, home hazard assessment and the provision of free, subsidised or loaned safety equipment. There was some evidence of a reduction in home hazards, but no good evidence of reduction in injuries could be ascribed to the interventions.

Play and leisure injuries

A number of effective interventions in the leisure environment have been reported,[7] including:

- a project to control firework distribution and sale and to clear unexploded fireworks from the street after celebrations, which was associated with substantial reductions in firework injuries
- interventions to increase the use of mouthguards in rugby players, which reduced the number of tooth fractures
- interventions to improve compliance with playground safety equipment, which reduced numbers of injuries
- interventions to improve safety in sports, which have been effective, for older adolescents in particular.[21]

Other injury groups

Product redesign and regulation have been shown to reduce mortality from suffocation and entrapment, to reduce burn and scald injuries in some circumstances and to reduce the incidence of unintentional poisoning and associated mortality.[6,7] Health and social care agencies can influence these areas for intervention through improving injury surveillance and reporting and through effectively advocating for safer products to be made and for appropriate legislation.

Cost-effectiveness

Economic analyses have shown that injury prevention measures can be cost-effective. There is a considerable cost to health and social care agencies and to society as a whole in managing the consequences of unintentional injuries. The cost of effective interventions should therefore be offset against their potential to save money in the wider community. Some interventions have been estimated to have a net cost-saving effect, even when only direct costs are considered, including child car safety seats, smoke detectors and bicycle helmets for 5–15 year olds.[1]

Surveillance

Good injury surveillance is a vitally important part of a comprehensive injury prevention strategy. Data on the epidemiology, causes and trends of childhood injuries can be used in a number of ways:

- to identify high-risk groups, for example in terms of age, gender, socio-economic status and geographical distribution
- to recognise patterns in injury causation, which may help to prioritise preventive interventions
- to identify trends in injuries, to monitor the effectiveness of interventions and identify new factors in the causation of injury, e.g. the use of a mobile phone while driving a car.

Injury data can be collected at national, regional and local levels. Primary care teams and local healthcare services have a key role, especially in the collection and dissemination of local data. Comprehensive data collection requires cooperation between several agencies, including primary and secondary healthcare services, local authorities, police forces, schools and leisure services. The use of local surveillance systems to target interventions, motivate participants and evaluate interventions is a feature of effective collaborative, community-based interventions.[7] The Accidental Injury Task Force has made detailed recommendations about the type and sources of injury data that should be collected.[22]

Priorities for intervention programmes

In reconciling the patterns of unintentional injury in the UK with the evidence for the effectiveness of the interventions, priority should be given to:

* area-wide road safety measures, including traffic calming, 20mph zones, safe crossings, parking restrictions, home zones, safe routes for walking and cycling and separation of pedestrians/cyclists from motor vehicles
* speed restrictions
* promotion of car safety seats for children and of rear-seat safety belt use
* fitting of smoke detectors, either hard wired or with long-life non-removable batteries
* sprinkler systems in the highest risk dwellings, e.g. houses in multiple occupation
* education and awareness raising, through home visits, parenting education or as part of child health surveillance, targeting families where risk is higher
* reducing smoking in households with children
* increasing use of child-resistant packaging for potentially toxic substances
* education programmes that address broad aspects of risk and risk-taking behaviour, which are appropriate for the developmental stage and experience of participants
* improving surveillance systems.

What primary care teams can do

Injury prevention is a multiagency task, requiring action across the five areas for health promotion set out in the Ottawa Charter[23] (see Box 12.3). Perhaps partly because of this, it often fails to make it into the priority areas of any single agency. This is unfortunate, given the strong evidence base for a range of injury prevention measures, outlined above.

Box 12.3: Levels of health promotion action described in the Ottawa Charter[23] and examples of injury prevention measures

* Healthy public health policy, including legislation and effective enforcement of road traffic laws.
* Creating supportive environments (including the family, school, leisure facilities and the built environment) through, for example, road engineering measures that protect child pedestrians and cyclists, especially in residential areas.
* Community action, such as supporting the enforcement of legislation in relation to the sale of potentially harmful products to minors, including fireworks and alcohol.

- Development of personal skills, such as programmes that make children and young people more aware of hazards, enable them to use appropriate self-protective skills and equipment and help them to develop social skills and self-esteem to enable them to avoid risk-taking behaviours.
- Reorientation of health services, which may include providing education and information directly to children, young people and families, both in health and in other settings and collaborating with other agencies to provide education.

Many effective injury prevention measures fall outside the traditional areas of direct responsibility of health and social care agencies, as traditionally defined. However, public health teams, led by directors of public health, now sit within PCTs and the public health role of community health professionals such as health visitors is expanding. These public health professionals should raise awareness of the issue of unintentional injury and enable greater priority to be given to implementing effective preventive measures.

Primary care organisations and social care agencies can work to:

- raise awareness of the issue of injury and help to make it a top public health priority
- identify, promote and support effective preventive interventions
- advocate for effective injury prevention measures through local strategic partnerships, local transport plans, community safety strategies, preventive strategies and other coalitions.

There are direct roles for health and social care in the implementation of preventive programmes, for example in:

- leading the development of comprehensive surveillance systems at all levels, providing data and information on patterns of injury and linking effectively with other agencies that collect injury data (see Box 12.4)
- providing education and advice on injury prevention to children, young people and families at appropriate times, for example at routine health surveillance, screening and prevention visits or at times of attendance for injury
- supporting education for children and young people in risk awareness and risk management, including first aid and immediate care
- helping to identify households or areas where there may be increased risk of injury and working to minimise these risks
- ensuring that families are given information about how to minimise the risk of injury to children, including the proper use of safety equipment and working to increase use of appropriate safety devices

- ensuring that health and social care settings minimise the risk of injury to staff and clients and foster an injury-prevention culture in the community
- where injury prevention fails, delivering effective trauma care, rehabilitation and support for those who suffer injury.

Box 12.4: The role of paediatric liaison health visiting in injury surveillance in Oxfordshire[24]

Injury surveillance – the use of a database to notify health visitors regarding children's attendance at emergency departments or minor injury units

The liaison health visitor service in Oxfordshire is well established and a dedicated injury database has been in use for the last 15 years. This records details of children age 0–4 years attending an emergency department and those 5–16 year olds who are admitted to hospital as a result of an injury. The cause of the injury, the treatment and outcome are all recorded.

The database is used to notify individual health visitors and school health nurses of children's attendance. The paperwork generated to inform the health visitors of the child's attendance also highlights any previous attendances as a result of an injury, stating the cause of that injury. This enables health visitors to identify families where there is an apparent need for injury prevention education and support.

Within the last five years the service has been extended countywide and now covers the minor injury units where children also present for treatment as a result of injury. While attendance at these units is generally for less severe injuries, some children will be referred to one of the two emergency departments within the county, if additional treatment is required. This helps to identify those children seen in several different treatment locations.

Additional information is available to primary care professionals and those in social services within the liaison health visitor injury database that is valuable in their work with families, to highlight the opportunities to support families, identify vulnerable children/groups and to address injury prevention.

Having this information on a database has also enabled the service to identify trends with regard to the types of injury, where the injury occurred and the outcomes and can be used to target specific areas for preventive interventions. The database is also used when reviewing non-accidental injury cases with a community paediatrician and hospital social worker.

The current stand-alone database is being reviewed to explore the possibility of integrating it with the main hospital computer system and with the injury surveillance work within the emergency department and to improve the data retrieval systems.

Areas for further research

There is good evidence for the effectiveness of a range of measures to reduce injury mortality and morbidity. But further research is needed in such areas as:

- effectiveness of interventions on reducing injury, disability and death rates, rather than proxy outcomes
- interventions to reduce injury in older children, adolescents and young adults (12–24 year age group)
- cost-effectiveness of injury reduction interventions
- socioeconomic patterns of injury-related morbidity
- effectiveness of interventions in reducing inequalities in injury-related mortality and morbidity
- effectiveness of interventions in different ethnic minority groups
- effectiveness of interventions in rural areas
- propensity for multiple risk and strategies for risk reduction
- better quality, larger studies are required from which more robust conclusions can be drawn across a range of potentially effective interventions.

References

1 Conway L and Morgan D (2001) *Injury Prevention.* BMJ Books, London.   **D**
2 Towner E (2002) Prevention of childhood injury. Background paper   **D** prepared for the Accidental Injury Task Force. In: *Preventing Accidental Injury – Priorities for Action.* Report to the Chief Medical Officer of the Accidental Injury Task Force. Department of Health, London.
3 UNICEF (2001) *A League Table of Child Deaths by Injury in Rich* **Statistics/** *Nations.* UNICEF Innocenti Research Centre, Florence. **data**
4 Road Accidents Great Britain 2002. **Statistics/** www.dft.gov.uk/stellent/groups/dft_transstats/documents/page/ **data** dft_transstats_024343.pdf
5 Department of Health (1999) *Saving Lives – Our Healthier Nation.* The   **P** Stationery Office, London.
6 NHS Centre for Reviews and Dissemination (1996) Preventing unin-   **A1** tentional injuries in children and young adolescents. *Effective Health Care.* **2 (5)**: 1–16.
7 Towner E, Dowswell T, Mackereth C *et al.* (2001) *What Works in*   **A1** *Preventing Unintentional Injuries in Children and Young Adolescents?* Health Development Agency, London.
8 Bunn F, Collier T, Frost C *et al.* (2003) Area-wide traffic calming for   **A1** preventing traffic related injuries. Cochrane Review. In: *The Cochrane Library.* Issue 4. John Wiley & Sons Ltd, Chichester.
9 Duperrex O, Roberts I and Bunn F (2003) Safety education of pedestrians   **A1** for injury prevention. Cochrane Review. In: *The Cochrane Library.* Issue 4. John Wiley & Sons Ltd, Chichester.

10 Frederick K, Bixby E, Orzal MN *et al.* (2000) An evaluation of the Injury Minimisation Programme for Schools (IMPS). *Injury Prevention.* **6 (2)**: 92–5.   **B2**

11 Department of Health (1992) *The Health of the Nation. A strategy for health in England.* The Stationery Office, London.   **P**

12 Kwan I, Mapstone J and Roberts I (2003) Interventions for increasing pedestrian and cyclist visibility for the prevention of death and injuries. Cochrane Review. In: *The Cochrane Library.* Issue 4. John Wiley & Sons Ltd, Chichester.   **A1**

13 Thompson DC, Rivara FP and Thompson R (2003) Helmets for preventing head and facial injury in bicyclists. Cochrane Review. In: *The Cochrane Library.* Issue 4. John Wiley & Sons Ltd, Chichester.   **A1**

14 DiGuiseppi C and Higgins JPT (2003) Interventions for promoting smoke alarm ownership and function. Cochrane Review. In: *The Cochrane Library.* Issue 4. John Wiley and Sons Ltd, Chichester.   **A1**

15 DiGuiseppi C, Roberts I, Wade A *et al.* (2002) Incidence of fires and related injuries after giving out free smoke alarms: cluster randomised controlled trial. *BMJ.* **325**: 995–7.   **B1**

16 Rowland D, DiGuiseppi C, Roberts I *et al.* (2002) Prevalence of working smoke alarms in local authority inner city housing: randomised controlled trial. *BMJ.* **325:** 998–1001.   **B1**

17 Rowland D, Afolabi E and Roberts I (2002) Prevention of deaths and injuries caused by house fires: survey of local authority smoke alarm policies. *J Public Health Med.* **24 (3)**: 217–18.   **C1**

18 Bass JL, Christoffel KK, Widome M *et al.* (1993) Childhood injury prevention counselling in primary care settings: a critical review of the literature. *Pediatrics.* **92 (4)**: 544–50.   **A1**

19 Roberts I (1996) Does home visiting prevent childhood injury? A systematic review of randomised controlled trials. *BMJ.* **312**: 29–33.   **A1**

20 Lyons RA, Sander LV, Weightman AL *et al.* (2003) Modification of the home environment for the reduction of injuries. Cochrane Review. In: *The Cochrane Library.* Issue 4. John Wiley & Sons Ltd, Chichester.   **A1**

21 Coleman P, Munro J, Nicholl J *et al.* (1996) *The Effectiveness of Interventions to Prevent Accidental Injury to Young Persons Aged 15–24 Years: a review of the evidence.* Sheffield Centre for Health and Related Research, University of Sheffield, Sheffield.   **A2**

22 The Measuring and Monitoring Injury Working Group (2002) Measuring and monitoring injury. Report to the Accidental Injury Task Force. In: *Preventing Accidental Injury – Priorities for Action. Report to the Chief Medical Officer from The Accidental Injury Task Force.* The Stationery Office, London.   **P**

23 World Health Organization (1986) *Ottawa Charter.* Division of Health Promotion, Education and Communication, World Health Organization, Geneva. www.who.dk/AboutWHO/Policy/20010827_2   **P**

24 Hill R (2004) Personal communication. John Radcliffe Hospital, Oxford.   **C2**

CHAPTER 13

Immunisation in primary care

Helen Bedford and David Elliman

Of all the preventive measures carried out in primary care, immunisation is the best researched and most cost-effective. Countries with effective immunisation programmes have seen dramatic falls in vaccine-preventable diseases. Indigenous measles, mumps and rubella have been eliminated from Sweden and Finland and polio has almost been eradicated from the world.

The guidance in the current edition of the publication *Immunisation Against Infectious Disease*[1] should form the basis of all immunisation practice in the UK. The printed edition is currently being revised (August 2004) whereas the web-based version is more regularly updated.

There are very few contraindications to most vaccines and so it ought to be relatively easy to deliver the routine programme to the whole population. As the evidence is so firmly in favour of immunisation, one would expect to achieve the targets of 95% set for public health purposes. Unfortunately, this is not always the case and the uptake of many vaccines in some areas is less than ideal. This is due, in part, to poor data collection so that uptake rates may be underestimated, but also because some children may be overlooked. Scares concerning whooping cough and, more recently, measles, mumps and rubella (MMR) vaccines have also resulted in reduced uptake. It is important that general medical practices are well organised and that all health professionals have enough knowledge to be able to answer parents' concerns.

There should be an individual within the practice who takes overall responsibility for immunisation issues. This includes arrangement of appointments, data collection, supply and storage of vaccines and clinical advice in difficult cases. It does not matter whether the practice's immunisation lead is a clinician or manager, so long as they have the ability and remit to coordinate the activities of all those involved with immunisation. Professionals within the practice should know who is the lead within the PCT from whom they can seek further advice. The role of the lead within the PCT is very similar to that of the previous district immunisation coordinator.[2]

Current vaccination programme

The routine schedule changes over time as a result of changing epidemiology and new technology. This can lead to the addition of new vaccines, alternative preparations or extra doses. For example, the change in autumn 2004 from live oral polio vaccine to the inactivated preparation was made because wild polio has been virtually eliminated worldwide and so the risk of vaccine-associated paralytic polio, although it is very small, is now unacceptable. The availability of a five-component acellular pertussis vaccine with efficacy comparable to the whole cell vaccine has allowed the use of a less reactogenic vaccine, while not compromising protective efficacy. This acellular vaccine can also be mixed with Hib vaccine without any reduction in the latter's efficacy, unlike the three component vaccine. The recommended programme (as at October 2004) is given in Table 13.1.[1]

Table 13.1: Recommended programme of vaccines in the UK

Age	Vaccines
0–8 months	BCG in high-risk groups (in some areas it is given to all)
0 months	Hepatitis B for babies of carrier mothers – may also need hepatitis B immunoglobulin
1 month	Hepatitis B
2 months	Hepatitis B
2 months	Diphtheria/tetanus/acellular pertussis (DTaP – 'triple') *Haemophilus influenzae* Type b (Hib) Inactivated polio vaccine (IPV) (These three preparations are usually combined at this age as one injection of DTaP/Hib/IPV) Meningococcal C conjugate (administered as separate injection)
3 months	As 2 months
4 months	As 3 months
12 months	Hepatitis B
12–15 months	Measles/mumps/rubella (MMR) 2nd MMR – may be given at any time as long as at least 3 months have elapsed after the first. Most commonly given with preschool booster at 3.5 years old
3.5 years	Diphtheria (may be low dose-'d')/tetanus/acellular pertussis/ IPV (dTaP/IPV or DTaP/IPV) ('preschool booster')
10–12 years	BCG, if tuberculin negative
15+ years	Diphtheria/tetanus/IPV (Td/IPV) ('school leavers' booster')

Immunisations underlined are normally only given to children and young people in high-risk groups

Knowing whether a vaccine is live or dead, makes it possible to predict, in general terms, the likely adverse effects and contraindications. Most vaccines may cause mild local reactions and systemic upset of varying degrees. Live vaccines may also produce the disease, but almost always in an attenuated form.

Table 13.2: Live and inactive vaccines

	Live (attenuated)	*Inactivated, component or toxoid*
Vaccines given as part of the routine childhood programme	BCG Measles/mumps/rubella (MMR)	Diphtheria *Haemophilus influenzae* type b (Hib) Meningococcal C conjugate Pertussis (whole cell and acellular) Polio (inactivated – IPV) Tetanus
Other vaccines	Polio (oral – OPV) Smallpox Typhoid (oral) Varicella Yellow fever	Anthrax Hepatitis A Hepatitis B Influenza Japanese encephalitis Meningococcal A and C Meningococcal A, C, W135 and Y Plague Pneumococcal (plain and conjugate) Rabies Tick-borne encephalitis Typhoid (inactivated)

Contraindications and children with problem histories

With increasing experience and research, it is evident that there are very few contraindications to most vaccines. What follows is a general outline of the current situation. The most up-to-date version of the Green Book should be consulted for further details.[1]

General contraindications

Except in rare circumstances, no vaccine should be given when an individual has an acute illness with systemic upset or is pregnant. Minor illnesses without fever or systemic upset, such as an upper respiratory tract infection, are not a contraindication to immunisation.

A vaccine is contraindicated if a person has previously had an anaphylactic reaction to the vaccine or a constituent.

Live vaccines

Administration of a live vaccine to some immunocompromised people may result in severe adverse reactions such as a severe form of the disease being vaccinated against. Examples of immunosuppression include: patients with congenital and acquired immunodeficiencies; those on immunosuppressive treatment, including high doses of systemic corticosteroids; those who have had a bone marrow transplant. However, this is not a blanket contraindication and depends on the particular vaccine and the nature of the immunosuppression. For example, MMR should certainly be given to someone with asymptomatic HIV infection and possibly to someone with AIDS. This is a complex field and advice should be sought from the consultant looking after the patient. More details can be found on the website of the Royal College of Paediatrics and Child Health.[3]

Pertussis

The traditional whooping cough vaccine was known as whole cell because it contained the entire organism. The vaccine now in use is known as acellular as it contains only a limited number of components. Depending on the preparation, it may contain three or five components. The three-component vaccine should be reserved for use only as a booster, as it has a lower efficacy than the five-component vaccine.

With increasing experience and research, there are now few contraindications to pertussis vaccine. The guidelines[1] are now much clearer. In the past a family or personal history of febrile convulsions or cerebral damage in the neonatal period were considered problem histories and reasons for special consideration, but now the only absolute contraindications are the same as for any killed vaccine. Children with well-controlled epilepsy should have the vaccine. Those who have what is termed an evolving neurological disorder should have the vaccination postponed until the condition is stable. If pertussis vaccination is to be postponed for only a matter of months, then as it is not possible to obtain pertussis vaccine by itself, it would be wise to postpone the DTaP/Hib/IPV as a whole.[4] Local or systemic reactions, unless anaphylactic, are not considered contraindications.

MMR vaccine

Combined MMR vaccine was introduced into the UK in 1988 to replace single-measles vaccine, used since 1968. It also represented a change in policy for the control of rubella. Prior to the use of MMR vaccine, rubella vaccine was offered to schoolgirls and susceptible adult women with the aim of providing them with individual protection against rubella infection in pregnancy. Although this selective immunisation policy was partially successful, cases of congenital rubella syndrome, as well as terminations of pregnancy for proven infection or contact with a case, still occurred. This was inevitable as the vaccine strategy had no impact on the circulation of the virus in the community and women who failed to be immunised or who, very rarely, lost their immunity were at risk of infection from young children. Single antigen mumps vaccine had never been used routinely.

The contraindications to MMR are as for any live vaccine. MMR vaccines in use in most countries contain small quantities of egg and so there has been concern about giving the vaccine to children who are allergic to egg for fear that they might have a serious reaction to it. However, there is considerable experience of using the vaccine in such children without any serious adverse effects. Therefore, most experts would advise that the vaccine should be given, but it may be appropriate to give it in a hospital setting when there has been a previous anaphylactic reaction to egg.[5] This is more to reassure the parents than from medical necessity. There is no good evidence that skin testing helps in the management of these children.

Mild measles occurs in about 5% of vaccine recipients, 5–11 days after immunisation. Some recipients may also develop mild mumps or mild rubella somewhat later. None of these are infectious and so would not pose a threat to a pregnant woman. More serious adverse events occur less frequently and include convulsions at a rate of one in every 3000 doses and idiopathic thrombocytopenic purpura (ITP) at a rate of one in every 32 000 doses.[6]

To prevent outbreaks of disease, particularly measles, 95% of the population have to be immune. Since 5–10% of individuals who have one dose of MMR vaccine do not produce protective antibodies to measles, two doses of the vaccine have been recommended since 1996. After a second dose of MMR vaccine, 90% of those who did not respond to the first dose will be protected. Adverse reactions are much less frequent after the second dose than after the first.[7] This two-dose policy has proved very successful and in countries with high uptake, such as the US, all three infections have become rare. In Finland, indigenous disease has been eliminated.[8] In the UK, there has been a decline in the numbers of reported cases with only one acute death, due to measles, in the 1990s. Since 1992 all deaths have been due to the late effects of measles infection, e.g. subacute sclerosing panencephalitis.[9]

Single antigen rubella vaccine is no longer available. Women found to be seronegative to rubella should be offered MMR vaccine.

Concerns over safety of MMR vaccine

In 1998, a paper was published describing a case series of 12 children with behavioural problems and bowel symptoms.[10] It was suggested that autism and bowel problems were causally linked. Many of the parents remembered their children's difficulties beginning soon after they had had MMR vaccine. The authors were very clear in stating: 'We did not prove an association between MMR vaccine and the syndrome described'. Subsequently, a minority of the authors have voiced their concerns that there may be a link and advised the use of separate antigens rather than combined MMR vaccine. This view has received disproportionate publicity and understandably many parents and health professionals are now confused and concerned about the safety of the combined vaccine. Since publication of this paper, a significant body of research has failed to find any evidence for a link between MMR vaccine and autism or bowel disease.[11-13] Despite this the uptake of MMR has been adversely affected with outbreaks of measles arising in some areas. At the time of writing (August 2004), the uptake of the vaccine is 82% on average in UK two year olds but lower in some areas such as London where the average is 70%.[14] There is evidence that measles is on the brink of becoming endemic again.[15]

Hepatitis B

The main use of this vaccine in childhood is for the infants of women found to be hepatitis B carriers during pregnancy or who have acute hepatitis B in pregnancy. Such infants should receive four doses of vaccine – at birth, one month, two months and 12 months. This can be given at any time in relation to other childhood vaccines.

BCG

The vaccine is routinely offered to children between 10 and 14 years of age following a negative Heaf test. It should also be offered to neonates at high risk of TB as defined in the Green Book.[1] In some high-incidence areas, it is offered to all neonates.

Travel vaccines

When they go abroad, children may be exposed to infectious diseases that are uncommon in the UK. They may therefore require travel vaccines. This subject is complex and advice should not be given lightly. Whether a particular vaccine is indicated will depend on the age of the child, the countries being visited, the part of the country in which the child will stay, the type of accommodation (especially eating arrangements), the duration of the visit, the time of year and any underlying medical disorders. Advice should be based on the most up-to-date information available and should also include topics such as the care of food and drink and, where appropriate, avoidance of malaria risks and malaria prophylaxis.[16,17]

New developments

Pneumococcal vaccine

A conjugate pneumococcal vaccine is licensed for use in children at high risk of invasive pneumococcal disease. Such children include those with sickle cell disease, non-functioning spleens and coeliac disease. It is not currently recommended for use at any age, whereas the plain polysaccharide vaccine is recommended for the elderly.[1]

Varicella zoster vaccine

This live vaccine is licensed for use in children at high risk of developing complications or severe disease. It is not currently recommended for routine use.

Meningococcal B

A vaccine to prevent meningococcal B infection is highly desirable but is proving difficult to develop. It is likely to be some years yet before one is available. In view of this it is important to remind people that the currently available meningococcal C vaccine will only cover about 40% of all cases of meningococcal disease.

Some questions parents ask

What about the mercury in vaccines?

Some vaccines include a mercury-containing preservative – thiomersal. This was often added because many vaccines were dispensed in multidose containers and it was important to prevent bacterial contamination. In other vaccines it was part of the manufacturing process. There are no recognised safety limits for the injection of mercury, but there are some for its oral ingestion. However, these vary widely. In 1999, it was noted that if an infant was given all the recommended vaccines in the US programme in the first six months, they would exceed one of these limits. However, the amount would still be below many other thresholds, including those set by WHO and the American Federal Drugs Agency.[18] Bearing in mind the precautionary principle and the fact that, in many countries, routine infant vaccines are rarely dispensed in multidose containers, manufacturers were asked to move towards thiomersal-free vaccines. In the UK, even if an infant had been given all the routine vaccines in the previous schedule, the amount of mercury received would not even exceed the lowest of the recommended safety levels. From autumn 2004 none of the routine childhood vaccines contain thiomersal.

Do too many vaccines overload the immune system?

Some parents and complementary practitioners have suggested that giving a number of vaccines together may overload the immune system, making children susceptible to other infections, autoimmune disorders and atopy. There is no scientific rationale behind this. Serious infections are no more common in children in the period immediately after they have been immunised.[19–21] There are a number of studies that show no association between atopy and immunisations.[22] It is more difficult to disprove a link with autoimmune disorders because of the long interval between vaccination and the onset of disease. However, there have been studies showing no link between Hib vaccine and diabetes and measles vaccine and multiple sclerosis.[23,24]

Would it be better to delay vaccines until the baby's immune system is more developed?

Most babies, even premature ones, produce an adequate immune response to the vaccines given at 8, 12 and 16 weeks. If anything, side effects such as fever and sore injection sites are more common when immunisations are delayed.[25] Diseases such as Hib, pertussis and meningococcal C are more prevalent in younger children. Therefore by delaying vaccines, infants are subjected to a double whammy – they are more likely to have side effects and protection against major infectious diseases is not there when it is most needed.

Very premature babies may not mount an adequate response to some vaccines, particularly hepatitis B and the polysaccharide conjugates. It may be appropriate to measure antibody levels in these babies to check whether they have achieved adequate levels.[26,27]

References

1 Department of Health (1996) *Immunisation against Infectious Disease*. HMSO, London. www.dh.gov.uk/assetRoot/04/07/29/84/04072984.pdf
2 Elliman D and Moreton J (2000) The District Immunisation Co-ordinator. *Arch Dis Child.* **82 (4)**: 280–2.
3 Royal College of Paediatrics and Child Health (2002) *Immunisation of the Immunocompromised Child.*
   www.rcpch.ac.uk/publications/recent_publications/Immunocomp.pdf
4 Ramsay ME, Miller E, Ashworth LA *et al.* (1995) Adverse events and antibody response to accelerated immunisation in term and preterm infants. *Arch Dis Child.* **72 (3)**: 230–2.

5 Lakshman R and Finn A (2000) MMR vaccine and allergy. *Arch Dis Child.* **82 (2)**: 93–5.

6 Miller E, Waight P, Farrington CP *et al.* (2001) Idiopathic thrombocytopenic purpura and MMR vaccine. *Arch Dis Child.* **84 (3)**: 227–9.

7 Virtanen M, Peltola H, Paunio M *et al.* (2000) Day-to-day reactogenicity and the healthy vaccinee effect of measles-mumps-rubella vaccination. *Pediatrics.* **106**: e-62.

8 Peltola H, Heinonen P, Valle M *et al.* (1994) The elimination of indigenous measles, mumps and rubella from Finland by a 12-year, two-dose vaccination program. *N Eng J Med.* **331**: 1397–402.

9 Health Protection Agency (2003) *Measles. Deaths, by Age Group, 1980–2002.* www.hpa.org.uk/infections/topics_az/measles/data_death_age.htm

10 Wakefield AJ, Murch SH, Anthony A *et al.* (1998) Ileal-lymphoid-nodular hyperplasia, non-specific colitis and pervasive developmental disorder in children. *Lancet.* **351**: 637–41.

11 Taylor B, Miller E, Lingam R *et al.* (2002) Measles, mumps and rubella vaccination and bowel problems or developmental regression in children with autism: a population study. *BMJ.* **324**: 393–6.

12 Madsen KM, Hviid A, Vestergaard M *et al.* (2002) A population-based study of measles, mumps and rubella vaccination and autism. *N Engl J Med.* **347**: 1477–82.

13 Anon (2003) MMR vaccine – how effective and how safe? *Drug Ther Bull.* **41 (4)**: 25–9.

14 Health Protection Agency (2004) *CDR Weekly.* **14 (26)**. www.hpa.org.uk/cdr/PDFfiles/2004/cdr2604.pdf

15 Jansen VAA, Stollenwerk N, Jensen HJ *et al.* (2003) Measles outbreaks in a population with declining vaccine uptake. *Science.* **301**: 804.

16 Department of Health (2001) *Health Information for Overseas Travellers.* HMSO, London. www.archive.official-documents.co.uk/document/doh/hinfo/travel02.htm

17 National Travel Health Network and Centre. www.nathnac.org/healthprofessionals/index.html

18 Ball LK, Ball R and Pratt RD (2001) An assessment of thimerosal use in childhood vaccines. *Pediatrics.* **107 (5)**: 1147–54.

19 Miller E, Andrews N, Waight P *et al.* (2003) Bacterial infections, immune overload and MMR vaccine. Measles, mumps and rubella. *Arch Dis Child.* **88 (3)**: 222–3.

20 Black SB, Cherry JD, Shinefield HR *et al.* (1991) Apparent decreased risk of invasive bacterial disease after heterologous childhood immunization. *Am J Dis Child.* **145**: 746–9.

21 Offit PA, Quarles J, Gerber MA *et al.* (2002) Addressing parents' concerns: do multiple vaccines overwhelm or weaken the infant's immune system? *Pediatrics.* **109 (1)**: 124–9.

22 Offit PA and Hackett CJ (2003) Addressing parents' concerns: do vaccines cause allergic or autoimmune diseases? *Pediatrics.* **111 (3)**: 653–9.

23 DeStefano F, Mullooly JP, Okoro CA *et al.* (2001) Childhood vaccinations, vaccination timing and risk of type 1 diabetes mellitus. *Pediatrics.* **108 (6)**: e-112.

24 DeStefano F, Verstraeten T, Jackson LA *et al.* (2003) Vaccinations and risk of central nervous system demyelinating diseases in adults. *Arch Neurol.* **60 (4)**: 504–9.

25 Ramsay ME, Rao M and Begg NT (1992) Symptoms after accelerated immunisation. *BMJ.* **304**: 1534–6.

26 Heath PT, Booy R, McVernon J *et al.* (2003) Hib vaccination in infants born prematurely. *Arch Dis Child.* **88 (3)**: 206–10.

27 Freitas da Motta MS, Mussi-Pinhata MM, Jorge SM *et al.* (2002) Immunogenicity of hepatitis B vaccine in preterm and full term infants vaccinated within the first week of life. *Vaccine.* **20 (11–12)**: 1557–62.

Further reading

- Chief Medical Officer (2004) *New Vaccinations for the Childhood Immunisation Programme.* 10 August. PL/CMO/2004/3. www.dh.gov.uk/assetRoot/04/08/73/47/04087347.pdf (accessed 12.8.04).
- Department of Health. *Immunisation: the safest way to protect your child.* www.immunisation.org.uk (accessed 31.7.04).
- Department of Health. *MMR The Facts.* www.mmrthefacts.nhs.uk/
- Health Protection Agency. *Vaccination of Individuals with Uncertain or Incomplete Immunisation Status* (accessed 31.7.04). www.hpa.org.uk/infections/topics_az/vaccination/uncertain_im_status.pdf
- Kassianos GC (2001) *Immunization: childhood and travel health.* Blackwell Science, Oxford.
- Offit PA and Jew RK (2003) Addressing parents' concerns: do vaccines contain harmful preservatives, adjuvants, additives, or residuals? *Pediatrics.* **112 (6 Pt 1)**: 1394–7.
- World Health Organization (2002) *International Travel and Health.* World Health Organization, Geneva. www.who.int/ith/

CHAPTER 14

Child health surveillance

David Elliman and Helen Bedford

Principles of screening

Child health promotion covers all activities designed to improve the physical or mental health of children.[1] A small but important component is child health surveillance, a top-down activity initiated by professionals and mainly aimed at the early detection of defects by using screening procedures. Immunisation can be considered as a primary preventive procedure because a disease is prevented, whereas screening is a secondary preventive procedure – a disease is not prevented, but its effects may be ameliorated. Many of the screening procedures are not carried out by primary care staff, but it is important that they are fully aware of the programmes as it is often the GP or health visitor to whom parents will turn if they have concerns.

Wald[2] defined screening as 'The systematic application of a test or enquiry, to identify individuals at sufficient risk to benefit from further investigation or direct preventive action amongst persons who have not sought medical attention on account of symptoms of that disorder'. A procedure is administered to a group of asymptomatic individuals in an attempt to identify those who are at greater risk of a condition. Common examples of procedures used are blood tests and physical examinations, but could also include a questionnaire. It is important to consider a screening programme as a whole, from the sending out of an invitation through to the initiation of treatment in those where it is indicated. This is a complex process, which can do harm as well as good.

In the past, screening programmes frequently arose out of the enthusiasm of an individual or group of individuals. This often resulted in considerable variation around the country (postcode screening) both in terms of which programmes were in operation and also in the details of how they were carried out. In an attempt to bring uniformity and to ensure a higher quality service, the National Screening Committee (NSC) was set up in 1996 to advise Ministers in England, Wales, Scotland and N Ireland. Soon after, child health and antenatal subgroups were established. The NSC has drawn up a list of criteria against which all current or proposed screening programmes should be judged.[3] They are summarised overleaf:

- the definition and natural history of the condition should be known
- the condition should be important in terms of its impact on individuals and society – a combination of severity and incidence
- there should be an effective management, e.g. diet for phenylketonuria, hearing aids for hearing impairment and the provision of reproductive choice in the case of antenatal screening for conditions such as Down's syndrome
- there should be a pre-symptomatic stage during which the initiation of treatment has a more favourable outcome than if initiated after the appearance of symptoms
- there should be a simple, inexpensive, accurate screening test
- there should be clear pathways for referral when an abnormality is suspected; there should be a diagnostic test that clearly distinguishes cases from non-cases
- there must be adequate resources for management of all detected cases
- the whole programme must be acceptable to the individuals being screened and society as a whole. Bearing in mind that the majority of people screened are not going to have the condition, it is very important that the effect on them is properly considered. In a screening programme for hypothyroidism, mothers whose babies had a positive screening test still had concerns when reviewed a year later, even though diagnostic testing proved to be normal.[4] Likewise, false-negative results, where conditions are missed, can be very distressing[5]
- all programmes should be properly monitored and audited to ensure that they operate to a high standard.

There are many screening programmes already in place in childhood and more may come in the next few years. Not all perform to a high enough standard, monitoring is often inadequate and audit infrequent. This particularly applies to the physical examination.[6] More effort will have to be put into this in future, at a local level by PCTs but also nationally.

Table 14.1 sets out the main recommendations of the National Screening Committee for neonatal and childhood screening (as at March 2004). These cover the whole of the UK except where countries are specifically excluded.[7]

Table 14.1: Main recommendations of the National Screening Committee for neonatal and childhood screening[7]

Age	Condition	Approximate incidence*	Test	Comments
6 days approximately	Phenylketonuria	10	Various, but all using the same blood spots	Already well established
	Hypothyroidism	30		
	Sickle cell disorders	Depends on ethnic origin – 1250 West African, 500 West Indian		To include all of the UK by the end of 2004
	Cystic fibrosis	40		To be rolled out throughout UK
Varies	Hearing impairment	100	Semi-automated testing	To include all UK by the end of 2006
In first 72 hours of life and again at 6–8 weeks	Ocular problems	30 (cataracts)	Inspection and red reflex	Already done as part of the routine neonatal and 6–8 week examination, but quality needs improvement
	Developmental dysplasia of the hips	120	Ortolani and Barlow tests	
	Congenital heart disease	800	Physical examination	
	Undescended testes	6000		
	Other congenital malformations	Depends on how broad is the definition		Not really a screening exercise
8 months	Hearing impairment	Accurate data not available	Infant distraction test	To be phased out as universal neonatal screening comes in
4–5 years old	Visual problems	5000–10 000, but depends on definition	Various	An orthoptist-led programme to be introduced as soon as practicable
School entry	Growth disorders	Accurate data not available	Height and weight	Needs to be done accurately and measurements plotted on a chart
	Hearing impairment	Unclear	Sweep test	Evidence is being sought for the value of this
	Visual problems	5000–10 000, but depends on definition	Various – commonest is measuring visual acuity with Snellen charts	Once the earlier orthoptist-led programme is in place, this should cease
Throughout school	Visual problems	Varies widely according to definition	Various – commonest is measuring visual acuity with Snellen charts	No changes to be made to what individual areas practise until further evidence becomes available

* Incidence per 100 000 children in cohort. This includes all cases, not just those newly detected by the programme at this point in time.

Summary of nationally recommended screening programmes

More detail on these recommendations as well as up-to-date information on the rollout of new programmes and quality standards can be found at the National electronic Library for Health Screening website.[7]

Neonatal blood spot programme

Testing for phenylketonuria and congenital hypothyroidism has taken place throughout the UK for decades.[8] Unfortunately, there are still occasional missed cases due to failings in the management of the system, particularly follow-up of missing results. It cannot be assumed that 'no news is good news'. Some areas in the UK already screen for sickle cell disease and cystic fibrosis and this will soon become universal. It will make use of the same blood spot. Training programmes will be instituted for relevant staff and national quality standards are being drawn up. The two new programmes will raise issues to do with the detection of a proportion of carriers and so it will be important that staff have a good understanding not only of the nature of all the conditions but also the relevance of the carrier state.

Neonatal hearing screening programme

Even when performed to the highest standards, the infant distraction test (a behavioural test of hearing, usually performed by the health visitor and another trained person at eight months of age) is far from perfect and it will not identify hearing loss until children are eight months old. There is emerging evidence that earlier detection and management improve the outcome for hearing-impaired children[9] and so a programme of neonatal hearing screening is being rolled out throughout the UK. This will detect most children with a congenital hearing loss. The screening will be performed by specially trained screeners or health visitors and may take place in hospital or in the community. Babies found to have a possible impairment will be referred for a diagnostic test (auditory brainstem response) and then, where appropriate, aids will be fitted. The median time of confirmation of hearing loss in infants where the programme is in operation is eight weeks in comparison with 12–20 months for the infant distraction test performed at 7–8 months. Hearing aids are being fitted at a median age of 14 weeks.

The proper functioning of this programme relies on the presence of a good tertiary audiology service, able to fit hearing aids in young infants, to monitor their performance and to change the moulds frequently. Once this programme is well established in a locality, the routine infant distraction test will cease. However, distraction testing will still be necessary for those infants who for one reason or another miss out on the neonatal testing or for those where concerns about their hearing arise later.

Neonatal and 6–8-week physical examinations

A superficial inspection should be performed immediately after birth to check for obvious physical anomalies. Within 72 hours a more detailed examination should be performed by a properly trained professional. This could be a doctor or a nurse[10] but, more importantly, whoever does it should be properly trained and updated. As with antenatal ultrasound, most components of this procedure do not fit the criteria for a screening test. The examinations of the eyes, hips and heart come nearest to such criteria. The eyes should be inspected and the red reflex tested, looking for structural anomalies, such as a cataract or any asymmetry. The Barlow and Ortolani tests for developmental dysplasia of the hips (previously known as congenital dislocation of the hips) should be performed. Any child with a suspected abnormality on these tests, or where there is a personal history of a breech presentation or a family history of a hip disorder in childhood, should have an ultrasound assessment of the hips (an X-ray is not appropriate as the femoral head will not be visualised at this age). Sometimes this is overlooked, so it is important that the primary care team ensure that it is arranged if it has not already been done. Assessment of the cardiovascular system includes noting the colour and respiratory rate of the infant, examination of the peripheral pulses and auscultation of the heart. As well as carrying out a general physical examination, the head circumference should be measured. The findings of the examination need to be recorded in the child's clinic record and in the personal child health record if it is available.[11]

Because of the natural history of most of these conditions, it is important that the neonatal examination is repeated at 6–8 weeks. The finding of an abnormality at this age does not necessarily imply incompetence on the part of the neonatal examiner. Although not fulfilling the criteria for screening tests, it is good practice to include, in both these examinations, a general physical examination of all the systems and measurement and plotting of the head circumference.

Vision screening at 4–5 years old

The testing of visual function under four years of age is very difficult and often requires retesting, tying up scarce resources.[12] Therefore, routine screening of visual function in children under four years old is not recommended. Even at four years old it is difficult and best done by an orthoptist. However, with current resources this would be impractical and so a compromise is that all children should have their visual function screened between their fourth and fifth birthdays by someone in a service that is led by an orthoptist. Abnormalities being sought are squint, amblyopia and reduced visual acuity. Once the orthoptist-led programme is in place, vision screening at seven years should cease. Evidence concerning screening at subsequent ages is lacking and so it is recommended that no new programmes should be implemented, but those already in place can continue, based in school settings.

Height and weight measurement

It is considered good practice to weigh children at routine contacts during infancy, e.g. at each of the two general physical examinations in the first 72 hours and at 6–8 weeks of age and at the time of immunisation.[13] It is also essential to measure the height and weight of any child suspected of having a chronic disorder or in whom there are concerns about their growth. However, there is a surprising lack of evidence to support routine monitoring of growth in otherwise healthy children. The consensus at a multidisciplinary meeting in 1998[13] concluded that height and weight should be measured and plotted on all children at the time of entry to school (that is, in the reception class). Subsequent routine measurements are not recommended. Although obesity is undoubtedly a major problem in children, there is currently no evidence to support routine screening for it in otherwise well children.[14]

School entry sweep test of hearing

Most children have a screening test for hearing impairment in the reception class at school. At present, there is little hard evidence to support this, but the consensus is that it should continue while further research is conducted. Children picked up at this age are most likely to have a conductive loss or, less likely, an acquired sensorineural problem. There will be some children who have a progressive sensorineural loss, which may not have been apparent at birth. This may be genetic in origin or acquired, e.g. following congenital rubella or cytomegalovirus infection. Routine screening for hearing impairment is not recommended at other ages, but children with high-risk conditions such as Down's syndrome and cleft palate should have their hearing assessed at intervals. All children who have had meningitis should have their hearing checked at least once.

Screening for emotional and developmental problems

Screening for emotional and developmental problems is not part of the recommended national programme. While these are important conditions, none of the widely used tests satisfy the standard criteria, not least because it is often difficult to define a case, i.e. what constitutes a significant abnormality and the natural history of some conditions is unclear.[15] Likewise, postnatal depression is a very important problem with major, sometimes permanent, adverse effects on the family. However, current evidence does not support screening using instruments such as the Edinburgh Postnatal Depression (PND) Scale.[16,17] Such instruments can have a useful place in the identification of PND when used properly as part of a larger programme.[18]

Data collection and audit

These programmes should all be properly audited to ensure that a high-quality service is maintained. Many of the conditions being sought are relatively uncommon and so, for the most part, monitoring of the process rather than outcome is what practitioners should concentrate on. National standards are currently in the process of being set for the timeliness of the performance of screening tests (as these become available they will be posted on the relevant section of the NeLH website[7]); return of the results to professionals and parents; number of false-positive results; speed at which diagnostic tests are performed after a positive screening result; and speed of initiation of treatment. Much of these data can be collected by using the forms in the personal child health record and all results should be recorded there for the parents.[11]

In view of the relatively small numbers involved, most audit is likely to be PCT rather than practice based. However, practices should be actively involved in this and where possible should be provided with their own data in comparison with others. Where cases are undetected by the screening programme or where standards are not met, further investigation is appropriate to ensure that any problems can be rectified and the programme improved.

Organisation within the primary care team

Ideally, one person should take responsibility for child health within the team. That person should oversee the organisation of the routine child health clinics, which would include routine contacts and immunisations. These should be run at a different time from the routine surgeries as it is not appropriate for well babies to be mixing with acutely ill children or adults. Clinics should be in a child- and family-friendly environment. The same person should be responsible for the monitoring and audit of the programme, although some of this will have to be on a population much larger than in an individual practice, however large.

It is likely that it will be the health visitor who ensures that individual children have had all the appropriate screening tests and that the results have been communicated to the parents. In spite of modern technology, many health visitors still feel more comfortable relying on their birth books rather than computers. However, as information technology improves, it should be possible to use it for managing individual children and checking their results, as well as producing aggregate data.

Coordinated teamwork will be key to the success of these programmes as many professionals are involved and there is a danger of people assuming someone else is getting on with a task, when it is not the case. This is important within the primary care team, particularly between health visitors and GPs, but also with school nurses, social workers and initiatives such as Sure Start.

Organisation within the primary care trust

Within a PCT there should be a person with lead responsibility for children's health. That person will need support from a wide variety of professionals and a standing child health group seems appropriate. PCT data need to be aggregated and compared with like PCTs as well as providing comparative data for practices within the PCT.

References

1 Hall DMB and Elliman D (eds) (2003) *Health for all Children* (4e). Oxford University Press, Oxford. www.health-for-all-children.co.uk
2 Wald NJ (1994) Guidance on terminology. *J Medical Screening.* **1**: 76.
3 National Screening Committee (2004) *The Criteria for Appraising the Viability, Effectiveness and Appropriateness of a Screening Programme.* www.nsc.nhs.uk/pdfs/criteria.pdf
4 Bodegard G, Fyro K and Larsson A (1983) Psychological reactions of 102 families with a newborn who has a falsely positive screening test for congenital hypothyroidism. *Acta Pediatr Scand Suppl.* **304**: 1–21.
5 Hall S, Bobrow M and Marteau TM (2000) Psychological consequences for parents of false negative results on prenatal screening for Down's syndrome: retrospective interview study. *BMJ.* **320**: 407–12.
6 Rahi JS and Dezateux C (1999) National cross sectional study of detection of congenital and infantile cataract in the United Kingdom: role of childhood screening and surveillance. British Congenital Cataract Interest Group. *BMJ.* **318**: 362–5.
7 National Screening Committee (2004) *Screening.* National electronic Library for Health. www.nelh.nhs.uk/screening/vbls.html
8 Streetly A and Corbett V (1998) *The National Newborn Screening Programme: an audit of phenylketonuria and congenital hypothyroidism screening in England and Wales.* Department of Public Health Medicine, Guy's and St Thomas's Medical Schools, London.
9 Yoshinaga-Itano C (2003) Early intervention after universal neonatal hearing screening: impact on outcomes. *Ment Retard Dev Disabil Res Rev.* **9 (4)**: 252–66.
10 Wolke D, Dave S, Hayes J *et al.* (2002) Routine examination of the newborn and maternal satisfaction: a randomised control trial. *Arch Dis Child Fetal Neonatal Ed.* **86**: 155–60.
11 Hall DMB (2003) *Personal Child Health Record.* www.health-for-all-children.co.uk

12 Snowdon SK and Stewart-Brown SL (1997) Preschool vision screening. *Health Technol Assess.* **1**: 1–83.

13 Hall DM (2000) Growth monitoring. *Arch Dis Child.* **82**: 10–15.

14 Hall DM (2001) *Child Growth Foundation seminar on the epidemic of obesity.* www.healthforallchildren.co.uk/pdf/epidemic_obesity/epidemic_of_obesity.pdf

15 Law J, Boyle J, Harris F *et al.* (1998) Screening for speech and language delay: a systematic review of the literature. *Health Technol Assess.* **2**: 1–184.

16 Shakespeare J, Blake F and Garcia J (2003) A qualitative study of the acceptability of routine screening of postnatal women using the Edinburgh Postnatal Depression Scale. *Br J Gen Pract.* **53**: 614–19.

17 Murray L, Woolgar M and Cooper P (2004) Detection and treatment of postpartum depression. *Community Practitioner.* **77 (1)**: 13–17.

18 National Screening Committee (2004) *Postnatal Depression.* National electronic Library for Health.
www.nelh.nhs.uk/screening/adult_pps/postnatal_depression.html

CHAPTER 15

Disabled children

Francine Bates

There are approximately 320 000 disabled children in England, the majority of whom live at home with their parents. In the past 10 years the prevalence of severe disability and complex needs in children has risen. Babies born prematurely are more likely to survive, as are children after severe trauma or illness. Up to 6000 children living at home are dependent on complex medical technology. Children and young people with learning disabilities have a greater prevalence of mental health problems than non-disabled children.

The great majority of disabled children live with their families and it is the families who assume day-to-day responsibility for caring for their child. Disabled children and their families want services that are prompt, convenient, responsive and of the highest quality and they want support from primary healthcare.

We need to address a number of issues in relation to caring for disabled children and their families in primary care. These are:

- promoting social inclusion
- early years provision of services
- providing direct support to families
- transition into adulthood
- commissioning services
- training and development of staff.

Promoting social inclusion

Exclusion from ordinary child and family activities and opportunities and services is commonly experienced by disabled children and their families. Many of the services that disabled children use are specialist services, which are not provided in the communities in which children live and do not offer opportunities for socialisation with non-disabled children.

Access to services

Parents of disabled children often complain about their exclusion from mainstream services. Families from minority ethnic backgrounds have particular difficulties in obtaining services. They report high levels of exclusion and unmet need and lower levels of receipt of services than white families.

PCTs must regularly review policies, practices and procedures to improve access and to ensure that disabled children and their families are not disadvantaged. Primary care providers should be aware of their responsibilities under the Disability Discrimination Act 1995 and other equality legislation. PCTs should ensure that services are culturally sensitive and responsive to the needs of minority ethnic communities.

Improving access to primary care

Parents of disabled children complain that staff often do not understand the impact that their child's disability has on their wider health needs. They need synchronised appointment systems so that families make a minimum number of visits to hospitals or clinics. Where multiple appointments are required, these should happen on the same day. They should be offered health appointments at school or outside school hours to minimise absence from school. Children with complex healthcare needs who are prone to health crises should be seen urgently on request.

Some children find it especially hard to wait, for example children with an autistic spectrum disorder or children with learning difficulties. This should be considered when booking appointments. You could offer double booking times or first/last appointment times for disabled children. Consider making facilities for private and personal care available to families with a child with personal/healthcare needs, e.g. changing mats.

Improving access to Child and Adolescent Mental Health Services (CAMHS)

Disabled children and young people have the same range of mental health needs as their peers and need access to services at all tiers (1–4) of CAMHS. There is a need for multiagency planning and commissioning of services to support families and minimise exclusion. Disabled children, particularly those with autism or learning disabilities, have often found it difficult to access CAMHS.

PCTs should work with mainstream and learning disability mental health services to ensure that appropriate services are accessible to all children and young people. Primary care practitioners should understand learning disability and children's mental health.

Improving access to palliative and terminal care

Palliative care is a vital part of care for all children with life-threatening or life-limiting illness and their families. It requires a comprehensive approach to the child and family. Some parents of disabled children find it hard to access children's palliative and terminal care services. It is important that these are provided in the setting of the family's choice.

PCTs should review provision of children's palliative and terminal care services. They should plan services for children with life-limiting conditions and/or complex health needs in partnerships with other independent providers such as the voluntary sector and children's hospices where these exist.

Improving access to therapy services and equipment

Inspections and research show that there are difficulties in obtaining therapy services for children, with long waiting lists in many areas. Children can wait up to two years before receiving support. The delays are partly the result of the different statutory responsibilities and priorities of the health service and local authorities, which often lead to a lack of clarity over funding.

Being able to communicate with others is central to social inclusion and an increasing number of disabled children use alternative communication systems, such as symbol boards/books and computer-assisted systems. Yet many children only have access to their communication systems at school, not at home or in other settings. Almost all families report unmet needs for equipment and assistive technology.

PCTs should build on plans to integrate community equipment services and develop multiagency protocols that set standards for the assessment and provision of children's equipment, including wheelchairs. Trusts should jointly agree plans for the provision and maintenance of both short-term and ongoing equipment supplies.

Practitioners should consider housing, community equipment and wheelchair needs when undertaking assessments. They should offer parents and other carers training and support in the use of the equipment and assistive technology being used by the child.

Improving access to education

Parents often complain that children with complex health needs are excluded from mainstream education because of the lack of appropriately trained staff on site. Many children who require tube feeding or regular medication wish to attend mainstream schools, but barriers are often placed in their way. Some parents lack confidence in the ability of schools to cater for the specific health needs of their child.

PCTs should deliver a range of services to schools in ways that support inclusion in mainstream education. They should establish joint local protocols for managing the needs of children with complex health problems in schools. Such protocols should include provision of a named health contact and a named teacher, who are jointly responsible for the preparation and regular review of a healthcare plan for each child.

Early years provision of services

Early identification

Early identification of disabilities is vital to a child's development and life chances. Health professionals are now being trained to identify impairments earlier than in the past. Yet practice is not consistent across the country and some parents continue to struggle to be believed and obtain a diagnosis. Problems remain in the manner in which the diagnosis is communicated to the family.

PCTs should implement the principles in *Together from the Start*.[1] They should ensure that practitioners working in the early years sector are provided with training to identify disabilities and inform parents in a sensitive manner, using the *Right from the Start* template.[2]

Integrated diagnosis and assessment process

Disabled children often have multiple needs and may be subject to multiple assessments by different people, each collecting similar information. Many parents complain about having to tell their story over and over again, but receive little practical help as a result.

PCTs should ensure that children with suspected or potential disability have prompt access to a diagnostic and assessment facility, which is as close to the child's home as possible. Where appropriate, multiagency assessments should be carried out in natural settings, such as the child's home or school. Wherever possible, services should be co-located to aid access for families, for instance in child development centres.

Assessment meetings should be child centred and give parents the time and space to think and to acknowledge their feelings. A written report of the diagnostic and assessment process should be given to families. Practitioners should record the child's abilities and strengths as well as their difficulties and plan how to maximise the child's progress and inclusion. They should assess the needs of parents and the wider family too.

Practitioners should produce a multiagency family service plan, which gives details of how the assessed needs of the child and family members will be met.[1]

Early interventions

Children are constantly developing. Delaying early intervention can result in irretrievable loss of function or ability (e.g. postural management) or the intervention being less effective (e.g. speech and language therapy). Early intervention has positive effects in terms of both promoting development and minimising decline or regression.

Practitioners should use the audit toolkits being developed as part of the *Early Support Pilot Programme* to jointly review and evaluate the standard of service they provide for disabled children under three years old and their families.[3] They should offer interventions to support optimal physical and cognitive development, such as physiotherapy, occupational therapy and speech and language therapy.

Providing direct support to families

General

Parents with disabled children have higher levels of stress than parents with non-disabled children. Many families have high levels of unmet needs for services. When services are fragmented and parents have to struggle to get their needs recognised, their contacts with services increase their distress. Too often services concentrate on the child's impairment, fail to see the child as a whole person and neglect the needs of other family members, including siblings.

Children's behaviour or sleep problems are key factors in creating parental stress. Disabled children, particularly those with learning disabilities, show greater levels of such problems than non-disabled children.

PCTs should offer a range of appropriate family support services. These services should be provided by both mainstream and specialist services and be available for all disabled children, including those with complex health needs, autistic spectrum disorders and multiple disabilities such as deaf and blind children.

Practitioners should offer support to parents in managing sleep and behaviour problems.

Health-based respite care

One of the most frequently reported needs by parents is a break from caring and many children also appreciate a break away from their family. Quality short-term break services are associated with reductions in maternal stress and reduction in marital problems.

Children for whom provision of respite care is most inadequate include those with complex health needs, challenging behaviour or autistic spectrum disorders and children from minority ethnic families.

PCTs should audit the current provision for children with complex health needs. This includes children receiving services and those waiting for them. PCTs should work with social services departments and voluntary sector providers to develop a broader choice of respite arrangements for children with health needs.

Key workers

Parents with severely disabled children want a single point of contact with services or a key worker to help them obtain the services they need. Studies of the benefits of key workers consistently report the positive effects on relationships with service providers, access to services, addressing unmet needs and family wellbeing. However, less than one-third of families with severely disabled children have a key worker.

PCTs should consider jointly commissioning key worker services to oversee the delivery of services from all agencies involved in the care and support of the child and family and ensure that a family has access to appropriate services. They should adopt best practice in the type of support a key worker should provide.[1]

Information for parents and children

Information is one of the most valued aspects of families' contacts with services, yet a substantial proportion of parents and disabled children and young people report receiving inadequate information about services and the child's condition and treatment. Parents from minority ethnic groups report unmet information needs. Parents and children want easily accessible and timely information in appropriate formats and language to be available through a single point of contact.

Practitioners should provide information to enable children and parents/carers to make choices about their treatment, the care and services they wish to use.

Listening to and responding to disabled children and their families

Like anyone else, disabled children and their parents want to be treated with respect and dignity. Children want staff to listen to them and give them choices. Parents want those providing services to listen to their child and all family members, meet the whole family's needs and respect their culture. A key theme of the NSF is the need for professionals to work in partnership with children and parents, to involve them in decisions about their care and about the development of services more generally. The government strategy paper *Building on the Best: choice, responsiveness and equity in the NHS* is designed to increase choice across the spectrum of healthcare, by service providers listening and responding to the views of children and adult users.[4]

Disabled children can contribute their unique and essential knowledge to decision making about their care. Involving children and their parents in planning results in more appropriate services. However, disabled children are less actively involved in decision making than non-disabled children. The lack of availability of communication aids to those children who rely on them limits their involvement in decision making.

PCTs should have a written user involvement strategy setting agreed standards. This should include an action plan for involving disabled children and their parents as equal and active partners and plans for targeted outreach work for families who are hard to reach, including consultation with black and minority ethnic families. PCT patients' forums should include representatives from local parents and disabled children and young people.

Practitioners should routinely involve disabled children and their parents and support them to make informed decisions about their treatment, care and services. Facilities, equipment and skilled workers should be available in all settings where services are provided to enable children who do not use speech, children who find engagement and interaction difficult and very young children, to participate in assessment and decision-making processes. Interpreting and translation services and bilingual advocates should be readily available too.

Transition into adulthood

Assessment and planning for transition from child to adult services is often unsatisfactory. There is a lack of coordination between the relevant agencies and little involvement from the young person. Some young people are transferred from children's to adult services without adequate care plans, which results in their exclusion from services. Some young people experience a deterioration in the services they receive as an adult. This can lead to a regression in their achievement and/or deterioration in their condition.

PCTs should participate in the locality-based transition group (e.g. learning disability partnership board transition subcommittee), set up to develop a multiagency transition strategy. They should develop interagency protocols on transition processes. They should commission appropriate adolescent/ young persons' services with a view to facilitating smooth transition to comprehensive multidisciplinary adult care.

Practitioners should offer young disabled people high-quality multiagency support, which allows them to have choice and control over life decisions. They should take a person-centred planning approach, as described in various guidance documents.[5–7]

Commissioning services

Multiagency strategic planning

Multiagency support to disabled children and their families is essential. Families with disabled children have contact with an average of 10 different professionals and can make over 20 visits per year to hospitals and clinics. Parents report a constant battle to find out what services are available and the roles of different agencies. The lack of a comprehensive database (at either local or national levels) pertaining to disabled children inhibits analysis of current levels of provision and multiagency strategic planning.

PCTs should play a leading role in developing local multiagency strategic groups, focusing on the needs of disabled children. They should develop joint commissioning of services with the various agencies, making maximum use of pooled budgets and other Health Act flexibilities. They should support the development and implementation of a locally based and nationally compatible multiagency database, containing core data on disabled children, based on shared and agreed definitions. Such a database will allow the sharing of core data about the population, current and projected needs (both met and unmet), and the outcomes of interventions. PCTs should contribute to the development and coordination of joint assessment systems.

PCTs should develop joint risk management protocols including guidance on invasive care, manual handling and management of challenging behaviour. They should develop local target waiting times to provide timely services agreed for the period between assessment and provision of services.

Training and development of staff

In order to meet the needs of disabled children, it is particularly important that PCTs work with other agencies to ensure that the workforce has the necessary skills and competencies. Knowledge and understanding of the particular needs of disabled children among frontline staff are often patchy and underdeveloped. There is often little training on disability awareness issues. The lack of specialist staff is one reason for unsatisfactory services, delays in service provision or inadequate levels of interventions.

PCTs should develop joint training initiatives, bringing together staff from different agencies and disciplines. Training should include disability awareness, equality and inclusion issues. They should ensure effective collaborative practice across primary care, including encouraging continuing professional development on a multidisciplinary basis.

References

1 Department of Health (2003) *Together from the Start: practical guidance for professionals working with disabled children (birth to third birthday) and their families.* DH, London.
2 SCOPE (2003) *Right from the Start – template document. A guide to good practice in diagnosis and disclosure.* Scope Publications, 6 Market Road, London N7 9PW.
3 Department for Education and Skills (DfES) (2002) *Early Support Pilot Programme.* DfES, London. www.espp.org.uk/pilot/index.html
4 Department of Health (2003) *Building on the Best: choice, responsiveness and equity in the NHS.* HMSO, London.
5 Department of Health (2002) *Towards Person-Centred Approaches.* DH, London.
6 Department of Health (2003) *Information Pack for Transition Champions.* The Valuing People Support Team, DH, London. www.valuingpeople.gov.uk/documents/TransitionChampionPackFull.pdf. Email: valuing.people.info@dh.gsi. gov.uk
7 Department for Education and Skills (DfES) (2001) *SEN Code of Practice.* DfES, London.

CHAPTER 16

Children in special circumstances: what that means for primary care

Margaret Lynch

Outcomes identified as important by children, young people and families[1] cover the following areas:

- being healthy
- staying safe
- enjoying and achieving
- making a positive contribution
- material wellbeing.

There is a compelling body of evidence from research and experience that some groups of children face barriers to achieving these outcomes. Not only do circumstances prevent them from reaching their full potential and participating fully in society, but their access to and use of services intended to promote their health, wellbeing and social inclusion are often impaired. For many, the inverse care law applies, with those children and families with the greatest needs having least access to services. If the gap in outcomes between these children in special circumstances and other children is to be narrowed, integrated action will be needed from a range of services at local level including health, social services, education, housing and the independent and voluntary sectors.

Policies set out in the Green Paper[1] are designed to safeguard children and maximise their potential. This too has been the aim of the NSF in respect of children in special circumstances. This chapter focuses on the role those working in primary healthcare can play in partnership with others who have responsibilities for providing services to children, young people, families and adults who are parents.

Defining children in special circumstances

The term children in special circumstances is intended to be an inclusive one, extending to all children at risk of achieving poor outcomes. Some, but not all, will be considered in need as defined in Section 17 of the Children Act, 1989.[2] For most, it is impossible to dissociate their mental and physical health needs from other unmet needs, which can impact upon their wellbeing and adversely affect their life chances. These are vulnerable children, many of whom will first come to notice through primary care and universal health services, giving health professionals a vital role to play in their recognition, alongside colleagues in education and social care. Sometimes it is the child's failure to present to universal or other services which first signals a problem. Some will be vulnerable because of parental attributes and will only be identified if those seeing the parent are aware of the potential impact of the adult's difficulties on their parenting capacity.

In any population, children in special circumstances could include:

- children and young people living away from home, including those looked after by local authorities, those privately fostered and young people living independently
- asylum-seeking and refugee children, with families and unaccompanied
- children with troubled parents, for example children of substance misusing parents, children living with domestic violence, children whose parents have mental health problems, children whose parents have a learning disability, children with parents in prison
- young carers
- children whose families are homeless
- children engaged, or who have been engaged, in antisocial or offending behaviour, including those who are in, or have been in, secure accommodation or young offenders institutions
- children not in school (not registered at a school or missing long periods of schooling, e.g. because of truanting, exclusion or family circumstances)
- teenagers who are parents themselves
- children who are abused, including those abused through prostitution and child trafficking.

Numbers of children living in special circumstances

Successive national surveys have revealed that between 300 000 and 400 000 children are known to social services in England as children in need at any one time (the total number of children in England is approximately 11 million). But there are many more children who are at risk of poorer outcomes in all areas of their lives, including health, compared with their peers. The following statistics give some idea of the dimensions of the challenge:

- The child poverty rate in the UK is one of the highest among industrial countries with a third of children living in households with an income below half the national average.[3]
- A report by Shelter[4] analysed government figures and suggested that around 100 000 UK children were living in hostels, bed and breakfast accommodation and shelters for the homeless, in 2001.
- English councils with social services responsibilities looked after 60 800 children as at 31 March 2003.[5]
- Around 10 000 children are privately fostered in England.[6]
- Home Office statistics indicate that asylum applications in 2002 included at least 15 000 children and young people under the age of 20 years (mainly under 15 years old) living with their families. Additionally, 6200 unaccompanied children under the age of 17 years made claims for asylum.[7]
- Runaway young people number 77 000 each year, including 20 000 young people who are under the age of 11 years.[8]
- Around 87 000 children in the UK have a teenage mother, 90% being unmarried.[9]
- Some 90 000 teenagers become pregnant in the UK each year. With 56 000 live births (over 7000 to under-16 year olds and over 2000 to under-14 year olds) the UK has the highest rate of teenage births in western Europe.[9] In addition, over 15 000 under-18 year olds have an abortion each year.
- Nearly 3000 juveniles were held in secure accommodation in March 2002.[10]
- Approximately 114 000 (1.4%) of children between 5 and 15 years old in the UK provide informal care to relatives (including 53 000 boys).[11] Eighteen thousand provide at least 20 hours and nearly 9000 provide 50 hours or more of care per week.
- There are almost one million UK children living in a family with a problem-drinking parent.[12]
- There are between 250 000 and 350 000 children of problem drug users in the UK (about 2%–3% of children in England and Wales and 4%–6% in Scotland).[13]
- The Nottingham psychiatric case register reveals that 10% of all new female referrals aged 15–60 years old have a child under the age of one year and 25% have a child who is under five years old.[14]
- Every year 150 000 children in England have a parent who enters custody and 7% of children will experience their father going to prison during their school life.[1]
- Up to 5000 young people are involved in prostitution at any one time in Britain, with a female/male ratio of 4 to 1.[15] The hidden nature of the activity means that accurate statistics are difficult to get.

At first glance these examples seem to include disparate groups of children. However, all are living in circumstances that pose a threat to their health and long-term wellbeing and unlike most children in the community, many do not have a parent or parents who are able to effectively advocate on their behalf to ensure that their needs are recognised and met. This may be because the child is not living with the parent (e.g. looked after children, unaccompanied asylum-seeking children and children in secure accommodation), the parent does not know how the system works (e.g. asylum seekers and refugees), the parent does not have the capacity because of their own predicament (e.g. mental or physical illness, substance abuse or domestic violence) or the parent has lost meaningful contact with the child (e.g. runaways and children involved in prostitution). For some children more than one reason for parental unavailability may coexist.

For most children the parent in effect acts as a coordinator of their child's contact with the health services and provides a safety net to ensure that planned interventions and follow-up take place. This will include accessing routine healthcare, for example immunisations and regular dental checks, seeking timely advice for acute illness and making sure diagnosis, treatment and follow-up all occur for more chronic conditions. Without an effective advocate this may not happen. For example, a study of looked after children showed that less than half of the healthcare plan recommendations were carried out.[16]

When a family moves, the effective handing on of the child's healthcare will be mainly dependent on the motivation of the parent. It is they who ensure that the child is registered with a general practice in the new area and that information about the child's health history is immediately available (for example, by not losing the parent-held record or copy letters from hospitals!). For some children in special circumstances moves are common, adding loss of medical history to the disadvantages they face. Electronic records should facilitate transfer of medical information, but general practices will remain dependent on knowing that the child has moved in the first place. Potentially the proposals for a lead professional and for information sharing contained in the Green Paper[1] should make coordination of care for children in special circumstances easier.

Disability and special circumstances

While disabled children are, by definition, children in need under the Children Act, they may additionally be in special circumstances. Some disabled children may be multiply disadvantaged. For example, a disabled child with a depressed parent may find that their parent is unable to meet some of their needs. Those working in primary care are well placed to ensure that those planning for the care of the disabled child understand and consider the needs of both parent and child. For a disabled asylum-seeking child the family may require additional support in understanding and accessing health, social care and education services. Primary care practitioners can play a valuable role, particularly at the time of referral by ensuring that the family know what to expect and that those who will be assessing the child are aware of the family's background and, where appropriate, the need for an interpreter.

Child protection and special circumstances

Many (though not all) children in special circumstances will be at increased risk of significant harm. One of your objectives in assessing and meeting their needs and those of their families should be to prevent significant harm. Some children in special circumstances will have already been identified as suffering significant harm. For example, most of the looked after children will have experienced parental neglect or abuse. In March 2001, 60% were looked after under court orders.[17] Links between child abuse and neglect and parental mental illness, substance abuse and domestic violence are well established.[18,19] Children involved in prostitution should be considered to be children in need of protection and guidance on multiagency involvement in their safeguarding is available.[20] Their considerable sexual health needs require special consideration and are best met by a genitourinary medicine (GUM) service where staff have experience of working with young people.[21]

Whenever a referral is made by a health professional to social services because of concerns over a child's welfare, details of any known special circumstances should be included in the referral. Similarly, when contributing to an assessment being undertaken by social services, such information will be needed to facilitate the process and inform planning. Usually, the reasons for sharing information should be explained to the child (appropriate to their age and understanding) and to their parents, seeking their agreement, unless to do so would place the child at risk of significant harm. Further guidance on consent can be found in the recently published *What to Do If You're Worried a Child is Being Abused*.[22]

The consequences

The consequences of these special circumstances will vary according to the resilience of the child or their families and social networks and the responsiveness of the services with which these children and their families come into contact. Research and experience show that many of these children face multiple challenges and without an early response to their predicament, their chances of a healthy and fulfilling life are predictably poor, as Box 16.1 shows.

Box 16.1: Evidence of health issues for children in special circumstances

- Children living in poverty have reduced life chances and poorer outcomes than other children.[3] Bringing up children in poor environments puts significant stress on parents.[23]
- Children in homeless households have poor long-term health and educational outcomes and have a reduced access to services.[24]
- Children in refuges have a high level of unmet health needs, especially in relation to mental health difficulties. Uptake of child health surveillance and immunisations is low.[25]
- There is a high prevalence of mental health problems of children coming into care. Despite a high level of referral, few receive treatment.[17]
- Looked after children fare worse than their peers for routine dental care, immunisation status and health-threatening behaviour.[17]
- A quarter of care leavers have a child by 16 years and 50% of girls were mothers within two years of leaving care.[9]
- The death rate for babies of teenage mothers is 60% higher than that for older mothers and they are more likely to be of low birth weight, have accidents and be admitted to hospital. The daughter of a teenage mother is one and a half times more likely to be a teenage mother herself than the child of an older mother.[9]
- The effect of parental problems such as mental illness, problem alcohol and drug use and domestic violence can adversely affect children through the parents' neglect of basic care, difficulty in controlling emotions and disruption of relationships.[18]
- Caring responsibilities can affect children's health, education and wellbeing, for example leading to lack of concentration, lower self-esteem and poor performance at school.[26]
- Juvenile prisoners have higher rates of mental illness and higher levels of drug and alcohol misuse. They are at serious risk from self-harm and suicide.[10] A significant proportion have previously spent time in care.
- Thirty per cent of prisoners' children suffer mental health problems compared to 10% among the general population of children.[1]

The aetiology of the range of poor outcomes experienced by children in special circumstances is rarely straightforward and difficulties often compound each other. For example, young runaways are likely to sleep in dangerous locations and put themselves at risk of sexual exploitation. Looked after children may be at risk from drug-abusing and neglectful homes and are more likely to become homeless as adults, teenage parents or young offenders. Children in homeless households are more likely than others to become homeless as adults. The girl excluded from school who has become pregnant will be reluctant to access antenatal care and advice and may well continue with behaviour that threatens her own health and that of the baby (e.g. poor diet, substance abuse and smoking).

Many children in special circumstances come from families who have not accessed effective early preventive health services – including child health surveillance and dental checks. Consequently, opportunities will have been missed for early identification of difficulties and the provision of prevention interventions, which could avoid the need for crisis interventions later. Interventions should therefore include strategies to facilitate and increase the uptake of universal services by children in special circumstances, including those living in poverty and areas of deprivation. Sure Start is an example of an initiative where this is already happening on a relatively wide scale across the country. The families of children in special circumstances may well need additional encouragement to participate fully in community- or school-based projects aimed at supporting parents and promoting the welfare and wellbeing of children. Before those working in primary care can give such encouragement they will have to familiarise themselves with what is on offer locally and extend the concept of referral beyond health-related services to include all services working with children and families, including those in education and the voluntary sectors.

Responding at the local level

Which children should be included within a children in special circumstances classification cannot and should not be rigidly defined. The overriding aim of identification should be to improve outcomes, not to ration services. Mapping at the local level is required to allow for variations between different populations and locations. Thus the population of children in special circumstances and the responses required may differ considerably between an inner-city PCT and one serving a remote rural location. If mapping is undertaken locally and involves both practitioners and the community, then the result should be a feeling of ownership and joint responsibility for vulnerable children. The process should be a multiagency approach and could well be undertaken under the auspices of local children and young people's strategic partnerships. Strengthening such cooperation between local authorities and other public, private and voluntary organisations should improve outcomes for children.[1]

Even within a PCT there may be variations in the make-up of the young population of 0–19 year olds. Individual general practices may wish to consider what this means for them. For example, do they cover homeless accommodation, a travellers' site or asylum hostel? How many looked after children are registered with the practice and are they easily identifiable? Where do the asylum seekers come from and what are the main languages spoken? Does someone in the practice understand the entitlements of asylum seekers and refugees and the difference in status between the two? (An asylum seeker is someone who has applied to be recognised as a refugee and if their application is successful will have all the same rights [welfare benefits, employment, etc.] as other members of the UK population.) Are routine enquiries made about any involvement a child may have in providing care to a chronically ill or disabled family member with a view to referring to local support networks? Is the identity of a child's primary carer recorded? Would it be known if a grandmother had taken over the care because the mother was in prison or that a child was being privately fostered? Are vulnerable young people accessing health promotion initiatives and mental health services and if not, why not? Have the young people themselves been consulted about the mode of delivery of such services?

Evidence suggests that poor access and take-up of services are influenced by a failure to adequately consider the diverse needs of local populations[27] and a national mapping of family support services in England and Wales revealed a lack of services to meet the needs of minority ethnic families.[28] Evidence also suggests that access to services and take-up are reduced for those living in rural locations. Distance and lack of transport[29] may be an issue, but so can confidentiality be. For example, how many young people will access a service in their village where they may know the receptionist and everybody in the waiting room? These factors have implications for service planning as well as for practitioners undertaking individual assessments of need.

Conclusion

Large numbers of children live in special circumstances. They achieve, on average, poorer outcomes than children in general and have a particular requirement for services, but often do not receive or use them. Unless all health and other services adopt a proactive approach to the early identification of these children, many will remain invisible until their problems cause distress and disruption to themselves, their families and the communities in which they live. Local mapping should identify children in special circumstances and services should be designed and delivered in ways that ensure that they reach all relevant children. All existing health services, whether universal, targeted or specialist services, should be accessible to children and families who may be in special circumstances. Support may be needed to enable children and families to make the best use of existing services and staff should be trained to work with children and families in special circumstances.

To be able to play a constructive role, health professionals working with children and/or their parents need to look beyond the immediate health needs of the child or parent/carer before them. They must also appreciate the wider impact on a child's development of the circumstances in which they live or lack of a parent's capacity to care for them. They should always enquire of any adult whether they care for children, gauge the likely impact of a parent's condition/behaviour on their parenting capacity and be able to make appropriate referrals for a more in-depth assessment of both the parent's and child's needs, if necessary.

It is essential that those working in healthcare appreciate the contribution special circumstances may be making to the origins of a child's health problems and take them into account when planning interventions, which could include referral to colleagues in social care or the voluntary sector. Conversely, it is important that those working in education or social care are aware that children in special circumstances may have unrecognised or unmet health needs that are contributing to a child's lack of wellbeing or progress.

References

1 Cm 5860 (2003) *Every Child Matters*. HMSO, London.
2 *Children Act 1989* (1989). HMSO, London.
3 Bradshaw J (2001) *Poverty: the outcomes for children*. Family Policies Studies Centre/National Children's Bureau, London.
4 Robinson B (2002) *Where is Home?* Shelter Publishing, London.
5 Department for Education and Skills (2003) *Children Looked After in England: 2002–2003*. Statistics Bulletin. HMSO, London.
6 Department of Health (2001) *Private Fostering: a cause for concern*. DH, London.
7 Research, Development and Statistics Directorate, Home Office (2003) *Asylum Statistics United Kingdom 2002*. The Stationery Office, London.
8 Social Exclusion Unit (2002) *Young Runaways*. SEU, London.
9 Social Exclusion Unit (1999) *Teenage Pregnancy*. SEU, London.
10 Social Exclusion Unit (2002) *Reducing Re-offending by Ex-prisoners*. SEU, London.
11 Doran T and Whitehead M (2003) Health of young and elderly carers; analysis of UK census data. *BMJ*. **327**: e1388.
12 Alcohol Concern (2001) Alcohol and the Family Information Bulletin. Alcohol Concern, London. **3 May**.
13 Advisory Council on the Misuse of Drugs (2003) *Hidden Harm: responding to the needs of children of problem drug users*. Home Office, London.
14 Oates M (1997) Patients as parents: the risk to children. *Br J Psych*. **170** (Suppl. 32): 22–7.
15 Barrett D (1998) Young people and prostitution: perpetrators in our midst. *Int Rev Law, Computers Technol*. **12 (3)**: 475–86.
16 Hill CM and Watkins J (2000) *Does the Statutory Medical Review Offered to Children by Southampton City Council Provide an Effective Means of Health Assessment?* SE Regional NHS Executive, Southampton.
17 Department of Health (2002) *Promoting the Health of Looked After Children*. DH, London.
18 Cleaver H, Unwell I and Aldgate J (1999) *Children's Needs – Parenting Capacity. The impact of parental mental illness, problem drug use and domestic violence on children's development*. HMSO, London.
19 Davidson LL and Lynch MA (2003) Domestic violence and child protection: issues for primary care. In: MJ Bannon and YH Carter (eds) *Protecting Children from Abuse and Neglect in Primary Care*. Oxford University Press, Oxford.
20 Department of Health, Home Office, Department for Education and Employment, National Assembly for Wales (2000) *Safeguarding Children Involved in Prostitution*. DH, London.

21 Thomas A, Forster G, Robinson A *et al.* (2003) National guidelines for the management of suspected sexually transmitted infections in children and young people. *Arch Dis Child.* **88**: 303–11.

22 Department of Health (2003) *What to Do If You're Worried a Child is Being Abused.* DH, London.

23 Ghate D and Hazel N (2002) *Parenting in Poor Environments: stress, support and coping.* Jessica Kingsley Publishers, London.

24 Vostanis P, Grattan E and Cumella S (1998) Mental health problems of homeless children and families: longitudinal study. *BMJ.* **316**: 899–902.

25 Webb E, Shankleman J, Evans M *et al.* (2001) The health of children in refuges for women victims of domestic violence: cross sectional descriptive survey. *BMJ.* **323**: 210–13.

26 Aldridge J and Becker S (2003) *Children Caring for Parents with Mental Illness: perspectives of young carers, parents and professionals.* Policy Press, Bristol.

27 Social Services Inspectorate (2000) *Excellence not Excuses: inspection of services for ethnic minority children and families.* DH, London.

28 Henricson C, Katz I, Mesie J *et al.* (2001) *National Mapping of Family Services in England and Wales.* National Family and Parenting Institute, London.

29 Social Exclusion Unit (2003) *Making the Connection: Final Report on Transport and Social Exclusion.* SEU, London.

CHAPTER 17

Child abuse: what you can do

Ruth Bastable

Child abuse is a disturbing and important subject – an area where we all have an important part to play.[1] There are some fairly simple things each of us can and should do well. Two of these are:

- to treat child abuse like any other life-threatening chronic illness
- to treat child protection as a clinical governance matter, for yourself, your practice and your PCT.

These suggestions and ideas about implementation are drawn from personal experience, so what is right in one area might not be exactly right for you, but you should get some good ideas to take forward in your own work.

Child abuse: an important cause of morbidity and mortality

Childhood illnesses cast long shadows forward and child abuse exemplifies this wisdom. Children who are abused may suffer prolonged effects on their health, which may be transient, situational, permanent or intermittent. Crucially, child abuse is preventable. A recent National Commission found that there is 'no doubt that most of the abuse children now suffer is preventable'.[2]

There are victims and survivors – how a child fares depends on the context, severity and persistence of abuse and features of the child itself. Some children are more robust than others and overcome difficulties. Billy, in Box 17.1, is one example.

Box 17.1: Pamela Stephenson, writing about her husband, the hugely successful comedian, Billy Connolly[3]

'Billy had another idiosyncrasy, one that was related to his earlier abuse. He could not bear to be touched by anybody at all and would jump in the air if another person got within eighteen inches of him. "Don't fucking touch me! Leave me alone!" Such flinching was quite understandable, considering how often and how brutally he had been attacked and beaten without warning.'

There is no single relationship between abuse and outcome – cruel treatment can produce a timid and crushed response or an angry and aggressive one, as the reports in Box 17.2 show.

Box 17.2: Extracts from letters from two abuse victims[2]

'I managed to block out all memory of the abuse. . . I didn't know why I behaved the way I did or why sex scared me so much, why it filled me with such self-loathing. I have already had two suicide attempts . . . '

'As soon as he was allowed back into the house it all started up again. For years I was rebelling against everything and everyone to the extent I was taken away from home and placed in the care of the county. A period of time in Holloway prison doing Borstal and still everyone thought I was just a crazy kid trying to get attention all the time by whatever means I could.'

Child abuse is common and is an important cause of child death (*see* Box 17.3).

Box 17.3: Incidence and prevalence of child abuse

Severe abuse

3/1000 children per year under the age of 18 years (widely acknowledged to be an underestimate). Prevalence is not really known, but an NSPCC[4] study of 2689 young people aged 18–24 years old found that:

- 7% had suffered serious physical abuse
- 6% had suffered serious physical neglect
- 6% had suffered serious emotional or psychological maltreatment
- 4% of children had suffered serious sexual abuse within the family (1% parent, 3% another relative, most often brother or stepbrother)
- 11% of the sample had suffered sexual abuse by another non-related but known person.

Child abuse deaths

- Child abuse is responsible for one to two deaths per week in England, 'but likely to be significantly higher'.
- Murder of a child by a stranger is rare (about five deaths per year).

How will the NSF help with child protection?

Safeguarding children and promoting their welfare are central to the NSF, as Box 17.4 describes. There are two important underlying goals of the NSF in respect of child protection.

- Promoting partnership between professionals and between professionals and parents and children is vital to child protection. Child protection absolutely depends on interagency working. The primary healthcare team (PHCT) cannot protect children on their own and children cannot be protected without the full engagement of the PHCT. Parents are overwhelmingly the perpetrators of abuse but most of the time, even though they are the perpetrators, they are also the best partners we have.
- Driving up standards: professional standards relating to child protection are notoriously variable and have been the subject of much criticism.[5,6] We cannot stop all child abuse, but we could stop some of it. Although some aspects of child abuse are very difficult and complicated, there are also simple things we could all do such as making sure we are educated about best practice in child protection, staying up to date and keeping good clinical notes.

Box 17.4: Key NSF principles as they apply to child protection

- Prevention and health promotion: much child abuse is preventable. We are in a good position in primary care to offer help and support with good parenting models.
- Early identification: appropriate and timely intervention. Some child abuse is out of the blue and there are no warning signs, but we may be able to offer timely support and stop serious difficulties developing.
- Child centred: this is vital to child protection. Child protection can be very complicated and it is easy to lose sight of the child's needs. This can be a special problem where we are supporting a parent with a mental health or drug or alcohol problem.
- Family oriented: although overwhelmingly the family are the perpetrators of the abuse, the best results are obtained by working in partnership with the family and supporting the child and the family.
- Inclusive: that is, sensitive to the individual needs of the child and taking account of race, gender, ability or disability. No one intervention in child abuse fits all. The child's needs must be assessed in the context of their development, the carers' parenting capacity and the wider environment in which the child lives.
- High-quality care, conforming to agreed standards: levels of professional engagement vary. GPs are traditionally regarded as unengaged, although there are encouraging signs that this is changing (see the Royal College of General Practitioners' position statement[7]).
- Informed by best evidence: often what we do in child protection is reactive rather than proactive and opportunities for primary prevention and early intervention are missed.

Every Child Matters[8]

The Green Paper *Every Child Matters* sets out the proposed organisational, educational and cultural changes to deliver the vision of the NSF. Central to the proposals are safeguarding as well as promoting the welfare of children.
Key proposed changes in primary care (Box 17.5) are:

- accountability and integration, with the formation of children's trusts
- information sharing and assessment with the removal of some of the legal barriers to information sharing and a common assessment tool. To support this, the government has published helpful guidance – *What to Do If You Are Worried a Child is Being Abused*[9] – to accompany existing guidance[10,11]
- training and standards, with clear and common standards for all those who work with children and common core training.[7]

Box 17.5: Changes proposed[8]

Accountability and integration

- Children's trusts will bring together social services, education, some health services (probably community paediatricians, teenage pregnancy coordinators, drug and alcohol teams as they relate to young people, also possibly speech therapy, health visitors and occupational therapists), Connexions and possibly youth offending teams. Each area will have a director of children's services who will be accountable for all local authority education and children's social services.
- There will be clear practice standards for each agency in relation to children.
- Local safeguarding children boards (LSCBs) will replace area child protection committees and will be statutory. LSCBs will be chaired by the director of children's services and constituent agencies will be obliged to contribute.

Information sharing and common assessment

- There will be a proposed minimum data set to which all professionals will contribute. Data will be held electronically as an information hub, managed by the local authority and for professional access. Projects such as information, referral and tracking (IRT) will be central.[12]
- Legal barriers to information sharing will be removed.
- Organisational boundaries to information sharing will be removed by the creation of children's trusts.
- The common assessment framework will be established for the assessment of children in need and their families.[11]

Standards and training

- All people working with children should be trained in child protection and there will be common core standards and training for all those who work with children.
- Safeguarding children will be brought within the clinical governance framework.
- There will be a duty to protect children and there will be relevant legislation relating to police, social services and health.
- Working with children will be made more attractive – better conditions, altered grading system based on responsibility, knowledge, skills and effort needed for the job rather than job title.
- There will be a review of the health visitor role, undertaken by the chief nursing officer.

The case of Victoria Climbié

Victoria's story and the lessons to be learnt from this are integral to the NSF and its implementation – as Box 17.6 describes.[13]

Box 17.6: Victoria's story

Victoria Climbié was born in Abidjan on the Ivory Coast on 2 November 1991. She died at St Mary's Hospital, Paddington on 25 February 2000, aged 8 years 3 months, after only 10 months in England. During her time in England, she was subjected to appalling abuse. In the last months of her life she was forced to lie in a plastic bag in a freezing bathroom with her hands bound. The subject of terrible beatings, she died from hypothermia and multiple organ failure. At post mortem, more than 128 separate inflicted injuries were noted. No part of her body was spared from torture.

The tragedy of Victoria lies not only in her appalling suffering, but also in the failure of the many services with which she came into contact to protect her. Victoria was known to many services in her short time in England and all of them, in varying ways, failed her. She had contact with three housing authorities, four social services departments, two police child protection teams, a specialist centre managed by the NSPCC and was admitted to two hospitals with a diagnosis of deliberate harm. She was also registered with a GP for most of her time in England.

On 12 January 2001, Victoria's great-aunt, Marie-Therese Kouao, and Carl John Manning were convicted of her murder.

Following her death, an inquiry chaired by Lord Laming was held.[13] It was found that the child protection system and the Childrens Act that underlies it are sound. What was not sound was the implementation and support of the system. Sadly, Victoria was one of many children to die in the way she did and there are many common features between Victoria's case and other child deaths (*see* Box 17.7).

Outstanding findings of the inquiry were:

- failure of basic good practice. In all, the inquiry made 108 recommendations. As soon as the findings of the inquiry were published, the then Secretary of State for Health identified half of the recommendations as relating to good basic practice and needing immediate action
- training: in particular, ill-trained and overworked staff who were poorly supported
- accountability: in particular, senior management who failed to take responsibility.

Box 17.7: Key points from the Victoria Climbié Inquiry relevant to primary care

Child protection is a part of safeguarding children and cannot be separated out from family support. There are recurrent themes from this and other inquiries that contribute to repeated failures. For primary care, the most relevant ones are:

- poor training, especially of staff who come into contact with children on a regular basis, but are not child protection experts
- poor note keeping
- child protection guidance may be out of date, inaccessible, not relevant to the professional's needs or not followed
- information sharing: many staff do not know when to share information, what information can and should be shared and under what circumstances.
- poor communication between agencies such as health and social services
- organisations (and therefore their staff) accord different levels of priority to safeguarding children and work to different standards. This makes working together very difficult
- the system does not always focus sufficiently on the child's needs
- accountability: senior management, including those in PCTs, do not take enough responsibility for what is happening.

What can we do in primary care?

Two suggestions about what you can do (Recommendations 83 and 82 from the Victoria Climbié Inquiry) placed in the context of the NSF and the Green Paper[8] are given below.

1 Protecting children proactively

Recommendation no 83 (13)

> 'The investigation and management of a case of possible deliberate harm to a child must be approached in the same systematic and rigorous manner as would be appropriate to the investigation and management of any other potentially fatal disease.'[13]

Child abuse is a chronic condition and involves vulnerable people who may not be able to speak for themselves. Implementing this recommendation will go a long way to ensuring basic good practice and driving up standards of care.

Not only is child abuse a major cause of ill health in adults, but abuse survivors and victims are also very frequent consulters in general practice. They consult frequently with symptoms for which there is no explanation and they may take years to disclose the origin of their malaise.[14]

Child abuse is a severe and life-threatening condition that behaves in some ways like a chronic illness. It has around about the same prevalence in the primary care setting as, say, diabetes (about 2% and another 2% we don't know about) and is just as corrosive. Those working in primary care have important roles at all stages of the problem. We should no more think of the referral of a child protection concern being the beginning and end of our role than we would think of admitting an elderly and vulnerable patient with diabetes to hospital as being the sum of our role. Just as in any other severe, life-threatening and chronic condition, we do not act alone but draw on the skills and expertise of the primary heathcare team and often the wider, multidisciplinary team (for example, those in social services and housing) as well.

We are proactive, we act as a safety net, we exhibit leadership skills and we are team workers. We gather information from a variety of sources: we do not just think about the patient in front of us, we think about them in the context of their family and their environment. We network, consult our colleagues, run things past them. We have a role at all stages of care: primary prevention, early identification, timely intervention, assessment, continuing management and secondary prevention (including mitigation of the difficulties as relayed in Box 17.8). We do this as part of primary healthcare and multiagency teams that are so essential to child protection.

Box 17.8: Opportunities to protect children in primary care

- Primary prevention and health promotion: for example, promoting models of positive parenting,[15] identifying and targeting vulnerable families for extra help such as home visiting programmes[16] early in the course of parenting difficulties.[17]
- Early identification: for example, the early identification and treatment of postnatal depression or other mental health problems or drug or alcohol problems in the parents or carers.
- Effective and timely intervention: for example, in recognising the significance of bruising in a pre-mobile child and taking appropriate and urgent action.
- Assessment: being well placed to contribute to the assessment of the child, within the context of parenting capacity and the context of the child's wider environment.[11]
- Continuing management: many agencies involved in protecting children have a transient contact. Part of the strength of primary care is in its continuing relationship with children and families.
- Secondary prevention: for example, in the management of survivors of abuse.

We are well placed to take up these opportunities in child protection because of the way in which we work in primary care within the PHCT.

- We are child centred: we see most of the children most of the time for most of the problems. For example, a GP will see the average child eight times per year between ages 0 and 4 years.
- We are family oriented: we see children in the context of the family and we may be best placed to offer early and timely help, for example where there are adult mental health problems or drug or alcohol misuse problems. We may also know a lot about the child and his or her family.
- Time: our contacts with children and families may be brief, but they often extend over years, sometimes even across generations. We are there before and after child protection concerns.
- Holistic: we are often very knowledgeable about the child, their family and the environment in which the child is being raised. A child's needs must be assessed in these contexts.[11]
- Relationships: we usually work with families in an atmosphere of trust and respect and often over a long period of time.
- We are team workers, through the PHCT and, increasingly, through wider, multidisciplinary teams.

To take up these opportunities, we need to tackle some important issues in primary care. These include developing a system-wide approach to child protection, being sufficiently trained and well educated in child protection and developing a better understanding of information sharing (*see* Box 17.9).

Box 17.9: Overcoming barriers in primary care

- We need to adopt a system-wide approach to the problem. No one professional can care for the patient on his or her own. Everyone has an important part to play and needs to know how to play that part, whether they are clinicians, managers or administrative/support staff. Like any other serious, life-threatening and chronic problem, we need standards, guidance and protocols for child protection that are implemented throughout the organisation, making clear the expectations from each member of the team.[7]
- We need sufficient education and training to do our job. This has to be sensitive to the environment in which we work and be relevant to primary care.
- We have to get much better at information sharing and communication, so as well as our own professional training, we also need common, interagency training. It is in the area of information sharing and communication where the proposed structural changes, such as children's trusts and the legislative changes, such as changes in the law on information sharing, will be most helpful.

---

2 Child protection within the framework of clinical governance

Recommendation no 82 (13)

> 'The Department of Health should examine the feasibility of bringing the care of children about whom there are concerns about deliberate harm within the framework of clinical governance.'[13]

Child protection has a high profile, mostly because of well-publicised cases such as that of Victoria Climbié. We need to avoid the temptation of making quick fixes. Every high-profile child death that occurs produces a flurry of activity and cries of 'never again', yet it does happen again and often for the same or similar reasons. Producing sustainable and lasting change will depend on making child protection an everyday part of practice. Placing child protection within clinical governance begins to tackle some of the difficulties over accountability, standards and training so strongly noted in the Victoria Climbié inquiry. Clinical governance is not just about what the primary care organisation does, it's about every one of us doing our part as individuals, within the practice, within the PHCT and within the context of the wider multiagency setting in child protection.

Clinical governance activities (*see* Table 17.1) lie in:

- performance management: such as the establishment of standards, audit with feedback, guidelines
- promoting clinical standards through education, mentoring, peer group review and participation in single agency and multiagency training and education
- risk management, through critical event reports relating to child protection incidents, getting the findings of serious case reviews into practice, making sure that up-to-date procedures are readily available
- user involvement, through consultation with healthcare providers and a full awareness of the child and parent perspectives.

Table 17.1: Putting the child's needs at the centre

Performance management:	Clinical excellence:
<ul><li>Child protection standards</li><li>Child protection audit with feedback and review</li><li>Clinical guidance</li><li>Practice protocols to cover education, communication, note keeping and procedures</li><li>Register of training (level, date)</li><li>Child protection education as part of annual appraisal</li><li>Management of underperforming doctors</li><li>Recognising good practice</li></ul>	<ul><li>Education – needs led, evidence based (content and process), progressive and developmental (part of lifelong learning), some preferably practice based (implementation, overcoming barriers to change). Education available in a variety of formats and support material available</li><li>Mentoring</li><li>Child protection education included in personal development plan</li></ul>

Attitude: the child's needs are paramount

Risk management:	*User* involvement:
<ul><li>Messages from serious case reviews into practice</li><li>Critical incident/significant event reporting</li><li>Practice to demonstrate reporting of child welfare event as critical incident</li><li>Ready access to up-to-date procedures</li><li>Ready access to up-to-date information on advice and referral</li><li>Police checking of staff in contact with children</li><li>PCT policy on accusations against staff</li></ul>	<ul><li>Engagement of GPs, practices, clinical governance leads, key players</li><li>Child protection educationally supported through PCT</li><li>Child and family perspective appreciated and valued</li></ul>

Some things you can do

As an individual: you can make sure you are adequately trained for what you do (*see* Box 17.10).

Box 17.10: Training and education: what do you need to know?

You need skills to be able to:

- *recognise*: child protection concerns as they occur in your job
- *refer*: understand how and where to get advice and how to refer a concern
- *understand your role*: as a health professional or administrator or manager and as a member of the practice and/or the PHCT and the PCT.

If you are in regular contact with children, particularly as a health professional, you will also need to know about:

- children in special circumstances: see child protection in the context of the overall response to vulnerable children (*see* Chapter 16). Child protection is an end game: it is the point at which opportunities for primary prevention and early intervention have been unsuccessful or missed. Child abuse is only one of the many ways in which children may be disadvantaged
- interagency working: both difficult and essential! Your local area child protection committee will put on courses and new training material is being developed.[9]

As a practice team: write a practice protocol (*see* Box 17.11). A lot of emphasis tends to be placed on the importance of recognising child protection concerns. This is important but within a practice, it is also important to think about communication, note keeping and procedures, as these are areas where problems also occur.

Your protocol needs to refer to your practice and how you do things. If you can interest and involve as many colleagues in the practice as possible, you will be much more successful in promoting ownership and, because of this ownership, adherence to the protocol.

Box 17.11: What should be in your practice protocol?

This is not an exhaustive list but it is in these areas that the problems commonly lie for general practice.

Education

- How practice members, including new staff, will be kept up to date about child protection issues.
- Person who will update and ensure the availability of local child protection procedures.
- Lead doctor or suitably trained nurse for child protection issues. If there is not a lead doctor or nurse, how will these tasks be allocated?

Note keeping and recording

- How you will identify the records of those children on the child protection register (and those of their parents and siblings).
- How you will record concerns to do with child protection issues that have not yet or may not result in registration. And how this will be recorded in the notes of the parent(s) and sibling(s).
- How case conference proceedings (which can be very bulky) will be stored.

Communication

- How and to whom non-medical staff report their concerns (e.g. reception staff or secretarial staff). What record is made of this.
- How clinical staff share their concerns with each other. What record is made of that sharing.
- How concerns are reported to social services. How telephone discussions are recorded.
- How requests for information (for example from social services) are dealt with.

Procedure

How the practice will ensure:

- familiarity of all clinical staff with local procedures as they relate to them
- clear knowledge of procedure for expressing and sharing concern within the practice
- clear knowledge on how to obtain advice from a specialist outside the practice. How and to whom to make a referral outside the practice.

As a PCT: sponsor practice-based child protection education as part of time to learn or other PCT clinical governance activity. User involvement is important in planning this. Organise the training and education to have an impact on changing practice and make people think and behave differently – as in the example in Box 17.12.

Box 17.12: Practice-based child protection training

One PCT audited child protection education for GPs and their employed staff. The PCT clinical governance lead and managers decided on a cascade system of education. Two members of each practice – one GP and one health visitor – attended a 'training the trainers' session and then, using PCT-sponsored material, delivered the training in their own practices.

At the end of 10 months, nine of the 18 practices in the PCT had completed the training and four more had a date arranged in their practice diary. Three had not yet got round to it, but knew they should; one asked for help and another had deferred the training due to internal practice problems (illness).

The training was favourably received. Some sample comments from clinicians and non-clinicians were:

'There are many forms of abuse.' 'It is better to do something/get involved rather than do nothing at all.' 'Action should be taken or matters could get worse.' 'It's everyone's job to recognise child protection issues and refer.' 'What I learnt today was not to be afraid of voicing concerns, to be aware of child protection issues in everyday life and who to refer to.'

Conclusion

Instigating child protection in primary care will not work without each of us playing our part. Child abuse is disturbing and it is easier to look away. Our part may only be a small one, but each of us can and must do it well.

Box 17.13: David Pelzer, abuse survivor, telling his story in *A Child Called 'It'*[18]

'Some readers will find the story unreal and disturbing, but child abuse is a disturbing phenomenon that is a reality in our society. Child abuse has a domino effect that spreads to all who touch the family. It takes its greatest toll on the child and spreads into the immediate family to the spouse, who is often torn between the child and their mate. . . Also involved are neighbours who hear the screams, but do not react, teachers who see the bruises and must deal with a child too distracted to learn and relatives who want to intervene, but do not want to risk relationships.'

References

1 Department of Health (2004) *The National Service Framework for Children*. DH, London.
2 Williams M (1996) *Childhood Matters*. National Commission of Inquiry into the Prevention of Child Abuse. HMSO, London.
3 Stephenson P (2002) *Billy*. Harper Collins, London.
4 National Society for the Prevention of Cruelty to Children (2000) *Child Maltreatment in the United Kingdom*. NSPCC, London.
5 Department of Health (2002) *Learning from Past Experience – a Review of Serious Case Reviews*. DH, London.
6 Department of Health (2003) *Keeping Children Safe – The Government's Response to the Victoria Climbie Inquiry Report and Joint Chief Inspectors' Report Safeguarding Children*. HMSO, London.
7 Carter YH and Bannon MJ (2003) *The Role of Primary Care in the Protection of Children from Abuse and Neglect*. Royal College of General Practitioners, London.
8 Cm 5860 (2003) *Every Child Matters*. HMSO, London.
9 Department of Health (2003) *What to Do If You are Worried a Child is Being Abused*. DH, London.
10 Department of Health (1999) *Working Together to Safeguard Children*. HMSO, London.
11 Department of Health (2000) *Framework for the Assessment of Children in Need and their Families*. HMSO, London.
12 Identification, Referral and Tracking (IRT)
www.cypu.gov.uk/corporate/services/identification.cfm
13 Laming H (2003) *The Victoria Climbie Inquiry*. Report of an Inquiry by Lord Laming. HMSO, London.
14 Smith D, Pearce L, Pringle M *et al.* (1995) Adults with a history of child sexual abuse: evaluation of a pilot therapy service. *BMJ*. **310**: 1175–8.
15 Phelan T (1995) *1–2–3 Magic. Effective discipline for children 2–12*. Child Management Inc, Glen Ellyn, Illinois.
16 Olds DL, Henderson CR Jr, Chamberlain R *et al.* (1986) Preventing child abuse and neglect: a randomised trial of nurse home visitation. *Pediatrics*. **78**: 65–78.
17 Scott S, Spender O, Doolan M *et al.* (2001) Multicentre controlled trial of parenting groups for childhood antisocial behaviour in clinical practice. *BMJ*. **323**: 194–8.
18 Pelzer D (2000) *A Child Called 'It'*. Orion, London.

CHAPTER 18

Listening to young people's perspectives in relation to adolescent health

Rob Chambers

Smoking

Box 18.1: Facts about smoking in England[1-3]

- 11% of 11–15-year-old girls and 9% of 11–15-year-old boys smoke regularly
- 1% of 11 year olds smoke regularly, rising to 23% of 15 year olds
- 30% of 16–24-year-old men and 26% of 16–24-year-old women smoke regularly
- Levels of smoking among 13–15 year olds are higher in households where at least one adult smokes (24%) than in households where no adults smoke (7%)
- 11–15 year olds with higher educational expectations are less likely to take up smoking[4]

The number of young people who smoke cigarettes has remained much the same over the last 10 years. We need to find more effective ways of conveying information to young people about the ill effects of smoking cigarettes, as Claire says in Box 18.2.

[Claire and other names given in boxes in this chapter are fictitious and box contents are anonymised reports of the views from various teenagers given to Rob, the chapter author.]

Box 18.2: Claire, 18 years old

'There is an obvious lack of educating children about the dangers and consequences of smoking which I experienced at school. Although I knew smoking was bad for you, I was never made aware of the results that various types of cancer caused by smoking have on a person. In my opinion children aged 10–13 years old must be educated at school about the harm smoking can do to someone.'

Ways to prevent children from starting to smoke present a huge challenge for health professionals and teachers. Young people whose friends and family members smoke are more likely to smoke themselves as the facts relayed in Box 18.1 describe. Smoking often starts as a social pastime with friends supplying the first cigarettes. So, social influence training can give young people skills such as refusing cigarettes when offered them by other young people.[5] School campaigns can teach children about the dangers of smoking to their health and how to resist the temptation to start smoking – at primary school as well as high school.

Box 18.3: Vin, 19 years old

'There is help for those who are addicted to smoking. Nicotine patches, gum and acupuncture are all effective ways to quit smoking, but the best way to quit smoking is cold turkey. In the long run it is the easiest and most effective technique of stopping smoking. Also you can try and stop by carrying around a list of reasons why you want to quit and keep reading it.'

Only informed adults should be allowed to smoke. The minimum age when young people should be able to buy tobacco products should be at least 18 years old.

One of the most effective methods of prevention is to ban advertising. There has been a ban on advertising in sport and on television and although these steps are a good start, there is still a lot more that can be done. There is advertising in magazines and banners on the roadside, but the worst case for promoting smoking has to be in films and television soap operas – in Box 18.4 Rob notes how common it is to see people smoking on TV.

> **Box 18.4:** Rob, 22 years old
>
> 'As a smoker who is trying to give up, I have only just realised how commonly tobacco products are used on the television. An average child in Britain watches many hours of television every day, so it surely does have a negative effect on them.'

Being overweight or obese

The increasing proportions of children and young people who are overweight or obese and the epidemic of inactivity among young people were described in Chapter 8. Research has shown that one-third of 14–15-year-old girls and one-sixth of 14–15-year-old boys believe that their weight is too high. Nineteen per cent of the girls and 4% of the boys in this age group were dieting at the time the research was carried out.[6] Graham captures the struggle that many teenagers have to control their weight, while having insight into the reasons for their weight being too high (*see* Box 18.5).

> **Box 18.5:** Graham, 19 years old
>
> 'For me personally I have struggled with being overweight since about age 15. This has always been a problem for me since then. I would put this down to lack of exercise as I used to be a regular rugby player and swimmer as a young teenager. More and more teenagers would prefer to come home from school or college and sit and watch television all night or go out for a drink with their mates, rather than go and play football with friends or do other forms of physical exercise. There is a general trend of laziness amongst the younger generation and it is slowly getting worse.'

Prevention of teenagers' weight problems lies in encouraging them to exercise regularly. To help a young person to exercise is quite a difficult prospect as they have to get off the sofa and motivate themselves. If they are reasonably active from a young age then they just need to keep a regular routine of exercise throughout their life.

Adolescents will make their first important choices in life as to what food they should eat when they are given options in the school dining-room. Family meals at home are an important base to work from. If a child is educated by their family about the correct types of food and good nutrition, this will set a good example to the child when they are making their own choices. It is all too easy to give a child a microwave ready-meal that is full of fat if the parent cannot be bothered to cook. Parents should make that extra effort to ensure that they set a good example to the child.

Young people are confused about where to go for reliable dietary advice – they need help to turn what they know about being overweight, having too little exercise, etc., into action.

Drinking alcohol

Box 18.6: Facts about drinking alcohol in England[2,7]

- The average weekly consumption of alcohol among 11–15 year olds has doubled over the last decade from 5.3 units in 1990 to 10.5 units in 2002, with boys drinking slightly more than girls.
- A survey in 2002 found that 24% of 11–15 year olds had had an alcoholic drink in the previous week.
- Children are starting to drink alcohol at an increasingly young age. Almost 20% of 13-year-old boys and girls drink alcohol at least once a week; at 14 years this rises to 34% and 31% respectively and at age 15 years around half reported drinking at least once a week.

Teenagers aged 13–16 drink mainly due to role models whom they copy. If it is acceptable for older teens and young adults to binge drink and drink excessively, then it is bound to have an effect on younger teenagers' opinions about drinking. A lot of role models in the music industry and from television are constantly shown in the tabloid newspapers to be drinking to excess, going to showbiz parties, etc. This can be translated as the norm to some teenagers.

It is hard to explain why it has become the norm to drink to excess. It is only in the last decade that drinking habits have changed – as the data reported in Box 18.6 show. Teenagers may be encouraged to drink by cheap readily available alcohol, which is sold in off-licences or in pubs and clubs (*see* Box 18.7).

Box 18.7: Tracey, 19 years old

'I see a number of younger people who are starting to drink at an earlier age than I did. Most often teenage girls as young as 14 years old can get into bars and clubs without any problem from door staff.'

Deals such as 'Happy Hour' and 'Two for One' are commonplace throughout Britain. Some local authorities are working with pubs and clubs to limit these kind of deals in an effort to reduce rowdy and criminal behaviour, fuelled by alcohol. We need to listen to young people to understand their perspectives (*see* Gaz in Box 18.8) to plan campaigns to impact on teenagers' drinking habits.

Box 18.8: Gaz, 19 years old

'In my opinion a big problem is "alcopops", which are marketed to appeal to teens and often to those who cannot legally buy them. When I first started drinking at about 14 years old I did not like the taste of beer so I would often buy alcopops, as they would taste like fizzy drinks. By getting used to drinking at such an early age I feel this led to stronger drinks, such as spirits (vodka, Jack Daniels) that I would consume on a weekly basis. After a few years of binge drinking, I have found that I have started to grow up and I am now more concerned about my general health and wellbeing. The other day I made an appointment at my local doctor's surgery to ask them if I could have a blood test of my liver, purely so I could determine if I had a serious problem due to excessive drinking.'

Illicit drug use

Box 18.9: Facts about drug use in England

- In one study, 11% of 11–15 year olds had taken illicit drugs in the previous month and 18% had used drugs in the previous year, the proportion of boys being slightly higher than that of girls. 6% of 11 year olds had used drugs in the previous year compared to 36% of 15 year olds.[2]
- 38% of teens had been offered drugs at some time, cannabis being the most common (21% had been offered stimulants such as ecstasy, cocaine or amphetamines and 17% volatile substances to sniff).[2]
- 13% of 11–15 year olds had used cannabis in the previous year.[2] 27% of 16–24 year olds had used cannabis in another major survey.[8]
- 4% of 11–15 year olds reported using Class A drugs in the previous year,[2] whereas 9% of 16–24 year olds had done so.[8]

The government's 1998 10-year strategy for tackling drug misuse[9] had four main aims:

1 helping adolescents to resist drugs misuse
2 protecting communities
3 improving treatment
4 stifling the availability of drugs.

Since then, the updated Drug Strategy[10] encompasses GPs and other primary healthcare professionals (as Tier 1 professionals – *see* Chapter 9) to become involved with helping drugs misusers. This may be by supporting teachers in delivering drugs education in primary schools or as part of personal social and health education in secondary schools. Fiona's and Dan's views emphasise the importance of such education in schools (*see* Box 18.10).

Box 18.10: Fiona, 17 years old and Dan, 17 years old

'There is not enough education in schools about the damaging effects of drugs. As a 15 year old I only had one half-hour lesson at school about the dangers of drugs. Looking back this was completely inadequate as drugs are widespread on the streets and I would not class myself well educated after just half an hour.' (Fiona)

'Peer pressure can have a huge impact on whether a teenager will use drugs. If you get in with the wrong crowd at school then you could end up in trouble whether it is to do with drugs, crime or general law breaking.' (Dan)

Limiting the supply of illegal substances is a main facet of the government's strategies.[9,10] But Greg in Box 18.11 has misgivings about the recent reclassification of cannabis to 'Class C' status.

Box 18.11: Greg, 18 years old

'My personal experience from growing up as a teenager is that drugs are always going to be a problem amongst teenagers; it is just how severe the problem is. I used to smoke cannabis on a regular basis and at the time I thought nothing of it. Looking back it was one of the biggest mistakes of my life. It would hamper my ability to work at school, ruined the relationship with my family for quite a few years and made me quite depressed. The government have decided to downgrade cannabis from a 'Class B' drug to 'Class C'. It would be naïve to say that smoking cannabis has no effect on teenagers deciding to experiment with harder drugs. From my personal experience the laws should remain as they are. It is as though the government is trying to make it acceptable to smoke cannabis.'

Sexual health

Box 18.12: Facts about sexual health

- 30% of men and 26% of women report sexual intercourse before 16 years. Most of these girls (70%) regretted having sexual intercourse before the age of 16 years.[1,11] For 30% first sex 'just happened' and 19% were drunk.
- Britain has the highest teenage pregnancy rate in western Europe. The conception rate for under-16 year olds has fallen from 9.3 per thousand in 1991 to 8.3 per thousand in 2000.[6]
- When asked why they did not use contraception when they had sex, the most common response (29%) was that the sexual activity was unplanned.[12]
- 54% of conceptions in 13–15 year olds lead to terminations, compared to 39% of conceptions ending in termination for 15–19 year olds.[6]
- The peak age of infection with chlamydia in men is 20–24 years old whereas in women it is 16–19 years old. As many as one in 10 sexually active women under age 25 may be infected with chlamydia.[6]

Peer pressure is often reported as one of the main reasons why teenagers have sex before they are 16 years old. But the teenager in Box 18.13 covers many areas that could all be addressed by those working in schools and primary care – and at strategic levels in the NHS and education sectors – by more accessible services, listening and responding to young people's concerns and delivering sex education in more appropriate and timely ways.

Box 18.13: A young person currently having unprotected sex herself[13] – Nat, 18 years old

Availability of condoms

'Why can't boys get them from their GPs? Do boys attend family planning clinics? They should be encouraged to attend clinics and GPs to get advice and condoms themselves.'

Sex education in schools

'I attended XX High School and the sex education was dead basic. We had sessions once a week with the school nurse. Girls and boys had a different session. I would have preferred it to be a joint session because I always sat with the lads, I get on with them better. It should be made more exciting than just advice about how to put a condom on. I don't like using condoms because I worry about them coming off and I don't enjoy sex as much with them on; I don't like the smell and feel of them. I don't think about infections and things like AIDS and I have a partner who I've been with for a year now. I don't have sex with strangers so I don't worry. I didn't like school at all and I didn't listen to what teachers had to say so I don't really think school is the best place for sex education.'

Contraception advice

'I have been to a family planning clinic once and I don't intend to go again. I thought I was pregnant, but they wouldn't do a test and just gave me condoms. I gave them away. I then went to my doctor for a test. The nurse was good. I think my GP listened to me properly and I felt like he cared about it. I was not embarrassed to talk to the doctor. I would feel more embarrassed going to the family planning clinic because everybody knows what you're there for. The waiting-room at the local clinic is the same one for the baby clinic and I had to walk right down the corridor and then I had to wait for the receptionist to give me the condoms (which I didn't even want!).'

Carly's poem describes the internal conflict many young people go through as their sexual urges are restrained by thinking ahead. The better informed the young person is and the more that they have to look forward to in the future, the more likely they are to be able to suppress urges to embark on risky behaviour.

Don't go losing your virginity (© Carly Stanford, 2004)[14]

Hold onto it as long as you can,
Don't go doing it with the wrong man!
Once it's given, you can <u>never</u> get it back-
You'll be known as a trollop in the sack!

Keep it safe, it's a gift;
If we don't do it, I'll be miffed!
Don't you lose it or give it away,
But it's OK on your wedding day.

It's very precious,
It may cause you pain,
You know you'll never be the same
<u>AND</u> you'll be guilty, you'll be to blame!

Only do it when you're in love,
Come on, come on, let's push and shove!
Everyone will know, you know,
Oooh, come on, I love you so!

You're slack if you do
And tight if you don't,
I can, I must, I will, I won't!

We've all done it,
You're the odd one out,
Oh! I want to scream and shout-
Just what on earth are they talking about?

If we do, I'll love you more,
I promise not to make you sore!
Don't you want to, just a bit?
God, he really is so fit!

My hormones tell me, Yes, Yes, Yes!
And I really must confess
I think I might – I think I will,
Perhaps I should go on the pill?

You must be pure and stay intact,
Come on let's do it, let's make a pact!
The dilemma grows, I must act,
But what I need above all – is fact!

After all what would I know,
I'm fifteen, a little so and so!
I've no knowledge, no great life plan,
I haven't even got a man!

Teenagers like me are judged on sight,
We must be doing it every night!
We're not like that, don't you hear?
Some of us are nowhere near!

All this talk, these words you see
Of self respect and dignity,
Why don't they just spell it out to me. . . .?
DON'T GO LOSING YOUR VIRGINITY!

Availability of healthcare for adolescents

Many teenagers may not be aware of how the healthcare system works from which they can get help and advice, as for Rebecca in Box 18.14. Look back at Chapters 2 and 3 for tips and suggestions on how to make your practice or clinic teen friendly and accessible to children and young people of all age groups.

Box 18.14: Rebecca, 18 years old

'As a young teenager I never knew how to get healthcare without going through my parents.'

Surveys of children and young people have shown that doctors, nurses and other medical staff feel that teenagers are still too young to understand medical issues and so will not explain in the same way that they would treat an adult.[15] So they do not give children and young people much say in their own care and treatment. Often young people may feel intimidated and frightened to ask certain questions, so there needs to be more of an understanding of their perspective from NHS staff. Continuity is important to children and teenagers who need to keep seeing the same doctor; changing doctors makes it hard for adolescents to communicate with somebody new, which can result in them not telling the full details about the severity of a certain problem, etc.

Young people need to be understood, respected, acknowledged and supported, instead of being patronised, smothered or blamed for their situation. Adolescents want to be taken seriously. Above all, they want to be listened to by medical staff, teachers, parents and to get supportive responses when they request help and advice.

Conclusion

There are two main causes of smoking, drinking alcohol, drug misuse and unprotected sexual activity among teens. First, peer pressure has a big influence on teenagers, as they can be forced into the risky behaviour to become socially accepted by their friends and others. Second, poor role models who smoke, drink, abuse drugs or are sexually promiscuous who appear on the television or in newspapers, or are from the music industry, may influence teenagers. Television programmes are filled with sex, drugs, crime, drinking and smoking. We must remember that all adults are potential role models, not just those in the public gaze. In today's society it is more acceptable to go out binge drinking and get intoxicated. Teenagers will always try to rebel and break rules, so unless something is done about the way the older generation behave then how can we expect teens to act differently?

Research to inform the national media campaign for combating teenage pregnancy has reached conclusions that can be generalised to other aspects of teenagers' risky lifestyle.[16] The most effective ways to provide a productive and healthy upbringing for children and teenagers are:

- parents need to communicate better with their adolescent children
- parents need to have more of an influence on the friends that their adolescents have, the places they go, what they watch on television and what they read
- parents need to have a greater interest in and encourage the leisure activities of their children from an early age
- parents and other adults should have regular discussions about morality and the sensible ways to react if their children are offered drugs, alcohol, etc. This will help them to build a good understanding of the issues and form their own sensible opinions
- humour and story-telling are often the best ways to communicate with young people and should be used for educational interventions.

References

1 Carter D (2003) *Adolescent Health.* British Medical Association Science and Education Department and the Board of Science and Education. BMA, London.
2 Blenkinsop S, Boreham R and McManus S (2003) *Smoking, Drinking and Drug Use among Young People in England in 2002.* HMSO, London.
3 Prescott-Clarke P and Primatesta P (1998) *Health Survey for England: the health of young people '95–'97.* HMSO, London.
4 Higgins V (1999) *Young Teenagers and Smoking in 1998: a report of the key findings from the Teenage Smoking Attitudes Survey carried out in 1998.* HMSO, London.
5 Coleman T (2004) ABC of smoking cessation. Special groups of smokers. *BMJ.* **328**: 575–7.
6 Coleman J and Schofield J (2003) *Key Data on Adolescence.* Trust for the Study of Adolescence, Brighton.
7 Department of Health (2003) *Health Survey for England 2002.* National Statistics. DH, London.
8 Aust R, Sharp C and Goulden C (2002) *Prevalence of Drug Use: key findings from 2001/2002 British Crime Survey.* Home Office, London.
9 UK Government (1998) *Tackling Drugs to Build a Better Britain.* HMSO, London.
10 Home Office (2002) *Updated Drug Strategy 2002.* Home Office, London.
11 Adler MW (2003) Sexual health – health of the nation. *Sexual Trans Infect.* **79**: 85–7.
12 Hill C (2000) *Sex Under Sixteen? Young people comment on the social and educational influences on their behaviour.* Family Education Trust, London.
13 Chambers R, Wakley G and Chambers S (2001) *Tackling Teenage Pregnancy: sex, culture and needs.* Radcliffe Medical Press, Oxford.
14 Stanford C (2004) *Don't go losing your virginity.* Presentation at Getting it Right for Teenagers: avoiding teenage pregnancy and promoting sexual health. Staffordshire University, Stoke-on-Trent.
15 Commission for Health Improvement (2004) *Children's Voices.* CHI, London. www.chi.nhs.uk/childrens_voices/index.shtml
16 Eborall C and Garmeson K (2000) *Research to Inform the National Media Campaign.* Teenage Pregnancy Unit, London.

National Service Framework for Children, Young People and Maternity Services

Standard 1: Promoting health and well-being, identifying needs and intervening early[1]

Vision

We want to see:
- all children and young people achieving the best possible physical and emotional health and well-being, both in childhood and into adulthood
- children, young people and families supported and able to make healthy choices in how they live their lives
- a measurable reduction in inequality of health outcomes for children and young people
- integrated services which provide effective checks and more targeted support for children and young people who need it

Standard: The health and well-being of all children and young people is promoted and delivered through a co-ordinated programme of action, including prevention and early intervention wherever possible, to ensure long term gain, led by the NHS in partnership with local authorities.

Standard 2: Supporting parents or carers[1]

> **Vision**
>
> We want to see:
> - parents or carers who are confident and able to bring up their children in a way that promotes positive health and development and emotional well-being
> - consistent information provided for parents or carers, which supports them in their role and is responsive to their needs
> - appropriate help and support provided for parents or carers who find it hard to access services and professionals.

Standard: Parents or carers are enabled to receive the information, services and support that will help them to care for their children and equip them with the skills they need to ensure that their children have optimum life chances and are healthy and safe.

Standard 3: Child, young person and family-centred services[1]

> **Vision**
>
> We want to see:
> - professionals communicating directly with children and young people, listening to them and attempting to see the world through their eyes
> - children, young people and their families having equitable access to high quality, child-centred health promotion, prevention and care services, which are responsive to their individual developing needs and preferences
> - the views of children, young people and families being valued and taken into account in the planning, delivery and evaluation of services.

Standard: Children, young people and families receive high quality services which are co-ordinated around their individual and family needs and take account of their views.

Standard 4: Growing up into adulthood[1]

Vision

We want to see:

- young people supported to make the transition to adulthood and to achieve their maximum potential in terms of education, health, development and well-being
- young people taking responsibility for their own health and making informed choices and decisions regarding their emotional and social development, and health and well-being both now and in the future
- services and staff who are able to respond in a sensitive way which encourages engagement and provides high quality support for young people.

Standard: All young people have access to age-appropriate services which are responsive to their specific needs as they grow into adulthood.

Standard 5: Safeguarding and promoting the welfare of children and young people[1]

Vision

We want to see:

- children and young people safeguarded from harm (maltreatment) and able to achieve their optimal outcomes throughout childhood, their teenage years and into adulthood
- children and young people growing up in circumstances where they are safe and supported.

Standard: All agencies work to prevent children suffering harm and to promote their welfare, provide them with the services they require to address their identified needs and safeguard children who are being or who are likely to be harmed.

Standard 6: Children and young people who are ill[2]

Vision

We want to see:
- children and young people who are ill receiving timely, high quality and effective care as close to home as possible
- children and young people who are ill and their families being cared for within a local system which co-ordinates health, social care and education in a way that meets their individual needs.

Standard: All children and young people who are ill, or thought to be ill, or injured will have timely access to appropriate advice and to effective services which address their health, social, educational and emotional needs throughout the period of their illness.

Standard 7: Hospital services for children[3]

Vision

To deliver hospital services that meet the needs of children, young people and their parents, and provide effective and safe care, through appropriately trained and skilled staff working in suitable, child-friendly, and safe environments.

Standard: Children and young people receive high quality, evidence-based hospital care, developed through clinical governance and delivered in appropriate settings.

Standard 8: Disabled children and young people and those with complex health needs[4]

> **Vision**
>
> We want to see:
> - children and young people who are disabled or who have complex health needs, supported to participate in family and community activities and facilities
> - health, education and social care services organised around the needs of children and young people and their families, with co-ordinated multi-agency assessments leading to prompt, convenient, responsive and high-quality multi-agency interventions that maximise the child's ability to reach his or her full potential
> - children and young people and their families actively involved in all decisions affecting them and in shaping local services.

Standard: Children and young people who are disabled or who have complex health needs receive co-ordinated, high-quality child and family centred services which are based on assessed needs, which promote social inclusion and, where possible, which enable them and their families to live ordinary lives.

Standard 9: The mental health and psychological well-being of children and young people[5]

> **Vision**
>
> We want to see:
> - an improvement in the mental health of all children and young people
> - that multi-agency services, working in partnership, promote the mental health of all children and young people, provide early intervention and also meet the needs of children and young people with established or complex problems
> - that all children, young people and their families have access to mental health care based upon the best available evidence and provided by staff with an appropriate range of skills and competencies.

Standard: All children and young people, from birth to their eighteenth birthday, who have mental health problems and disorders have access to timely, integrated, high quality, multi-disciplinary mental health services to ensure effective assessment, treatment and support, for them and their families.

Standard 10: Medicines management for children[6]

Vision

We want to see:
- all children and young people receiving medicines that are safe and effective, in formulations that can easily be administered and are appropriate to their age, having minimum impact on their education and lifestyle
- medicines being prescribed, dispensed and administered by professionals who are well trained, informed and competent to work with children to improve health outcomes and minimise harm and any side effects of medicines
- children and young people and their parents or carers who are well-informed and supported to make choices about their medicines and are competent in the administration of medicines.

Standard: Children, young people, their parents or carers, and healthcare professionals in all settings make decisions about medicines based on sound information about risk and benefit. They have access to safe and effective medicines that are prescribed on the basis of the best available evidence.

Standard 11: Maternity services[7]

Vision

We want to see:
- flexible individualised services designed to fit around the woman and her baby's journey through pregnancy and motherhood, with emphasis on the needs of vulnerable and disadvantaged women
- women being supported and encouraged to have as normal a pregnancy and birth as possible, with medical interventions recommended to them only if they are of benefit to the woman or her baby
- midwifery and obstetric care being based on providing good clinical and psychological outcomes for the woman and baby, while putting equal emphasis on helping new parents prepare for parenthood.

Standard: Women have easy access to supportive, high quality maternity services, designed around their individual needs and those of their babies.

References

1 Department of Health (2004) *Core Document, National Service Framework for Children, Young People and Maternity Services.* Department of Health, London.
2 Department of Health (2004) *Ill Child Standard, National Service Framework for Children, Young People and Maternity Services.* Department of Health, London.
3 Department of Health (2003) *Getting the Right Start: National Service Framework for Children, Standard for Hospital Services.* Department of Health, London.
4 Department of Health (2004) *Disabled Child Standard, National Service Framework for Children, Young People and Maternity Services.* Department of Health, London.
5 Department of Health (2004) *Child and Adolescent Mental Health (CAMHS) Standard, National Service Framework for Children, Young People and Maternity Services.* Department of Health, London.
6 Department of Health (2004) *Medicines Standard, National Service Framework for Children, Young People and Maternity Services.* Department of Health, London.
7 Department of Health (2004) *Maternity Standard, National Service Framework for Children, Young People and Maternity Services.* Department of Health, London.

Index

Page numbers in italics refer to tables or figures.